This book is concerned with the role of economic philosophy ('ideas') in the processes of belief-formation and social change. Its aim is to further our understanding of the behaviour of the individual economic agent by bringing to light and examining the function of non-rational dispositions and motivations ('passions') in the determination of the agent's beliefs and goals. Drawing on the work of David Hume and Adam Smith, the book spells out the particular ways in which the passions come to affect our ordinary understanding and conduct in practical affairs and the intergenerational and interpersonal transmission of ideas through language. Concern with these problems, it is argued, lies at the heart of an important tradition in British moral philosophy. This emphasis on the non-rational nature of our belief-fixation mechanisms has important implications: it helps to clarify and qualify the misleading claims often made by utilitarian, Marxist, Keynesian, and neo-liberal economic philosophers, all of whom stress the overriding power of ideas to shape conduct, policy and institutions.

BELIEFS IN ACTION

BELIEFS IN ACTION

Economic philosophy and social change

EDUARDO GIANNETTI DA FONSECA

University of São Paulo

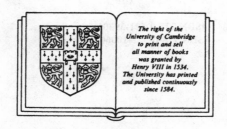

The right of the
University of Cambridge
to print and sell
all manner of books
was granted by
Henry VIII in 1534.
The University has printed
and published continuously
since 1584.

CAMBRIDGE UNIVERSITY PRESS

Cambridge

New York   Port Chester

Melbourne   Sydney

CAMBRIDGE UNIVERSITY PRESS
Cambridge, New York, Melbourne, Madrid, Cape Town, Singapore, São Paulo, Delhi

Cambridge University Press
The Edinburgh Building, Cambridge CB2 8RU, UK

Published in the United States of America by Cambridge University Press, New York

www.cambridge.org
Information on this title: www.cambridge.org/9780521393065

First published 1991
This digitally printed version 2008

A catalogue record for this publication is available from the British Library

Library of Congress Cataloguing in Publication data
Fonseca, Eduardo Giannetti da, 1957–
Beliefs in action : economic philosophy and social change /
Eduardo Giannetti da Fonseca.
p.   cm.
Based on the author's thesis (Ph.D.)–University of Cambridge.
Includes bibliographical references and index.
ISBN 0–521–39306–X (hardcover)
1. Economics–Philosophy.   2. Social change.   I. Title.
HB72.F64   1991
330'.01–dc20   90–15006
CIP

ISBN 978-0-521-39306-5 hardback
ISBN 978-0-521-10060-1 paperback

To Phyllis Deane

Contents

Preface and acknowledgements

This book is basically about the role of political and economic philosophy ('ideas') in the processes of belief-formation and social change. I have tried to bring out and examine in more detail a point which economic philosophers of all persuasions have largely taken for granted in their works, and to address an issue – the relations between ideas, interests and behaviour – about which sweeping and confident claims have only too often been made, but which has rarely been subjected to critical and sustained discussion. The object of this work is to further our understanding of the behaviour of the individual economic agent by bringing to light and examining the function of non-rational dispositions and motivations ('passions') in the determination of the agent's beliefs and goals.

Drawing on the economic psychology put forward by David Hume, Adam Smith and a few other 'enlightened sceptics', I suggest that agents act on the basis of what they believe is their own self-interest, but that this opinion of interest is best understood as being determined by the non-rational or sensitive rather than by the rational or cogitative part of the human mind. Man, according to this view, is *not* a rational animal, but something altogether more tentative, affective, unstable and perhaps interesting too: an animal which has the *capability of reason*. To exercise and live up to this capability, I hold, is an endless and sometimes tricky struggle.

In the crucial chapters of the book, I have tried to spell out the mechanisms and particular ways in which the 'passions of the imagination' come to affect (i) our ordinary understanding and conduct in practical life as consumers, producers and decision-makers, (ii) the intergenerational and the interpersonal transmission of 'ideas' through language, and (iii) to show how a concern with this problem lies at the heart of an important tradition in British moral

xi

philosophy. The emphasis on the non-rational input of our belief-fixation mechanisms, it is also argued, has one important implication. It helps to clarify and heavily qualify what I believe are the exaggerated and misleading claims often made by utilitarian, Marxist, Keynesian and neo-liberal economic philosophers, all stressing the overriding power of 'ideas' – persuasion and the clash of rival ideologies – to account for and to change human conduct and the institutions of practical life.

The book is divided in two parts. Part I ('The war of ideas') examines the limits of economic philosophy and the constraints bearing on the autonomy or 'freedom to do' of the individual economic agent. Part II ('Patterns of misunderstanding') deals with belief-forming processes and, in particular, with problems and pitfalls in the transmission of abstract systems of economic and political thought. The aim in part II is to develop an illustrated taxonomy of misunderstandings in intellectual exchanges, along with an analysis of the distinct misapprehension mechanisms involved.

The main problems discussed, the overall structure of the argument and the relations between both parts are set forth in the introductions to parts I and II. In both parts I have tried (a) to adhere to the principle of methodological individualism, and (b) to put the discussion in historical perspective by mobilizing and bringing in, as far as possible, the resources embedded in the history of ideas on the subject at issue. A further methodological assumption underlying the argument in both parts is (c) the view that the best approach to rationality and good communication is through the study of non-rationality and misunderstanding. It may also be useful to note that parts I and II have been deliberately structured so that they can be read independently of each other. This should enable readers with a more particular interest to read one part without necessarily having to go through the other.

Over many years of research and composition I have accumulated many debts. First, I wish to express my gratitude to Professor Phyllis Deane, to whom this book is dedicated. She guided my very first steps in academic research. Her patience, kindness and enthusiasm made this work possible. I should also like to thank Bob Rowthorn, who supervised the Ph.D. thesis on which this book is based, for his unfailing help, encouragement and criticisms.

Early drafts of particular chapters were tested out as seminar papers or lectures for the Faculty of Economics at the University of Cambridge and the Instituto de Pesquisas Econômicas at Universidade de São Paulo. A number of people have read one of the many drafts of this work and have generously helped me to improve the argument, avoid errors and misconceptions, clarify the text and persist in my task. I am particularly grateful to Renford Bambrough, Roberto Viana Batista, Richard Brent, John Broome, Peter Clarke, Partha Dasgupta, Jayati Ghosh, Geoff Harcourt, Keith Hart, Wilfried Hinsch, Peter Kriesler, Gay Meeks, Antônio Delfim Netto, Hans-Martin Niemeier, Hugo Tucker and an anonymous referee for the Press. They are of course in no way responsible for my obstinacy and the final outcome. Lúcio Castilho kindly helped me to check the references and compile the bibliography.

The financial support for my graduate training and research (1981–4) was given by the Brazilian Conselho Nacional de Desenvolvimento Científico e Tecnológico, CNPq. A three-year research fellowship at St John's College, Cambridge (1984–7) enabled me to pursue my studies with undreamed of concentration and depth; I am grateful to the Master and Fellows of the College for this unique opportunity and for their generous support. Finally, a British Council grant helped me to visit Cambridge in the winter of 1989–90 and to make the final revision of the manuscript.

My greatest debt is to Christine and Joel.

Abbreviations

Works by David Hume

THN	*A Treatise of Human Nature*
1stE	*An Enquiry Concerning Human Understanding*
2ndE	*An Enquiry Concerning the Principles of Morals*
E	*Essays Moral, Political, and Literary*

Adam Smith

TMS	*The Theory of Moral Sentiments*
WN	*An Inquiry into the Nature and the Causes of the Wealth of Nations*
EPS	*Essays on Philosophical Subjects*

John Stuart Mill

CW	*The Collected Works of John Stuart Mill*

Alfred Marshall

PEc	*Principles of Economics*

Periodicals

JHI	*Journal of the History of Ideas*
HOPE	*History of Political Economy*

References to these works are made in parentheses in the text and in the notes at the end of the book. The abbreviations are followed by the volume (where appropriate) and by the page number. For example: CW8,57 = Mill's *Collected Works*, vol. 8, p. 57. Details of the editions used are given in the bibliography.

PART I

The war of ideas

Part I is organized into seven chapters. The main questions tackled concern the role of ideas in social action and the problem of autonomy in the economic behaviour of the individual agent. The logical structure of the argument is as follows.

Chapter 1 states what is perhaps the single key premiss shared by economic philosophers influential in the evolution of economic ideas and belonging to conflicting poles of the ideological spectrum – the notion that the ideas put forward by economists and political philosophers powerfully affect social behaviour and the actual conduct of human affairs. Textual evidence is then produced in order to support and detail empirically this claim.

Chapters 2 to 4 give an account of the main challenges posed by the growth of scientific knowledge to the basic assumption of economic philosophy (chapter 1). Particular attention is devoted (chapters 3 and 4) to the origins and nature of the 'economic man' concept, that is, the normalization of human behaviour developed by economic science and leading to the complete abstraction of the beliefs and opinions of the individual agent in the explanation of his ordinary transactions. Chapter 4 gathers up the threads of the preceding chapters in an attempt to consider how the 'economic man' concept (chapter 3) fits in with the 'man-machine' doctrine (chapter 2).

Finally, I go on to suggest two qualifications which seem required to revise the economic philosophers' claim that 'Ideas rule the world of human affairs and its events':

(i) The economic process in any complex society sets significant constraints on the autonomy of the individual agent or his 'freedom to do'. Economic actions (e.g. wage-earning and managerial activities) become largely instrumental, i.e. a matter of doing things one would not otherwise do, so as to secure the means to satisfy one's wants; the agent's behaviour in the system is thus determined not by his own beliefs and opinions but by the logic of the economic situation (chapter 5).

(ii) There is also the psychological constraint on individual autonomy. Agents are not entirely aware of the workings of their own minds or able to fully regulate them; hence they may have beliefs and opinions which affect their behaviour as producers and consumers and yet escape their attention and are in effect sealed off from rational consideration (chapters 6 and 7). The discussion of (ii) in particular draws heavily on the Humean–Smithian philosophy of action, with its emphasis on the passions of the imagination and its implications as regards the limits of economic philosophy.

The main contention of part I is that the arguments put forward in chapters 5 to 7 provide grounds: (a) to qualify and revise the central assumption of economic philosophy and (b) to protect it rationally and effectively from the ever more sophisticated challenges to its survival arising from scientific mechanism in economics and elsewhere. The chief aim is to spell out the two basic reasons why it is so markedly easier to believe in one's moral autonomy than to translate it into action in ordinary practical life. 'Free time', I conclude, can only be conducive to greater autonomy in individual behaviour if the hard-earned 'freedom to do' is supplemented by the quest for self-knowledge and self-command.

Socrates. Come now, Protagoras, uncover for me this part of your mind as well; how do you stand as regards knowledge? Do you agree with the majority there too, or do you think otherwise? The opinion of the majority about knowledge is that it is not anything strong, which can control and rule a man; they don't look at it that way at all, but think that often a man who possesses knowledge is ruled not by it but by something else, in one case passion, in another pleasure, in another pain, sometimes lust, very often fear; they just look at knowledge as a slave who gets dragged about by all the rest. Now are you of similar opinion about knowledge, or do you think that it is something fine which can rule a man, and that if someone knows what is good and bad, he would never be conquered by anything so as to do other than what knowledge bids him? In fact, that intelligence is a sufficient safeguard for a man?

Plato's *Protagoras*, 352b–c

CHAPTER I

From Hume to Hayek
Economic philosophy and the role of ideas in social action

There is at least one clear point on which philosophers influential in the evolution of economic ideas agree, even when they are otherwise radically at odds with each other: they all believe in the power of ideas to transform human conduct and institutions. An explicit agreement on this point unites economic philosophers as far apart on values and principles as D. Hume and W. Paley in the eighteenth century, J.S. Mill and K. Marx in the nineteenth or, more lately, J. Robinson and F.A. Hayek. But what are these ideas, and how do they interfere with human action in ordinary life?

A good starting-point to answer these questions is Hume's assertion that 'though men be much governed by interest, yet even interest itself, and all human affairs, are entirely governed by opinion' (E,51). There is no interest without 'opinion of interest'. By opinion of interest, Hume means that the very self-interest which supposedly motivates social agents into action is in fact a certain perception of interest, that is, an ordering of preferences grounded on expectations and beliefs. The pre-eminent example of opinion shaping the perception of interest for Hume is the fact that a great number of agents are prepared to give up their individual, self-centered pursuit of advantages when the benefit of their own family is at stake.[1] Even the most staunch cases of selfishness usually stop short of family knots.

Other examples of the ways in which opinion governs interest are: the agent's judgements as to the desirability of disregarding his more immediate and visible interests in order to pursue remote and less probable ones, his estimation as to the relative weight of bodily *vis-à-vis* intellectual pleasures as ends of action, and the voluntary 'abstaining from the possessions of others' which springs from what Hume called 'a general sense of common interest' and the belief 'that it will be for my interest to leave another in the possession of his goods,

7

provided he will act in the same manner with regard to me'
(THN,490).

It was the extraordinary variability of opinions concerning what is
one's self-interest that Hume had in mind when he remarked that
'Nero had the same vanity in driving a chariot, that Trajan had in
governing the empire with justice and ability' (E,86). The relevant
questions are: (a) what are the determinants of distinct perceptions of
interest?, and (b) how far is it possible to influence opinions of self-
interest and common good by means of rational and moral
argument?

But, although declaring himself impressed by the 'sudden and
sensible change in the opinions of men within these last fifty years, by
the progress of learning and of liberty' (E,51), Hume's primary
concern as a moral philosopher was not trying to foster or reverse such
a change. He wanted, instead, to understand the moral interpretation
of phenomena. Not to moralize human conduct by striving to 'make
us feel the difference between vice and virtue', but rather to
anatomize the different operations of the human mind and 'with a
narrow scrutiny [to] examine it, in order to find those principles
which regulate our understanding, excite our sentiments, and make
us approve or blame any particular object, action, or behaviour'
(1stE,6). (As I shall try to argue in chapter 6 below, Hume's decision
not to join, as a belligerent party, in direct contests for the convictions
and opinions of mankind (the 'war of ideas') sprang from his far-
reaching conclusion that 'belief is more properly an act of the sensitive,
than of the cogitative part of our natures' (THN,183). This move, I
will suggest, seriously restricted the role assigned to philosophy and
ethical argument as factors in the process of belief-formation; it
seriously called into question the causal efficacy of the 'war of ideas' in
its relation to human behaviour and social change.)

Hume's attempt to bring forth a thoroughly positive 'mental
geography' of the cognitive and evaluative faculties of the human
mind soon attracted the criticism of his contemporaries. Apart from
his more orthodox and hostile critics (like Rev. W. Wishart, then
Principal of Edinburgh University, and the Scottish 'common sense'
philosophers T. Reid and J. Beattie), two of the most prominent
eighteenth-century British moral philosophers – F. Hutcheson and
W. Paley – objected to Hume's 'mental geography' on the grounds of
its failure to provide also a 'compass rose' showing the true north of
virtue.

Hutcheson – the teacher and predecessor of Adam Smith as Professor of Moral Philosophy at the University of Glasgow, to whom Hume submitted the manuscript of the still unpublished Book III ('Of Morals') of *A Treatise of Human Nature* (1739–40) – criticized his treatment of moral philosophy in that work, remarking that it 'wants a certain Warmth in the Cause of Virtue'.[2] And Paley, the Archdeacon of Carlisle who, in the words of Keynes, had been 'for a generation or more an intellectual influence on Cambridge only second to Newton' and also 'the first of the Cambridge economists',[3] followed up this criticism in his *Principles of Morality and Politics* (1785).

For Paley, the practical relevance of moral philosophy was its *raison d'être*. He defined moral philosophy straightforwardly as 'that science which teaches men their duty and the reasons of it', and then censured Hume – particularly referring to the fourth appendix of *An Enquiry Concerning the Principles of Morals* (1751) – for failing to advance reasons 'sufficient to withhold men from the gratification of lust, revenge, envy, ambition, avarice, or to prevent the existence of these passions'.[4]

Yet there is an underlying agreement between Paley and Hume concerning the paramount force of opinion, especially unquestioned and uncritically assimilated opinion, as a determinant of behaviour in practical life. 'We appear astonished when we see the multitude led away by sounds', argued Paley in the opening remarks of his *Principles*, 'but we should remember that, if sounds work miracles, it is always upon ignorance', the 'influence of names' being 'in exact proportion to the want of knowledge'. What really differentiates Paley's enterprise from Hume's, is his trust that cogent argument and persuasion – it was not for nothing that Charles Darwin once referred to Paley as 'the Euclid of the moral sciences' – are able to supply the knowledge wanted for dissipating the fog of 'sounds', 'names' and 'ignorance', and thus to effectively fortify the will of men in the exercise of virtue.

Each and every individual human being, indeed every single living creature, held Paley, has the centre of gravity of his own existence in himself. Living organisms exist for their own sake and are actively engaged in pursuing their own good, rather than for the sake of any other organism or species and simply in order to cater for its needs or desires. It is the peculiar condition of man that each separate individual has to work his way and use his understanding to find out what is his own good.

The task of moral philosophy, according to Paley, is to ensure that an ever increasing proportion of men will not flee from the duty of 'caring for their souls', that is, will be able and resolute enough to think for themselves and to use their own understanding in seeking an opinion of their own and the communal good. The public discussion of political and socio-economic arrangements was singled out by him as the sphere of social life in which people are most prone to surrender to the seduction of 'sounds', 'names' and equivocal words: 'Indeed, as far as I have observed, in political, beyond all other subjects, where men are without some fundamental and scientific principles to resort to, they are liable to have their understandings played upon by cant phrases and unmeaning terms, of which every party in every country possesses a vocabulary'.[5] Clear and principled moral thinking – based of course in his own blend of Christianity and utilitarianism – were for him the best antidotes against semantic pollution, doctrinal contamination and institutional decay.

The Philosophic Radicals, just like Paley, were not content merely to interpret the world. They were keen to change it and, as one historian of their reformist toils put it, did not wish to be seen by society at large as 'men of crochets, fitter for the study than the platform'.[6] Their stated goal was the greatest happiness of humanity as a whole, and their means to achieve it was a vigorous, far-reaching and philosophy-based program of reform which was meant to affect virtually every aspect of social life, from the penal, legal and educational systems to the position of women in society, the reproductive behaviour of the working class and the use of ordinary language.

Linguistic reform was indeed one of their key targets. In a passage which clearly echoes Paley's strictures on the misuse of language in public debate, and which came out in a work on educational reform published in 1817, J. Bentham stated: 'What if . . . the import of all words, especially of all words belonging to the field of Ethics . . . should one day become fixed? What a source of perplexity, of error, of discord, and even bloodshed, would be dried up!' Similarly, criticizing the 'rhetorical and mischievous nonsense' of the 'natural law' and 'natural rights' language used by the French National Assembly in its 1791 Declaration of Rights, Bentham concluded: 'In a play or a novel, an improper word is but a word . . . In a body of laws – especially of laws given as constitutional and fundamental ones – an improper word may be a national calamity: – and civil war may be the consequence of it. Out of one foolish word may start a thousand daggers'.[7] The hope that philosophy could gradually pave the way for 'undistorted communication' in public affairs is at the heart of the utilitarian enterprise.

In the eyes of an eager 'subversive' and 'questioner of things established' like J.S. Mill, Hume's combination of a bold intrepidity in philosophical analysis with a resigned timidity in socio-economic reform entitled him to the epithet of 'the profoundest negative thinker on record' (CW10,80). He praised Hume's razor-sharp powers of analysis and logical criticism, remarking that 'German subtlety alone' could hope to thoroughly comprehend or match them, but he surely did not share Hume's moral scepticism as to 'whether virtue could be taught' or whether it is part of the business of a philosopher trying to put a vision of what he thinks is a desirable state of affairs and then set about persuading whoever cares to listen about it.

'Questions of ultimate ends are not amenable to direct proof', wrote Mill in *Utilitarianism* (1861). There is no prospect of ever coming to a true, final and definite answer to the question of how one should live. Yet, he went on to argue, 'considerations may be presented capable of determining the intellect either to give or to withhold its assent' (CW10,207–8). Questions of ultimate values shaping conduct are not to be ruled out and put aside as wholly arbitrary and beyond the scope of rational consideration. In fact, it was precisely losing sight of such questions and handing them over to 'blind impulse' or 'arbitrary choice' that was seen by Mill as one of the greatest menaces demanding unyielding resistance from philosophical quarters – the menace of 'a tame uniformity of thought, dealings and actions', of giving a free, unrestrained rein to 'the habit of our time to desire nothing strongly' and to smuggle in, as the 'ideal of character', simply 'to be without any marked character . . . to maim by compression, like a Chinese lady's foot, every part of human nature which stands out prominently, and tends to make the person markedly dissimilar in outline to commonplace humanity'.[8]

Contrary to what might be at first expected, Mill's genuine and paramount concern to promote the cause of utilitarian justice, and to practically improve what he called the 'business part of the social arrangements', did not imply a corresponding neglect of abstract philosophical speculation. For he also set great store on the power of outstanding philosophical opinion-shapers to bring about practical change, and he was in one mind about the decisive role of general views and ideas in determining the course of events in human affairs. One of the many – and perhaps the clearest – of his statements to this effect comes up in the essay on 'Bentham' (1838):

Speculative philosophy, which to the superficial appears a thing so remote from the business of life and the outward interests of men, is in reality the thing on earth which most influences them, and in the long run overbears every other influence save those which it must itself obey. (CW10,77)

What we think determines how we act. 'Speculative philosophy' plays a decisive, though unacknowledged, role in our ordinary practical thinking; hence it has controlling force upon our actions. And as he put it elsewhere, 'one person with a belief, is a social power equal to ninety nine who have only interests'.[9]

To the old Socratic question 'whether virtue can be taught', Mill returns a clear, confident and unambiguous 'yes'. 'It is for those in whom the feelings of virtue are weak', he argued against moral sceptics in 'Remarks on Bentham's philosophy' (1833), 'that ethical writing is chiefly needful'. And the 'proper office' of ethical writing, he continued, 'is to strengthen those feelings': 'It is by a sort of sympathetic contagion, or inspiration, that a noble mind assimilates other minds to itself, and no one was ever inspired by one whose own inspiration was not sufficient to give him faith in the possibility of making others feel what he feels (CW 10, 15–6). As I shall try to show in chapters 3 and 4 below, in his mature work on political economy, and especially in his discussions on the institution of property and in his advocacy of a 'stationary state', Mill did not shrink from making use of this notion and trying out its efficacy as a weapon to produce social change in the desired direction.

A basically similar emphasis on the practical implications of philosophical speculation with respect to down-to-earth economic practices permeates the school of thought stemming from the works of Marx. As it will be presently seen, when it came down to the question of the reception and use of his own theories (or those of his closest rivals), Marx did not find anything amiss with the view that ideas powerfully affect the actual conduct of human affairs. He did not believe that this view, which belonged to the dialectical side of his 'dialectical materialism', was in any way dependent on supposedly idealist premises of thought.

As it is well known, early in his intellectual journey Marx boldly concluded that 'hitherto philosophers have only interpreted the world in various ways', whereas 'the point is to change it'. The well-meaning but sterile verbiage of the German mid-nineteenth century young Hegelians had provoked him to write that 'the weapons of criticism obviously cannot replace the criticism of weapons' and that 'material force must be overthrown by material force'. Nevertheless, he then immediately added, 'theory also becomes a material force once it has gripped the masses'.[10] And Marx himself clearly found no better way of changing the world than interpreting it anew. Only that now the 'critique of heaven', i.e. the philosophical criticism of Christian theology and of its 'written heaven', gives way to the more worldly 'critique of earth' – the no less philosophical criticism of British political economy and of the economic system it had attempted to portray.

Evidence about Marx's belief in philosophical theories becoming 'material forces' when they have managed to 'grip the masses' may be drawn from a variety of sources and periods of his life.

Clearly, it was part and parcel of his approach to political militancy from the early days of the Communist League in the 1840s up to the *Critique of the Gotha Programme* (1875), one of Marx's last major writings. Already in 1846, in one of the first of his many clashes with fellow-revolutionaries over points of doctrine, Marx rebuked in strong and revealing terms a German agitator (W. Weitling) for his lack of attention to theory:

To call to the workers without any strictly scientific ideas or constructive doctrine, especially in Germany, [is] equivalent to vain and dishonest play at preaching which assumes an inspired prophet on the one side and on the other only gasping asses . . . People without constructive doctrine cannot do anything and have indeed done nothing so far except make a noise, rouse dangerous flares and bring about the ruin of the cause they had undertaken.[11]

In his detailed analysis of the programme adopted in 1875 by the newly created German Social-Democratic Workers' Party, Marx put forward a bitter indictment of the party's leadership for its doctrinal shortcomings and its acceptance of mistaken (i.e. F. Lassale's) economic principles, which had led to (as F. Engels put it) 'the bending of the knee to Lassalleanism on the part of the whole German socialist proletariat'. Marx's own philosophical *practice* betrays his firm and intimate conviction that ideas matter.

But perhaps the most forceful illustration of how far Marx was prepared to go to demonstrate that beliefs are the ultimate cement of any socio-economic order is his discussion of the basis of slavery in the *Grundrisse* (1857–8), the copious notebooks from which *Das Kapital* (1867) would eventually emerge: 'With the slave's awareness that he cannot be the property of another, with his consciousness of himself as a person', argued Marx, striking here a peculiarly Hegelian chord, 'the existence of slavery becomes a merely artificial, vegetative existence, and ceases to be able to prevail as the basis of production'.[12] What was true for the slaves of antiquity was of course even more so to the modern, 'factory wage-slaves'.

The argument that any social order only holds together in so far as a set of beliefs obtains in the bulk of its working members applies *a fortiori* in the context of an economic system like capitalism, in which the physical coercion of workers is not regularly deployed and the bonds of personal dependence are largely inoperative. 'Individuals are now ruled by abstractions, whereas earlier they depended on one another', wrote Marx of the economic order based on the generalized exchange of commodities and the sale and purchase of labour-power. It is Marx's intention to 'unveil' the social relations lurking under the 'abstractions' now ruling the economic actions of individuals; and to show that now, as before, they do depend on one another, and in such a way that one group of them benefits from the labours of the other group without providing any suitable equivalent in exchange.

This is why capitalist society, for Marx, more than any other previous social formation, has a certain belief-system as a condition of existence. But, as he puts it in *Capital*, 'reflection begins *post festum*'. And Marx is out – armed with the sophisticated arsenal of dialectical 'tongue-wrestling' – to dispel the 'fetishism of the commodity', to decipher the 'social hieroglyphic' in which 'every product of labour' is transformed when production for exchange predominates, and to lay bare 'the secret of profit-making' under capitalism. Indeed, the very outburst of intellectual activity which led to the composition of the *Grundrisse* in the winter of 1857–8 was in fact prompted, as Marx himself related to Engels and Lassale, by his fear that the Revolution might occur *before* he had given to the world his great economic masterpiece: 'I am working like mad all night and every night collating my economic studies so that I at least get the outlines clear before the *deluge*'.[13] The 'deluge' of course did not come. But the illusion that it was imminent worked miracles.

In a motion approved by the Congress of the International Working Men's Association (First International) held in Brussels in September 1868, Marx's erudite critique of British political economy (published in German a few months earlier) was recommended to the attention of socialists in all countries and described – in a suggestive and since then amply used catchphrase – as 'the Bible of the working class'.[14] Whatever might be said about the existence of a degree of tension in Marx's thinking on this question or the materialist strain in his thought, there can be no denying of the fact that he was not merely trying to make his ideas understood by readers (like, say, astronomers or molecular biologists do), but was deeply steeped in the business of exposing and producing belief, i.e. winning converts to his truth and showing the way forward to mankind.

Further evidence about this point is the interview given by Marx to the New York *World* in July 1871, just after the violent suppression of the Paris Commune uprising. There was rumour (incidentally false) that Marx had been the 'spiritual leader' of the French workers, and the London correspondent of the American newspaper wanted to know his views about the recent events in Paris and the prospects for the labour movement in general. 'It seems to me', remarked the journalist inviting a comment, 'that the leaders of the new international movement have had to form a philosophy as well as an association for themselves'. Marx's reply was to the point:

Dr. K.M. – Precisely. It is hardly likely, for instance, that we could hope to prosper in our war against capital if we derive our tactics, say, from the political economy of Mill. He has traced one kind of relationship between labour and capital. We hope to show that it is possible to establish another.[15]

The reference to Mill here is apposite. Marx was aware that *he* was in fact his most formidable rival in the field of economic and social philosophy among English classical economists. Marx's jealousy of the enormous success of Mill's *Principles* (1848) was indeed thinly veiled.[16]

But Marx's reply establishes also that he still held on, in his mature years, to the belief of his youth according to which: 'Just as philosophy finds its material weapons in the proletariat, so the proletariat finds its intellectual weapons in philosophy'.[17] And it would not perhaps be too far-fetched after all to claim that, sustaining Marx's lifelong philosophical endeavours, was the conviction (or hope) once expressed by G.W.F. Hegel in a private letter, to the effect that:

'Theoretical work, as I am becoming more convinced everyday, accomplishes more in the world than practical work: once the realm of notions is revolutionized, actuality does not hold out'.[18]

Twentieth-century economic philosophy has been no less clear or emphatic in stressing: (a) the power of general beliefs and opinions to shape action and (b) the power of systematic thinking and persuasion to change them. The 'crisis of our times' and the 'problems of the age', it has often been argued, have philosophical origins. And the implication is that, therefore, they have a philosophical cure.

J. Robinson draws a parallel between the capacity of the human brain to learn language (not only the lexicon but also how to weave words and sentences into a grammatical text) and its capacity to internalize a code of moral values and metaphysical beliefs – an 'ideology' – which is at once highly malleable and no less indispensable in the domain of practical life, whatever its cognitive status may be thought to be. The absence of such a code, suggests Robinson in *Economic Philosophy* (1962), would imply the abolition of human society altogether: 'A society of unmitigated egoists would knock itself to pieces'.[19]

Values change through time and they account for real change in socio-economic life. This is the reason why, as she put it elsewhere, 'to eliminate value judgements from the subject-matter of social science is to eliminate the subject itself, for since it concerns human behaviour it must be concerned with the value judgements that people make'.[20] At the same time, dissenting from the ruling code and trying to disseminate alternative values and beliefs logically implies the recognition of a common ground from where change must take place – a shared 'battlefield' where the challenge must occur if it represents a genuine disagreement rather than being at cross-purposes. For not only is a rebel 'influenced by what he rebels against' but, just as important, he is forced to recognize and understand the object of his rebellion if he has any desire to be successful and turn it to good account.

The task of economic philosophy however, according to Robinson, is *not* trying to set forth any new (or restore some neglected) set of values and beliefs of little or no cognitive worth. Its purpose should be rather to seek after positive knowledge about human agency in order 'to find out the causes, the mode of functioning and the consequences of the adoption of ideologies, so as to submit them to rational criticism'. The challenge, she states, is 'to puzzle out the mysterious way that metaphysical propositions, without any logical content, can yet be a powerful influence on thought and action'.[21]

Thus, she seems to have come nearer to Hume's more positive stance, first by assigning greater emphasis to the need for a better understanding of belief-formation processes, and second by expressing her misgivings about engaging in the business of manufacturing and putting up new values and doctrines for society (or resurrecting old ones). But what distinguishes her position from Hume's, however, is her underlying assumption that the ideas of economists and political philosophers – the unfalsifiable 'ideologies' and 'metaphysical propositions' put forward by a few professional intellectuals – have in fact exerted an overriding influence on the processes of belief-formation and ordinary behaviour in society at large. This latter view, whose *locus classicus* is surely the much quoted concluding paragraph of J.M. Keynes' *General Theory* (1936), has found widespread support in twentieth-century economic philosophy and, as I shall try to show next, its acceptance has cut right across the political spectrum and is by no means peculiar to the Keynesian camp.

In *The Great Depression* – a book published in 1935, just one year before the appearance of Keynes' *General Theory* – L. Robbins addressed the issue of the causes of the economic problems of the inter-war period in Europe and of the prolonged depression of the 1930s. As it is well known, Robbins was by then Keynes' most formidable academic opponent in England. He concluded his work arguing that the real cause of the depression did not have to do with any supposed inherent flaw in the workings of the market mechanism, but could be traced to the self-defeating economic policies and institutions adopted by 'Governments all over the world'. And he maintained further that these policies and institutions were, in turn, the result of the intellectual sway of 'detached and isolated thinkers' over the minds of 'the masses':

The policies which at present prevail have been adopted, not because they have been forced on politicians by the masses, but because the masses have been taught to believe them. The masses, as such, do not think for themselves; they think what they are taught to think by their leaders. And the ideas which, for good or for bad, have come to dominate policy are the ideas which have been put forward in the first instance by detached and isolated thinkers . . . The measures of the last decade have been the result, not of spontaneous pressure by the electorate, but of the influence of a number of men whose names could be counted on the fingers of two hands. We do not appreciate fully the tragedy of this aspect of the present situation unless we realise that it is essentially the work of men of intellect and good will. In the short run, it is true, ideas are unimportant and ineffective, but in the long run they can rule the world.[22]

The resemblance between Robbins' phrasing here and the better-known passage by Keynes (cf. p. 183 below) is simply too strong to be missed. But what should also be noticed is that in his claim that 'ideas rule the world' – as indeed in much of his diagnoses of and prescriptions for the 1930s economic troubles – Robbins was himself following closely in the footsteps of the Austrian neo-liberal school.

The belief that political and economic philosophy – or 'ideology' – works as the overriding factor in the processes of belief-formation and social change runs a distinct thread in the thinking of all leading Austrian neo-liberals. L. von Mises, for example, an early exponent of the movement, had already suggested in his *Liberalism In The Classical Tradition* (1927) that:

The decisive question, therefore, always remains: How does one obtain a majority for one's party? This, however, is a purely intellectual matter. . . In a battle between force and an idea, the latter always prevails . . . It is ideas that group men into fighting factions, that press the weapons into their hands, and that determine against whom and for whom the weapons shall be used. It is they alone, and not arms, that, in the last analysis, turn the scales.[23]

But the most forceful, systematic and committed supporter of this thesis within the neo-liberal tradition has surely been the Austrian economic philosopher F.A. Hayek, the man whom, incidentally, Robbins had brought to teach and work at the London School of Economics in 1933.

It is interesting to observe initially that Hayek, for all his admiration of Hume ('perhaps the greatest of all modern students of mind and society'), in his actual philosophical practice treads a path markedly divergent from that observed by the Scottish thinker.

Like Hume, Hayek declares himself impressed by the change in the opinions of educated men during his lifetime. But whereas Hume, on the one hand, stepped back from normative and prescriptive engagements, and clearly distanced himself from what he called the 'easy and obvious philosophy' engaged in 'alluring us into the paths of virtue by the views of glory and happiness' (1stE,5–6), Hayek, on the other, does not hesitate to plunge into an open and full-blooded moral crusade, aimed at counteracting what he sees as the 'devastating effects' brought about by 'the progressive destruction of irreplaceable values by scientific error'.[24] Indeed, nothing could be farther from the Humean ice-cold, detached standpoint than the Hayekian zeal for convincement, reform and ideological warfare.

Hume, as seen above, had sought to bind himself to the ideal of mental discipline of the Newtonian scientist in order to anatomize the act of believing, i.e. to 'know the different operations of the mind, to separate them from each other [and] to class them under their proper heads' (1stE,13). He had hoped, among other things, to throw some light upon what he considered the most peculiar phenomenon of social life, viz. 'the easiness with which the many are governed by the few'. Nothing, he held, 'appears more surprising' than this, 'to those who consider human affairs with a philosophical eye' (E,32). But his Austrian admirer, on the contrary, is all out for capturing the 'spirit of the age' and by any means ousting from it what he saw as the ruling 'unfounded superstition' of his own generation: 'this belief that processes which are consciously directed are necessarily superior to any spontaneous process'.[25] In his work on political and economic philosophy, Hayek has never refrained from making the very transition from 'is' to 'ought' which Hume thought was the characteristic feature of 'all the vulgar systems of morality' (THN, 469–70).

In point of fact, Hayek's central concern with changing the world makes it a matter of crucial relevance for him to enquire into the ways and mechanisms through which change takes place. And although the substantive goals of his 'holy war' on behalf of the spontaneous order allegedly responsible for the prosperity and freedom of the 'Great Society' surely differ from those informing the utilitarianisms of Paley and Mill (not to speak, of course, of Marx's communism), it is possible to say that Hayek's strategy for changing the world springs from a diagnosis of how change takes place that is substantially in line with the one adopted by his fellow-travellers in the art of seizing the 'spirit of the age' and carving their own opinions and beliefs into it. He musters great conviction when it comes to estimating the power of ideas – i.e. persuasion and the clash of 'ideologies' – in the processes of belief-formation and social change.

'Few contentions meet with such disbelief from most practical men', wrote Hayek in the first volume ('Rules and Order') of *Law, Legislation and Liberty* (1973), 'as that, what is contemptuously dubbed as an ideology, has dominant power over those who believe themselves to be free from it even more than over those who consciously embrace it'. Elaborating on this great – and supposedly unacknowledged – power of 'highly abstract and often unconsciously held ideas' to impinge upon the course of 'social evolution', he added:

It is certainly humbling to have to admit that our present decisions are determined by what happened long ago in a remote specialty without the general public ever knowing about it, and without those who first formulated the new conception being aware of what would be its consequences, particularly when it was not a discovery of new facts but a general philosophical conception which later affected particular decisions.

Finally, he concluded that not only ordinary behaviour but also scientific disciplines fall prey to such general philosophical ideas which, as he put it, 'not only the "men in the street", but also the experts in the particular fields accept unreflecting and in general simply because they happen to be "modern"'.[26]

The normative implication he naturally derives from this account is that 'it is our special duty to recognise the currents of thought which still operate in public opinion, to examine their significance, and, if necessary, to refute them'.[27] In a statement which may be seen as epitomizing the standpoint of Austrian neo-liberalism, K. Popper refers to Hayek and argues that 'we must not underrate the power of the intellect and the intellectuals': 'It was the intellectuals – the "second-hand dealers in ideas", as F.A. Hayek calls them – who spread relativism, nihilism, and intellectual despair. There is no reason why some intellectuals – some more enlightened intellectuals – should not eventually succeed in spreading the good news that the nihilist ado was indeed about nothing'. 'The power of ideas', Popper claimed elsewhere, 'and especially of moral and religious ideas, is at least as important as that of physical resources'.[28]

So, there is a substantial agreement among economic philosophers through time and across the political spectrum regarding the power of ideas to influence the behaviour of agents in socio-economic life. Not all of them, however, and pre-eminently Hume, took this to imply: (a) that philosophical ideas in the long run rule the world, or (b) that normative moral philosophy and a belligerent part in the 'war of ideas' are therefore fruitful and far-reaching intellectual enterprises.

In chapters 6 and 7 below an attempt will be made to bring out the reasons why Hume came to side with the 'majority view' (see epigraph to part I), and so to diverge, on this issue, from the economic philosophers discussed above. As I shall try to argue when discussing the 'enlightened scepticism' of Hume and Adam Smith, there are good reasons to suggest that their views about the existence of a 'natural order', and in particular their emphasis on the role of the 'passions' as determinants of belief, lend support to the alternative view, viz. that the influence exerted by political and economic philosophers and their 'metaphysical propositions' upon the course of human affairs is in effect rather limited.

The following chapters present an outline of the scientific case for the view that the agents' beliefs and opinions, *qua* mental states, are of little or no significance in the explanation of their outward behaviour. Chapter 2 charts the origins of science-based physicalism in the eighteenth-century Enlightenment and the formulation of the 'man-machine' doctrine. Chapter 3 retraces the development of the 'economic man' concept in modern economic science and assesses some conceptual implications of the 'pleasure-machine' construct associated with the advent of neo-classical economics. In chapter 4, I shall try to bring together the argument of the two former chapters, and discuss some logical parallels and contrasts between the 'man-machine' and the 'economic man' concepts. Finally, the remainder of part I (chapters 5, 6 and 7) is devoted to a critical assessment of the economic philosophers' claims regarding the power of their own trade ('ideas') to shape social behaviour and rule the world.

CHAPTER 2

The scientific challenge to economic philosophy, I Physicalism and the birth of the 'man-machine' doctrine: La Mettrie

All these variations, from Paley to Hayek, around the theme 'Ideas rule the world of human affairs and its events', suggest a number of questions. It might be interesting, for example, to examine in more detail the place and the precise function of this specific thesis in the particular intellectual campaign undertaken by each of its diverse proponents. But my main concern here, however, will not be with any particular economic philosophy; what I shall try to do, instead, is to raise a few questions of a more general and philosophical scope, in order to consider not the substantive content but rather the basic assumptions underlying this wide and reasonably clear-cut agreement between economic philosophers. What kinds of arguments or approaches may be brought forward in order to support the alternative view, viz. that ideas and theories have only a very limited effect, if any, in the determination of man's actions?

In this chapter, I will consider some of the most radical attempts to dismiss ideas entirely from the picture and thus to explain human behaviour in purely mechanical terms – the 'man-machine' thesis. The aim is to reconstruct some of the critical moments in the history of the scientific challenges – via increasingly refined *physical* explanations of *all* observed phenomena – to the assumption which first made (and still makes) moral and economic philosophy intellectually viable enterprises. Then, in chapter 3, I shall turn to the history of economics in order to trace out the parallel and belated assimilation of the mechanical model of explanation by the moral sciences, with special reference to the rise of neo-classical economics and the notion of 'economic man'.

The first and most obvious general question suggested by the claims about human action and social change reviewed in chapter 1 is, are they true? And, if so, to what extent? On what grounds would it be possible to argue that the economic philosophers have, in general, just taken for granted and grossly overestimated the influence of ideas in the processes of belief-formation and social change? Most people, the Aristotelian dictum runs, are bad judges in their own case: are economic philosophers any different? Are they not simply trying to enhance the importance of their own trade? And is it not possible to discern, in their claims, an air of self-pleading and self-aggrandizement in front of a world which has been largely indifferent to, and independent of the wares they put up for sale? Is it not the case here that, to borrow Adam Smith's phrasing (EPS,47), they 'naturally explained things to themselves by principles that were familiar to themselves'?

The challenging and toning down of claims regarding the practical implications of *opinions* with respect to human conduct in ordinary life has itself a long tradition. It appears to be in fact directly related to the birth and rise of moral philosophy in Greek thought. Socrates himself, as Plato reports in the *Phaedo*, found it necessary to dismiss what would be a purely physical account of human action in general, and of his own predicament in particular, and to stress, instead, the element of moral autonomy – the choice of what is best – governing his conduct: 'As the Athenians have decided that it is better to condemn me, I for my part have thought it better to sit here, and more right and proper not to run away, but to undergo whatever penalty they may impose'.[1]

Earlier in this same dialogue, Socrates had already described how in his youth, when his mental activity and curiosity – his 'love of truth' – was at its height, he had found himself utterly disappointed and dissatisfied with the mechanistic explanations put forward by the then leading students of *phusis*, that is, of the 'true reasons' (*aitia*) of coming-to-be and of destruction in natural processes. It was basically as a response to this experience of disappointment – 'these marvellous hopes of mine were dashed' (98b–7) – and to the ensuing cognitive dissatisfaction – 'to call such things "reasons" is quite absurd' (99a–5) – that Socrates set off on his 'second voyage' in quest of the 'true reasons' of change and, as a result, came to the formulation of the teleological mode of explanation: essentially, the programme of explaining change in both the natural and the human worlds in terms of ends ('what is best'), i.e. of purposeful and, for mankind, self-given, moral choice.

But the question apparently remained a lively one in Greek philosophy up to the post-Aristotelian period. It is noteworthy, in this respect, that even Epicurus, for all his attack on superstitious beliefs and his adherence to an atomic, thoroughly anti-teleological view of the universe (including man's soul), could not bring himself to accept the stark physical determinism upheld by some of the pre-Socratic Greek atomists.

'Opinion says hot and cold', held the early Greek atomist philosopher Democritus, 'but the reality is atoms and empty space'. For the Epicureans, however, even the mild fatalism of popular religion would be preferable to the doctrine of absolute determinism and the principle according to which human ideas and decisions are mere epiphenomena, that is, essentially idle in the physical world and incapable of altering the necessary and unbreakable course of events: 'For, indeed, it were better to follow the myths about the gods than to become a slave of the destiny of natural philosophers: for the former suggests a hope of placating the gods by worship, whereas the latter involves a necessity which knows no placation'.[2]

The Epicurean way out of the deterministic implications of early Greek atomism, it may be interesting to note, which took the form of an obscure and *ad hoc* proviso that atoms do not necessarily fall in a 'straight line' but may also 'swerve' slightly and deviate from the 'fated' linear path, constituted the central topic tackled by Marx in his doctoral thesis contrasting the Democritean and the Epicurean philosophies of nature. The very early Marx – 'human self-consciousness [is] the highest divinity' – warmly supported the Epicurean standpoint and defended it from its ancient and modern detractors. For it was through the hypothesis of the swerving of the atom from the straight line, he held, that Epicurus had in effect provided a much needed loophole for human autonomy within the materialist camp. He had thus vindicated the precedence of ethics (human self-given ends) over physics (the realm of 'blind necessity' to be mastered and made subservient to human good).[3]

The scientific achievements of seventeenth-century physics, which were partly inspired by a revival of interest in early Greek atomism and Epicurean philosophy, obviously did much to encourage increasingly sophisticated attempts to explain human action without having recourse to the supposed beliefs, desires, intentions and moral judgements of the agents. Why not extend to the study of living creatures the methods and mode of abstraction which had proved so fruitful in explaining and predicting physical phenomena ranging from the movements of the heavenly bodies to local motion and the reflection of light? The eighteenth-century Enlightenment, as it will be seen, went further and used the growth of scientific knowledge as an antidote against the poison of enforced theological dogma and arbitrary authority in matters of belief.

Already in the first half of the seventeenth century, R. Descartes made a move to investigate 'dumb animals' as if they differed from the artefacts produced by engineers not in character but only in degree. 'I am not disturbed by the astuteness and cunning of dogs and foxes, or all the things which animals do for the sake of food, sex, and fear', he wrote in a reply to the Cambridge Platonist H. More in 1649. 'Thought in animals', Descartes conceded, cannot be disproved or otherwise, 'since the human mind does not reach into their hearts'. But at the same time, he went on to argue (rejecting implicitly More's attempt to vindicate Platonism and the notion of 'anima mundi' or 'spirit of nature' as an explanatory principle in the study of living natural bodies), 'it seems reasonable, since art copies nature, and men can make various automata which move without thought, that nature should produce its own automata, much more splendid than artificial ones. These natural automata are the animals'.[4]

What Descartes made of 'dumb animals' – i.e. those capable of experiencing and communicating sensation, but not of 'real speech' in the sense of 'indicating by word or sign something pertaining to pure thought' – would soon be made of man. 'My opinion is not so much cruel to animals as indulgent to men', he pointed out to More, since seeing the former as automata at least acquitted the latter 'from the suspicion of crime when they eat or kill animals'.[5] But others, of course, were not prepared to display the same indulgence towards man, at least in the sense of granting him that privileged uniqueness which he still possessed in the Cartesian system, thanks to the 'thinking substance' ('res cogitans') he was presumed to encapsulate.

It is worth noting that a roughly similar metaphysical dualism can also be found in the Baconian campaign for the regeneration of the empirical sciences on pragmatic grounds. 'If a man meditate much upon the universal frame of nature', wrote Bacon in a revealing passage of *The Advancement of Learning* (1605), 'the earth with man upon it (the divineness of souls except) will not seem much other than an anthill, whereas some ants carry corn, and some other their young, and some go empty, and all to and fro a little heap of dust'.

Bacon's short parenthesis, in this passage, on the soul of man as being 'immediately inspired from God', is no less significant than his striking insect metaphor. The view clearly conveyed here is that, as he put it, '[no man can] marvel at the play of puppets, that goeth behind the curtain, and adviseth well of the motion'.[6] But although scientific knowledge ('going behind the curtains') undermines our primitive enchantment with natural phenomena ('the play of puppets'), still the special metaphysical status of the human soul or mind redeems the whole business by bringing practical improvement to the anthill. The task ahead is the science-based recreation – through technology – of the Garden of Eden, and Bacon's most distinguished seventeenth-century follower, the experimental scientist R. Boyle, was very much in tune with the spirit of the Baconian philosophy when he declared himself 'disposed to think the soul of man a nobler and more valuable being, than the whole corporeal world'. 'Beasts', it followed, 'inhabit and enjoy the world; man, if he will do more, must study and spiritualize it'.[7]

But of course science would not stop where the Baconian and the Cartesian breakthroughs had left it. One of the obvious ways out of the uneasy metaphysical dualism postulated by the Cartesian system was precisely to make away with the intractable 'res cogitans' by explaining it as yet another outcome of the combination of certain types of motion obtaining in ordinary extended matter ('res extensa'). This move, pioneered in England by T. Hobbes in direct opposition to the Cartesian split,[8] paved the way to an analysis of the human mind and psychology from a strict materialist – i.e. physico-chemical or, in current terminology, neurophysiological – standpoint.

A further and radical step in the transition from the 'beast-machine' to the 'man-machine' was carried out in the eighteenth century by the French materialist 'philosophe' J.O. de la Mettrie, author of *L'Homme Machine* (1747). A physician by training, but thoroughly educated in metaphysics and aware of his debt to the iatrochemistry school (from *iatros*: physician) and to Cartesian biology, he maintained that 'from animals to men the transition is not violent': 'Man is a machine, and there is nothing in the entire universe but a single substance diversely modified'.[9] The basic idea is to see human beings and their actions as objects and events in the physical world, that is there to be described and accounted for, like all the rest, in purely objective terms; in terms in which moral thinking and mental processes in general – the agent's subjective experiences – have no place.

The sixteenth- and seventeenth-century pioneers of modern

science had laid great stress on the principles of simplicity (*Natura simplicitatem amat*) and of parsimony (*Natura semper agit per vias brevissimas*) as guiding or regulative principles of the scientific understanding. In the eighteenth century, the principle of continuity (*Natura non facit saltum*) finds a place with the two others, and begins to make its fruitfulness and directive power felt in scientific research. The Cartesian 'bifurcation of nature', reserving for the human soul a privileged, unique and ultimately bewildering place in an otherwise thoroughly mechanical physical universe, did not seem a satisfactory foundation for the project of furthering the scientific understanding of man. The task ahead, it was held, was to carry through the total elimination of anthropocentric myopia from the understanding of natural phenomena, so as to eventually deanthropomorphize man's self-understanding itself.

La Mettrie and other enlightened French materialists like Baron d'Holbach, author of *Système de la Nature* (1770), held the view that all psychological phenomena from sensation and feeling to memory and highly abstract thinking have determinate physiological causes and are properties of organized matter in the same way as other physical phenomena, like, for example, weight, magnetism or electricity are properties of inert matter. As d'Holbach put it, building on La Mettrie's path-breaking work, 'Man always makes himself the centre of the universe', but in reality, he went on, 'everything he does, everything that passes within himself, are the effects of inert force, of self-gravitation, of the attractive or repulsive powers contained in his machine':

Man occupies a place amidst that crowd, that multitude of beings, of which nature is the assemblage . . . His life itself is nothing more than a long series, a succession of necessary and connected motion, which operates perpetual and continual changes in his machine; which has for its principle either causes contained within himself, such as blood, nerves, fibres, flesh, bones, in short, the matter, as well solid as fluid, of which his body is composed – or those exterior causes, which, by acting upon him, modify him diversely; such as the air with which he is encompassed, the aliments by which he is nourished, and all those objects from which he receives any impulse whatever by the impression they make on his senses.[10]

One of the consequences of the 'man-machine' concept was a complete reassessment of the nature of language. The assembling of 'a being with the power of speech' ceases to be regarded (as in the Cartesian philosophy) as a metaphysical impossibility, and starts to be seen as a feasible project, hanging solely on the ingenuity and dexterity of the artificer. Moreover, the moral autonomy of human beings is explained away as a delusion analogous to the one indulged in by St Francis in the thirteenth century, when he preached to flowers, stones, worms and bees, calling them 'brothers' and urging them to join in and 'praise the Lord'. 'A man as he ought to be' sounds to La Mettrie, the physician, as insipid as, say, 'a tree as it ought to be'.

In *L'Homme Plante* (his first work exploring the consequences of the 'man-machine' philosophy for morals and for the individual in society), La Mettrie pointed to the basic structural and physiological similarity of the human, the animal and the vegetable machines, in order to sustain the view that the traditional 'chain of being' concept – asserting the principles of continuity and plenitude in the natural world – should be interpreted not after seventeenth-century neo-Platonic rationalism, but in a materialist way, that is, according to the model of scientific explanation Descartes had deployed and worked up in his physics.

The implications he derived from this move were severe: remorse and guilt, no less than fear of eternal punishment and Hell and other religion-inspired terrors, were to be seen as absurd notions, and discarded as causes of idle suffering. Medicine – meaning here straightforward psychiatric, drug-based therapy – should become, in this context, the key to morality and the prevention of social anomy, and all criminal judges, accordingly, should be qualified physicians: 'I am, and I am proud of it, a zealous citizen; but it is not in this quality that I write, it is as a philosopher; as such, I see that Cartouche was Cartouche and Pyrrhus, Pyrrhus: counsels are useless to one born with a thirst for carnage and blood'.[11] As d'Holbach were to put it, following closely (and eloquently) in La Mettrie's footsteps, 'had man fairly studied himself, everything should convince him that during every moment of his life he is but a passive instrument in the hands of necessity':

[Man's] birth depends on causes entirely outside of his power; it is without his permission that he enters this system where he has a place; and without his consent that, from the moment of his birth to the day of his death, he is continually modified by causes that influence his machine in spite of his will, modify his being, and alter his conduct. Is it not the least reflection enough to prove that the solids and fluids of which the body is composed, and that the hidden mechanism that he considers independent of external causes, are perpetually under the influence of these causes, and could not act without them? Does he not see that his temperament does not depend on himself, that his passions are the necessary consequences of his temperament, that his will and his actions are determined by these same passions, and by opinions which he has not given to himself? His blood more or less heated or abundant, his nerves more or less braced, his fibres more or less relaxed, give him dispositions either transitory or durable, which are at every moment decisive of his ideas, of his desires, of his fears, of his motion, whether visible or concealed.[12]

Thus, according to this view, the Cartesian dualism is to give way to a strictly materialist monism. Mechanical causation overrules the teleological explanation of behaviour. And 'moral man' – the offspring of man's self-conceit before nature – drops, sinks and melts away into the 'physical man'.

It is not surprising, given the radicalism and awkwardness of this picture, to find that it provoked equally strong and odd reactions. The German poet and naturalist J.W. von Goethe, for example, on first reading d'Holbach's work by the end of the eighteenth century, recoiled in disgust at its contents. In his autobiography, he recalls how he and his friends had once turned to the *Système de la Nature* in search for knowledge about the natural world but then had found themselves utterly disappointed:

We did not fathom how such a book could be dangerous. To us it seemed so gray, so Cimmerian, so deathly that we could scarcely bear the sight of it and shuddered as though it were a ghost . . . The word 'freedom' has such a lovely sound that we could not have dispensed with it even if it denoted an error. Not one of us finished the book, for the expectations we had upon it were disappointed.[13]

Their reaction, we may note, parallels to a certain extent the young Socrates' rejection of early Greek atomism and More's misgivings about the Cartesian 'natural automata'. But the most explosive and symptomatic reception was no doubt the one afforded to La Mettrie's 'ghost'.

The publication of *L'Homme Machine* in late 1747 immediately set in motion a remarkable flow of angry (and no less revealing) intellectual reactions in Europe.[14] The author – probably anticipating the adverse furore that his rather outspoken and provocative scientific pamphlet was bound to raise – had taken careful measures to preserve his anonymity. But his Dutch publishers, though going as far as to claim ignorance of the author's name in the 'Avertissement de l'imprimeur' which opens the book, had to bear the brunt not only of religious intolerance (in this case the united efforts of the Calvinist, Catholic and Lutheran Churches) but also of official persecution. The book was immediately banned in France and copies burnt by Protestants – who were known in those days for their 'tolerance' in matters of belief – in a public square of The Hague. The publishers were summoned by the Dutch authorities and compelled to give up for destruction all the available copies, disclose the identity of the author (which they apparently refused to do on the grounds of ignorance), and to apologize for having made public the work, while committing themselves never to relapse.

When the authorship of the book finally came to light in early 1748, La Mettrie, who was already an exiled dissident from France, was expelled from his adopted country, Holland. He then sought and found refuge as a physician-philosopher serving in the 'enlightened court' of Frederick the Great in Potsdam (Prussia). There, he enjoyed for a while time to speculate further on the moral and political implications of the scientific understanding of man and also to defend himself from some of the charges and misunderstandings provoked by his little book. But, in spite of the King's protection, his *Oeuvres Philosophiques* (1751) were banned by the Prussian censors as well, and in less than three years after his moving to Potsdam he died. (The very peculiar circumstances surrounding his death – 'At the home of the French ambassador to Prussia, Lord Tyrconnel, whom he had recently cured of a troublesome ailment, La Mettrie consumed a prodigious amount of "pate de faisan aux truffes", fell gravely ill, and died a few days later', – would be exploited to the full by his eighteenth-century enemies. Such an end, thought many of his religious and lay opponents, represented somehow a fitting practical conclusion to the line of reasoning set forth in the pages of *L'Homme Machine*, and, while some of them saw in his death the punishment reserved for atheists, others preferred to believe that it exemplified the 'natural penalties' associated with *libertinage* and lack of moderation: an illustration of Bishop Butler's contention that 'the effects of a dissolute course of pleasure are often mortal'.)

The striking oddity of La Mettrie's position in the history of ideas deserves to be noted. Exiled from two countries and censored in nearly all of the European continent, he typifies a somewhat familiar figure in the 'war of ideas': the man who finds himself victimized not for anything he *did*, but for holding and propagating undesirable views and opinions. The intellectual persecuted on account of writings which are felt (and feared) by members of the theological, academic and/or political establishments as 'dangerous' and potentially subversive of the social order.

The irony in his particular case, however, is that one of the logical implications of his mechanical picturization of the workings of the human mind was precisely the notion that it is pretty foolish to suppress speculative opinions, however unorthodox, if only because (as a La Mettrie scholar has put it) 'they had almost no practical effect either on existing moral notions or on social behaviour'.[15] Thus La Mettrie came to clash, as a victim, with one of the very beliefs – viz., in the power of ideas to subvert human institutions – which his philosophy was set on refuting.

In his so-called 'philosophical testament', the essay 'Discours preliminaire' which opens his suppressed 1751 *Oeuvres Philosophiques*, La Mettrie defended his scientific views and contributions by concentrating precisely on the thesis of the practical innocuity of all – including of course his own – philosophical speculation or what he called 'l'innocence de la Philosophie'. Scientific writers, he argued, may prove as well as it can be proved that human beings are essentially automatic machines, and that each individual mind is like a self-performing piano listening to (and amused by) its own playing. Yet practical men, i.e. the ordinary 'citoyen' as opposed to the 'philosophe', will never believe in this; for the same instinct which binds them to life, food and sexual reproduction will endow them with enough vanity to seal off and sustain at any price the belief that the destiny of the human soul is in some way special. It is therefore mistaken (and even ridiculous) to blame the 'philosophes' for effects which are completely beyond their power to bring about:

I believe that I have proved that remorse is a prejudice instilled by education, and that Man is a machine subject to an imperious and absolute fatalism. I may have been mistaken, as I would like to believe: but supposing, as I sincerely believe, that this is philosophically true, and so what? All these questions belong to the same category as the mathematical point, which does not exist save in the head of the geometers.

'Let us not fear then', La Mettrie went on to conclude, 'that the minds of the "peuple" should ever mould themselves upon those of the "philosophes", which are too far above their reach'.[16]

The interesting thing about this position is that, in his attempt to minimize the power of ethics, metaphysics and ideas in general over men's beliefs and feelings, La Mettrie surely was not as isolated as he had been, at least in his own time, in his adherence to a strict form of physicalism. For at least on this point his views were shared by other leading members of the European Enlightenment, even if (as discussed in chapter 6 below) their reasons for doing so were essentially distinct and did not depend on the extreme form of mechanical materialism he had pioneered and advocated.

Thus Voltaire, for example, though rejecting La Mettrie's atheism and rigid scientific mechanism, had already argued in his *Lettre Philosophique* on Locke (1733) to the effect that philosophical writings and theories had little or no influence on what ordinary people believe or how they behave. 'Divide the human race into twenty parts', suggested Voltaire:

Nineteen of them are composed of those who work with their hands, and will never know whether there is a Locke in the world or not. In the remaining twentieth part how few men do we find who read! And among those who do read there are twenty who read novels for one who studies philosophy. The number of those who think is exceedingly small, and they are not aiming to disturb the world.[17]

La Mettrie's rather crude physicalism may thus be seen as only one of the roads leading to 'l'innocence de la Philosophie' thesis in eighteenth-century thought.

In chapter 4, I shall consider in more detail some logical implications of the physicalist doctrine associated with the growth of science, referring to more recent views on the subject by leading scientists, economists and philosophers of science and asking how far the 'man-machine' construct may be said to fit in with the 'economic man' of modern economics. But before that, in chapter 3, I shall examine the mechanization of human agency in the evolution of economic theory and the conceptual prearrangement underlying the idea of economics as a 'mechanics of utility and self-interest'.

The scientific challenge to economic philosophy, II Economics and the rise of 'economic man': Jevons and Edgeworth

Modern economic enquiry, as I shall try to show in this chapter, did not remain aloof from the scientific developments outlined in the last chapter. But there was, however, a considerable time-lag. The eighteenth-century founders of modern economics, F. Quesnay and Adam Smith, still kept their accounts of human behaviour as essentially distinct from the explanations of natural processes modelled after the achievements of seventeenth-century physics. It was only by the last quarter of the nineteenth century, with the advent of the Jevonian 'mechanics of utility and self-interest', that the mechanical model of explanation of human behaviour made a decisive headway in the province of economics.

It is highly probable that Adam Smith had no other than La Mettrie in mind when, in his important posthumous essay on the psychology of scientific discovery illustrated by the history of astronomy (1795), he referred to 'a learned physician' who, as he put it, 'lately gave a system of moral philosophy upon the principles of his own art, in which wisdom and virtue were the healthful state of the soul; the different vices and follies, the different diseases to which it was subject; in which the causes and symptoms of those diseases were ascertained; and, in the same medical strain, a proper method of cure prescribed' (EPS,47).[1] Doing this, held Smith, was no doubt consonant with our spontaneous tendency to reduce the unknown to the already known and to explain anything that appears to us surprising or strange by referring it back to those principles with which we are most familiar. But it was also carrying much too far, and in a clumsy way, the use of analogy in scientific thinking.

Another 'learned physician' of the French Enlightenment was of course Quesnay, the surgeon and distinguished medical practitioner in the court of Louis XV to whom Adam Smith seemingly intended to dedicate the *Wealth of Nations* (1776).[2] But, as it will be presently seen, the leader of the physiocrats (the first school of thought in the history of economics) surely left no doubts concerning his belief in the moral autonomy of economic agents.

The key passage comes up in the third chapter of the essay in which Quesnay had set out to present the philosophical foundations of the economics of physiocracy, 'Observations sur le droit naturel des hommes réunis en société' (1765). 'Freedom, that inherent attribute of man', he maintained, '[is] the intellectual faculty which examines and weighs up objects in accordance with the disposition of the mind'. It was not arbitrary choice, i.e. choice which is supposedly independent of the motives operating upon the will, and it was not the satisfaction of appetite, or even the multiplying of the means by which appetite may be satisfied, i.e. standing face to face with a wider range of possible objects from which to choose. Indeed, he stated: 'It is in this [latter] sense that uncultured men concern themselves only with extending further and further the use of their freedom, and with satisfying their passions with as little discernment as moderation'.

On the contrary, freedom for Quesnay was the choice of what is best: the exercise of deliberation, discernment and moderation in order to arbitrate between the motives operating upon the will. It did not necessarily conduce to the best course of action, and it may be used improperly by men. A few people, he conceded, are altogether incapable of exercising it, due to physical causes – 'any man who is mad owing to the faulty structure of his brain is in the power of a *physical law* which does not allow him to make the best choice or to conduct himself wisely'. But in his dealings with the 'laws of nature', he went on to state,

The man endowed with intelligence has the special privilege of being able to contemplate and understand them, so as to draw from them the greatest possible benefit, avoiding any rebellion against these supreme laws and rules . . . The natural order which is most advantageous to men is perhaps not the most advantageous to the other animals; but included in man's unlimited right is that of making his lot the best possible.[3]

The overriding concern of the physiocrat school was to ensure that the 'moral order' and the 'positive laws' of society would conform to, rather than clash with, the 'natural order which is most advantageous to men'.

Thus, obedience to 'Nature', that is to say, conformity to the way of life to which the *Phusis* (Latin: *Natura*) herself would point her finger – hence the name 'physiocrats', i.e. adherents to the rule of Nature – is only one of the many courses of action open to man: a 'special privilege' and 'unlimited right' which rational beings should not miss. Ignorance of this 'natural order' was the root cause of public and private distress, seeing that 'transgressions of natural laws are the most widespread and usual causes of the physical evils that afflict men'. And this is the reason why, according to Quesnay and his school, the 'private and public instruction in the laws of the natural order' would form the basis of a good society, for 'without this fundamental institution', the argument ran, 'governments and the conduct of men can be characterized only by obscurity, aberration, confusion and disorder'.[4]

It must also be noted that in his last revision of *The Theory of Moral Sentiments*, published just before his death in 1790, Adam Smith maintained his criticism of B. de Mandeville's attempt to posit an abstract, undifferentiated and all-explaining concept of individual self-love in order to account for both selfish and *prima facie* altruistic forms of human behaviour in private and public life.

The problem with this 'in almost every respect erroneous' doctrine of 'Private Vices, Publick Benefits' – as in the subtitle of the satire through which Mandeville made popular his 'licentious system' – was that it blurred all distinction between moral and non-moral action, while ascribing to egocentric 'self-love' an absolute and irremissable primacy upon human behaviour. 'All public spirit, therefore', argued Smith, 'all preference of public to private interest, is, according to him [Mandeville], a mere cheat and imposition upon mankind; and that human virtue which is so much boasted of, and which is the occasion of so much emulation among men, is the mere offspring of flattery begot upon pride' (TMS,309).[5]

Adam Smith rejected this doctrine outright. He maintained that there exists such a thing as genuinely moral action, and that even self-love itself may frequently be a virtuous, praiseworthy motive of behaviour. His argument here, as elsewhere, bears the stamp of the Aristotelian tradition in ethical thought. The good man ought to act out of self-love, since by so doing he will benefit both himself and his fellow-citizens, and 'love of virtue', as Smith says, is 'the noblest and the best passion in human nature'. But the wicked man should not be a lover of self, for in this way 'he will hurt both himself and his neighbours, following as he does evil passions'.[6] (In the Aristotelian view of the 'good life', happiness is primarily a function of moral virtue and intellectual fulfilment ('goods of the mind'), but a role is also given to the possession of 'external goods', like good birth, wealth and connections with people holding positions of power; pleasure is part of the good life and external goods are seen as instrumental in the execution of good deeds. Thus we have (a) a qualification of the more austere and lofty Platonic view, where external goods have no place, and (b) a partial reconciliation between self-interested activities – e.g. the pursuit of external goods – and the good life for man.)

By freezing, as he had done, the concept of individual self-love, and then crowning it with tyrannical powers upon our ordinary behaviour, Mandeville had in effect blocked the road of moral enquiry (knowledge of good and evil), and hence ruled out any possibility of discriminating good, really praise-worthy behaviour from, say, the conduct of that most typical (i.e. 'obvious and vulgar') of the Smithian actors, the man who is eager to outshine economically his fellow-men and 'who sets his character upon the frivolous ornaments of dress and equipage, or upon the equally frivolous accomplishments of ordinary behaviour' (TMS,309).

'It is the great fallacy of Dr. Mandeville's book', summed up Adam Smith, 'to represent every passion as wholly vicious, which is so in any degree and in any direction'. Yet for all that, he then pondered, it was far from clear what had been the real impact of his 'licentious' moral philosophy on men's lives, and one should take care not to overestimate it. 'Such', he finally concluded, 'is the system of Dr Mandeville, which once made so much noise in the world, and which, though, perhaps, it never gave occasion to more vice than what would have been without it, at least taught that vice, which arose from other causes, to appear with more affrontery, and to avow the corruption of its motives with a profligate audaciousness which had never been heard before' (TMS,312–3). A conclusion no doubt worthy, one might add, of the philosopher who had stated in Book V of the *Wealth of Nations* (drawing here explicitly on his extensive classical background), that 'there is nothing so absurd which has not sometimes been asserted by some philosophers' (WN,876).[7]

By the beginning of the nineteenth century the pressure to simplify and mechanize human behaviour in economic thought was clearly on the rise. Introducing his *Principles of Political Economy* (1820), T.R. Malthus was already finding it necessary to stress that 'the science of political economy bears a nearer resemblance to the science of morals and politics than to that of mathematics'. He objected to the 'precipitate attempt to simplify and generalize' prevailing 'at present among the scientific writers on political economy' – D. Ricardo's main theoretical work had been published three years earlier – and justified this statement by drawing attention to the fact that economic actions lacked the relative regularity of ordinary physical phenomena inasmuch as they depended 'upon the agency of so variable a being as man, and the qualities of so variable a compound as the soil'.[8] And nearly two decades later J.S. Mill would remark about his former private tutor, Bentham, that 'man, that most complex being, is a very simple one in his eyes' (CW10,96).

The young Mill, it is true, in his 1830 essay on economic method, had gone a long way towards 'economic man' in his attempt to examine and vindicate the tacit premiss permeating Ricardian economics – the assumption that no motive of action other than the desire for material gain and capital accumulation need be much considered by the economic scientist. This, he argued, was no more than a hypothetical premiss, and 'no political economist was ever so absurd as to suppose that mankind are really thus constituted'. Yet the 'desire for wealth' and the primacy of the money-motive in ordinary economic transactions, he insisted, were in effect 'the nearest to truth' of all equally simple starting-points for abstract economic analysis, and were therefore able to provide 'a nearer approximation' in theory, than would otherwise be feasible, 'to the real order' of our economic affairs.[9]

But by the time he got down to the composition of his own economic treatise, the epoch-making *Principles of Political Economy* (1848), Mill had already moved a long way from both, the orthodox Ricardianism and the crude Benthamite utilitarianism he had been forced to swallow in his boyhood and early youth. In particular, he had grown out of the rigid adherence to the assumption of Ricardian 'economic man' which he had so eagerly tried to justify in his early programmatic essay. And as a result (as Marshall very perceptively pointed out), in his own *Principles* Mill 'made no attempt to mark off by a rigid line those reasonings which assume that man's sole motive is the pursuit of wealth from those which do not' (PEc,632n).

So, in Book I ('Production') of that work, for example, Mill explained the marked propensity of the English middle classes to save and accumulate by referring to non-economic factors including, in the case of England, 'that extreme incapacity of the people for personal enjoyment which is characteristic of countries over which puritanism has passed' (CW2,171). And in Book IV ('Influence of the Progress of Society on Production and Distribution'), he not only advocated the cessation of economic growth and capital accumulation, on the grounds that 'It is only in the backward countries of the world that increased production is still [1848] an important object: in those most advanced, what is economically needed is a better distribution', but he went on to dare to assess the money-motive at its true value, evoking first the formidable economic advantages and achievements of the northern states of the United States and then remarking that, though 'they have no poverty', yet 'all that these advantages seem to have yet done for them is that the life of the whole of one sex is devoted to dollar-hunting, and of the other to breeding dollar-hunters' (CW3,754-5).[10]

Mill's perception of the 'restless spirit of the Americans in the midst of their prosperity', it may be noted, had much in common with the remarks made by the French political philosopher A. de Tocqueville in *Democracy in America* (1835):

A native of the United States clings to this world's goods as if he were certain never to die; and he is so hasty in grasping at all within his reach, that one would suppose he was constantly afraid of not living long enough to enjoy them. He clutches everything, he holds nothing fast, but soon loosens his grasp to pursue fresh gratifications. In the United States a man builds a house to spend his latter years in it, and he sells it before the roof is on: he plants a garden, and lets it just as the trees are coming into bearing: he brings a field into tillage, and leaves other men to gather the crops: he embraces a profession, and gives it up: he settles in a place, which he soon afterwards leaves, to carry his changeable longings elsewhere . . . Death at length overtakes him, but it is before he is weary of his bootless chase of that complete felicity which is for ever on the wing.[11]

But what is distinctive about the Millian stance is his trust that 'mental cultivation' and the 'moral education' of agents would bring about the desired change, i.e. a society approaching to the 'all equal and cultivated' goal. The prospect of the future, held Mill referring to the labouring classes, 'depends on the degree in which they can be made rational beings': 'The progress indeed has hitherto been, and still is, slow. But there is a spontaneous education going on in the minds of the multitude, which may be greatly accelerated and improved by artificial aids' (CW3,763). Furthermore, he added:

In the present stage of human progress, when ideas of equality are daily spreading more widely among the poorer classes, and can no longer be checked by anything short of the entire suppression of printed discussion and even of freedom of speech, it is not to be expected that the division of the human race into two hereditary classes, employers and employed, can be permanently maintained. (CW3,766–7)

Thus, and oddly enough, the work which is still seen by many as a classic in the liberal tradition and to which 'the bourgeoisie', as J. Schumpeter observed, 'accorded such a [favourable] reception', actually 'carried a socialist message and was written by a man palpably out of sympathy with the scheme of values of the industrial bourgeoisie'.[12]

But the central point to stress is that Mill, unlike Adam Smith, never expressed serious doubts about the power and efficacy of ideas, philosophical campaign and moral persuasion. Smith, as just seen, rejected the Mandevillian 'licentious' and wrong-headed dismissal of moral philosophy and vigorously objected to what he saw as its attempt to explain away the reality of moral conduct by positing an all-ruling and homogeneous 'self-love'. But he was also careful to suggest that the amount of 'vice' in our ordinary behaviour may not have (and probably had not) increased a hair's breadth on account of this doctrine 'which once made so much noise in the world'. If virtue cannot be taught, neither can vice. (The philosophy of action underlying this notion shall be examined in chapters 6 and 7 below.)

Similarly, in the *Wealth of Nations*, Smith had argued: (a) that the single most important factor accounting for the economic prosperity and the 'progress of opulence' in civilized nations, viz. the division of labour and the associated process of technical change, had been the 'result of human action, but not the execution of any human design':

This division of labour, from which so many advantages are derived, is not originally the effect of any human wisdom, which foresees and intends that general opulence to which it gives occasion. It is the necessary, though very slow and gradual consequence of a certain propensity in human nature which has in view no such extensive utility; the propensity to truck, barter, and exchange one thing for another. (WN,25)[13]

And (b), he suggested that, even though human institutions and wrong-headed systems of political economy could eventually 'thwart' or retard the 'natural inclinations of man' and the 'natural course of things', their real effect was limited and should not be overestimated.

'The natural course of things', as Smith put it in the *Theory of Moral Sentiments*, 'cannot be entirely controlled by the impotent endeavours of man: the current is too rapid and too strong for him to stop it' (TMS,168):

The uniform, constant, and uninterrupted effort of every man to better his condition, the principle from which publick and national, as well as private opulence is originally derived, is frequently powerful enough to maintain the natural progress of things toward improvement, in spite both of the extravagance of government, and of the greatest errors of administration. Like the unknown principle of animal life, it frequently restores health and vigour to the constitution, in spite, not only of disease, but of the absurd prescriptions of the doctor (WN,343) . . . in the political body, the natural effort which every man is continually making to better his own condition, is a principle of preservation capable of preventing and correcting, in many respects, the bad effects of a political economy, in some degree, both partial and oppressive. Such a political oeconomy, though it no doubt retards more or less, is not always capable of stopping altogether the natural progress of a nation towards wealth and prosperity, and still less of making it go backwards. If a nation could not prosper without the enjoyment of perfect liberty and perfect justice, there is not in the world a nation which could ever have prospered. In the political body, however, the wisdom of nature has fortunately made ample provision for remedying many of the bad effects of the folly and injustice of man; in the same manner as it has done in the natural body, for remedying those of his sloth and intemperance. (WN,674)

It is perfectly consistent with this view that, in his criticism of the 'agricultural system of political oeconomy' put forward by Quesnay and his school, Smith took great care not to overstate the practical consequences of its theoretical shortcomings. He described the economics of physiocracy, much as he had depicted Mandeville's ethical thought, as a doctrine which 'at present exists only in the speculations of a few men of great learning and ingenuity in France . . . a system which never has done, and probably never will do any harm in any part of the world' (WN,663).

But Mill, on the contrary, amplified as much as he seems to have been able to the reality of the practical mischief resulting from mistaken views in ethics and political economy. Thus, criticizing Bentham's persistent confusion of individual interest with the selfish, 'purely self-regarding' principles of action in human nature, he went on to argue:

By the promulgation of such views of human nature, and by a general tone of thought and expression perfectly in harmony with them, I conceive Mr

Bentham's writings to have done and to be doing very serious evil . . . It is difficult to form the conception of a tendency more inconsistent with all rational hope of good for the human species, than that which must be impressed by such doctrines, upon any mind in which they find acceptance. (CW10,15)

Conversely, as seen above (chapter 1), Mill had also gone out of his way to stress the overriding power of philosophy to promote socio-economic reform. And in his mature economic writings he did not forsake his ethical thought by remaking man ('that most complex being') as a Benthamite 'push-pin playing simpleton'. As he made clear in his discussion of property-rights and in his advocacy of the stationary state in the *Principles*, he believed (i) that self-interest is not always enlightened or equivalent to selfish behaviour, and (ii) that opinions of interest were liable to being altered and deflected in the desired direction through rational and moral arguments. Agents were not to be seen as essentially unresponsive or immune to enlightened assaults.

So it was not until the last quarter of the nineteenth century, with the reaction against Millian orthodoxy led in England by W.S. Jevons, and with the rise of neo-classical economics, that a full-blooded 'economic man' – in some limited respects analogous to the 'man-machine' concept – finally set a more permanent and definite foot in the province of economics.

True, Ricardo and some of his followers, as Marshall pointed out, had worked out their economic theories 'on the tacit supposition that the world was made up of City men': They regarded man as, so to speak, a constant quantity, and gave themselves little trouble to study his variations. The people whom they knew were chiefly City men; and they took it for granted tacitly that other Englishmen were very much like those they knew in the City'.[14] But Mill had put aside this Ricardian assumption, and Marshall himself still believed that, in modern economic science, 'the human as distinct from the mechanical element is taking a more and more prominent place'. Economists, he suggested, were 'getting to pay every year a greater attention to the pliability of human nature, and to the way in which the character of man affects and is affected by the prevalent methods of the production, distribution and consumption of wealth' (PEc,631–2). As I shall try to argue in the remainder of this chapter (and most of the next one) it would be hard to conceive of a more erroneous prediction.

In his early 1862 paper setting out the foundations for a 'general mathematical theory of political economy', Jevons had already been very clear and straightforward about what he thought was needed. 'A true theory of [political] economy', he wrote, hinting at the Benthamite framework of his proposal, 'can only be attained by going back to the great springs of human action – the feelings of pleasure and pain'. 'There are motives', he conceded, 'nearly always present with us, arising from conscience, compassion, or from some moral or religious source'. But these, he went on to say, are motives which a general mathematical theory of economics 'cannot and does not pretend to treat': 'These will remain to us as outstanding and disturbing forces; they must be treated, if at all, by other appropriate branches of knowledge'.[15]

It was through this conceptual move, I shall now argue, and the consequent specialization of 'pure theory' on the 'economic man' assumption as defined by Jevons, that the mathematical working up of the 'mechanics of utility and self-interest' became a viable research programme in economics. The leading motive and some of the peculiar features of this move are perhaps nowhere clearer than in the idea of a 'Mecanique Sociale' put forward by F.Y. Edgeworth in his *Mathematical Psychics: An Essay on the Application of Mathematics to the Moral Sciences* (1881).

The fundamental aim of the work – as the full title bears out – was to explore the possibilities of mathematical handling with respect to the subject-matter of the moral sciences, i.e. human practical conduct. Edgeworth's own justification for this aim was that the mathematical treatment of human action in socio-economic life would allow for a more precise statement and tackling of the utilitarian problem: 'the realisation of the maximum sum-total of happiness', where happiness is defined as equivalent to the units of pleasure-intensity experienced by each agent during a unit of time.

However, the costs of increasing a certain form of precision and analytical sharpness in this context are, as we shall presently see, far from negligible. For the application of the mathematical tools of physics to the analysis of our economic transactions exacts a formidable price from the moral scientist. In short, it requires the absolute normalizing of human conduct in economic life so as to make it machine-like, in the sense of requiring automatic and consistent responses of agents to the price signals of the economy, irrespective of the moral and aesthetic opinions which they may hold.

A wide gap is opened up separating *moral* action from *economic* action, i.e. action which is *not* affected by the ideas of duty, beauty, sympathy or moral obligation, and is subjected purely to calculations of return given the constraints of civil and public law.[16] The province of economics is, in this way, neatly disentangled from the province of morals (choice of what is best), and also from the province of instinct (impulsive action aimed at the immediate satisfaction of appetite), to become the realm of expedient maximization of the means necessary for the pursuit of the 'higher' and 'lower' ends established in the context of the two other provinces, of morals and of instinct respectively.

It is this piece of abstraction concerning what is the economic type of action which enables Edgeworth to postulate, as 'the first principle of economics', that 'every agent is actuated only by self-interest'.[17] What is really presupposed by the postulate of self-interest is the definition of economic action as one in which the moral and non-economic concerns of the agent, his beliefs and opinions, have no say. The great benefit yielded by such definition is this. By filtering out all questions of non-economic values and ultimate ends from the notion of economic action, it is now possible to handle the behaviour of all agents as if amounting to no more than partnership in a computational game, not dissimilar to the partnership involved in, say, chess-playing or the purely operational aspect of a military confrontation.

Indeed, the postulate in itself 'rules out neither the saint nor Genghis Khan'.[18] All that is required is that the behaviour of both the saint and Genghis Khan *qua* economic agents be normalized and made morally neutral – both equally trading their leisure and endowments in exchange for the means which shall enable them to effectively pursue their respective visions of the good, and so maximize the units of pleasure-intensity per unit of time. There is, of course, winning and losing in this game. And a Genghis Khan ('Very Mighty Ruler') type of character is, perhaps, likely to fare somewhat better than the saint in the 'harmless' art of shifting resources to activities yielding higher rates of return. But in so far as they refrain from overstepping the law of the land, it is assumed, there is no right or wrong, good and evil in their deals. It is, one might say, 'moral holiday' in the province of economics.

Like any piece of abstraction, this one simplifies its object. Of course, it is impossible to think without abstractions, and science works not by trying to get rid of them but by critically selecting a few promising modes of abstraction and then working out, in a highly specialized way, their logical and empirical implications. Further, the simplicity and generality of theories are highly desirable properties. To be a thinker means, as it has been said, 'to know how to make things simpler than they are'. The real question, therefore, is not so much one of 'lack of realism', as it is of cognitive and practical purchase. This, in effect, is the standpoint of the Baconian philosophy of science:

It may be that there are some on whose ear my frequent and honourable mention of practical activities makes a harsh and unpleasing sound because they are wholly given over in love and reverence to contemplation. Let them bethink themselves that they are the enemies of their own desires. For in nature practical results are not only the means to improve well-being but the guarantee of truth. The rule of religion, that a man should show his faith by his works, holds good in natural philosophy too. Science also must be known by works. It is by the witness of works, rather than by logic or even observation, that truth is revealed and established. Whence it follows that the improvement of man's mind and the improvement of his lot are one and the same thing.[19]

Thus, the true test of a set of positive statements about the world is not the claims their proponents will no doubt make on their behalf, nor the logico-mathematical refinement of the theory they frame, and not even their degree of empirical support. The true cognitive test of a scientific theory are its fruits: its ability to help us bridge the disagreement between our goals, on the one hand, and the course of the world on the other. Its contribution, in other words, towards filling that huge – and according to many ever enlarging – gulf separating our human potential from our attainments.

And the fact of the matter is that not all neo-classical economists, particularly Marshall and some of his followers (as it will be seen in chapter 4), viewed this specific simplification of the economic object as a fruitful foundation for economic science. Edgeworth himself readily admitted to the seemingly 'Laputan' or 'chimerical' nature of the conceptual move leading to the abstraction of economic actions as such from all the values and beliefs of those who perform them. 'The concrete nineteenth-century man', he wrote, 'is for the most part an impure egoist, a mixed utilitarian'. Yet, as he candidly confessed, 'at least the *conception of Man as a pleasure-machine* may justify and facilitate the employment of mechanical terms and Mathematical reasoning in social science'.[20]

The paradox of the enterprise is that what starts off as an attempt to increase the rigour and conclusiveness of moral enquiry by the use of the techniques and notation of mathematical physics, turns out to entail depriving moral science of its constitutive object, namely the diversity and malleability of human conduct in the economic as in any other sphere of action, and the dependence of any socio-economic order on a set of values and beliefs shared by the bulk of its members. The ideal of a 'Mecanique Sociale' envisaged by Edgeworth amounts in effect to the self-annihilation of economics as a moral science:

'Mecanique Sociale' may one day take her place along with 'Mecanique Celeste', throned each upon the double-sided height of one maximum principle, the supreme pinnacle of moral as of physical science. As the movements of each particle, constrained or loose, in a material cosmos are continually subordinated to one maximum sum-total of accumulated energy, so the movements of each soul, whether selfishly isolated or linked sympathetically, may continually be realising the maximum energy of pleasure, the Divine love of the universe.[21]

Plainly, the issue at stake here is not so much (as it is often taken to be) the neglecting of 'a bit more room up top' for the motives prompting economic agents to action, but rather the doing away with all room for autonomy and responsibility in ordinary economic transactions.

The distinctive feature of the 'economic man' as a 'pleasure-machine' is that he is not a moral agent in his dealings, but a player. His psychology and motivations (whether they are 'high' like Marshall's 'free choice by each individual or that line of conduct which after careful deliberation seems to him the best', or 'low' like e.g. Keynesian 'animal spirits'), just as much as his values and beliefs, are seen as irrelevant in the analysis of his transactions and the scientific description of behaviour. But whatever the scope for establishing 'theorems of intellectual and aesthetic interest'[22] afforded by this decontamination of economic action from all that concerns man, two important points arise.

The *first* one is this. Economics ceases to be a moral science. The view that the agents' value judgements and general beliefs shape their economic conduct is disqualified for the purpose of explaining their outward behaviour in the system. Strictly speaking, it becomes pointless trying to dissuade economic agents from a certain course of action in order to bring them to see and to follow a more desirable one. It is only by changing some rules of the economic game and managing the appropriate price signals that it is possible to alter the behaviour of the agents concerned and bring about the required adjustments. There is no room for moral persuasion once the economic stage is set and the actors begin their dealings.

From this point of view, it is a moot question whether Marshall was right when he maintained that 'No doubt men, even now, are capable of much more unselfish service than they generally render'; but he surely was voicing an illusory goal when he concluded from this that 'the supreme aim of the economist is to discover how this latent asset can be developed most quickly, and turn to account most wisely' (PEc,8). Indeed, Marshall's wish that his *Principles* would be 'read by businessmen' – just as much, we may note, as Marx's to make of *Capital* 'the Bible of the working class' – becomes now, as Schumpeter put it, 'a strange ambition'.[23]

The *second* point is this. Nothing prevents what was originally worked up as a potentially fruitful piece of scientific abstraction from being taken (or misunderstood) as though it were a moral precept or a desirable state of affairs. Hume's proposition that no set of non-moral premises can logically entail a moral conclusion is also a reminder of just how easy and all too common it is for the human mind to risk the step. If, for example, the simplifying assumption that animals behave like 'natural automata' has proved a very fertile starting-point in ethology, then one may go on and conclude *à la* Descartes (see the letter to the Neoplatonist More quoted above) that therefore men *should* be cleared from the suspicion of wrongdoing when they mistreat them. There is no harm in 'mistreating' or 'being cruel' to an automaton ('res extensa').

The same applies to the decontamination of economic actions from the moral and aesthetic opinions of those who perform them, for the purpose of model-building and forecasting. Is it desirable that such disentangling of the economic circuit from morality should be striven after by those actively engaged in economic activities? Plainly, it is not possible to wholly translate this piece of abstraction into our ordinary behaviour – human life *as it is* simply is not amenable to the neat subdivisions of abstract analysis. But certainly it is still possible to go a long way in this direction. And if there is any truth in the notion that 'the best way to persuade consists of not persuading', then it is an obvious yet not irrelevant question to ask, whether modern economics continues to function as a moral science (in Paley's sense), although presumably in spite of itself.

If this is the case, then the 'moral holiday' enjoyed by agents trading in the province of 'pure economic theory' (standard neo-classical economics) is in effect rather more than a possibly fertile starting-point for analysis. It is a piece of abstraction that easily lends itself to a normative reading – an essay in moral persuasion which, though-not like Marshall's notorious preaching or Marx's occasional invective, is in fact no less effective for that. As it has been recently suggested, 'Standard textbook economics stops about there: the prescription is self-interest, constrained by the law'; the supposition, of course, is that, in the economic sphere of action, 'It is only necessary for each individual to act egoistically for the good of all to be attained', and that 'the best results would follow if people did not think in moral terms at all, and merely acted selfishly'.[24] The 'invisible hand' at work here transmutes *is* into *ought*. And the legal minimum (calculations of return within the framework of law) stands promoted to the status of a moral maximum (the good of all).

So, the mechanization of the economic picture advanced by Jevons, Edgeworth and some of their contemporaries can be seen as combining two divergent tendencies:

1 There is the simplification of economic action so as to make it independent of moral ends. The central feature of the metamorphosis of economic agents into 'pleasure-machines' is that they cease being moral persons and become players, each one computing his way – always within the legal framework – towards the means that shall enable him to fulfil his desires and commitments once he steps out of the purely economic sphere of action.

2 There is the metamorphosis of the economic agents into 'pleasure-machines' as constituting in itself an end. Economic actions, the argument runs, ought to be purely instrumental rather than ends in themselves. And it is a good thing, given the nature and properties of a pure market economy, that agents should suspend their moral beliefs and opinions as they try to amass at lowest cost the maximum of the means necessary for the satisfaction of their highest preferences. The disengagement of the economic life from morality turns out to be not only a promising starting-point for abstract analysis, it becomes a moral end-point too, that is, a desirable state of affairs.

CHAPTER 4

Economic man and man-machine
Some logical parallels and contrasts between the two concepts

The argument so far has set forth three basic approaches to the question of the role of beliefs and opinions in the economic behaviour of the individual agent. Chapter 1 put forward the position predominant in economic philosophy: 'Ideas rule the world of human affairs and its events'. The stress falls squarely on the power of beliefs and opinions to determine conduct, and these are themselves largely explained (except Hume) as resulting from the 'war of ideas' waged by intellectuals, in particular those who deal directly with economic and political issues.

Chapter 2 outlined the radical challenge to this view associated with physicalism and the 'man-machine' doctrine: 'Mental events are caused phenomena with no causal efficacy'. The beliefs and opinions of agents, in so far as they correlate with their bodily actions, are assumed away as epiphenomena, i.e. a subclass of physiological events which is devoid of true explanatory power.

Finally, chapter 3 retraced the formulation of the concept of 'economic man' in the history of economic science, focusing on the rise of standard neo-classical theory and its attempt to work out a 'mechanics of utility and self-interest' or 'Mechanique Sociale'. A central feature of this move, it is argued, was the normalization of economic behaviour, so that the actions of the individual agent could be explained as automatic responses to the changing price signals in the economy.

In this chapter, I shall try to gather up the threads of the two preceding chapters and examine some logical parallels and contrasts underlying the *rapprochement* between modern economics ('economic man') and modern science ('man-machine'). I shall then proceed to argue that: (a) though there may be nothing in the nature of things to rule out in principle the individual agent's autonomy or his capacity for genuine self-government in practical life – as the physicalist thesis, if true, would entail – (b) the 'ideology man' of economic philosophy is based on a rather intellectualist account of human agency and of the ways in which the relevant belief-fixation mechanisms operate; hence it must be strongly qualified. Finally, I go on to suggest two fundamental qualifications to the economic philosophers' claim that 'Ideas rule the world of human affairs'; these two qualifying arguments are stated at the close of this chapter and then taken up at length in chapters 5 and 6–7 respectively.

The transition from classical political economy to standard neo-classical economics is marked by a vigorous attempt to enhance the clarity, rigour and precision of economic theorizing. As it is well known, by the last quarter of the nineteenth century, dissatisfaction with the Millian orthodoxy was widespread and many-sided. And, although the critics were unable to refute or crush head-on the ruling system (the refutation of the wage-fund doctrine being the notorious exception), they were out to lay down new foundations for the discipline as a whole and to replace its methods of reasoning, argument and presentation.

The neo-classical breakthrough was based on: (i) a new emphasis in economic analysis on the theory of consumption and the value in use or utility-aspect ('ophelimity') of goods – in a radical shift away from the classical preoccupation with production theory, accumulation and economic development; (ii) the rediscovery – in the path pioneered by A. Cournot, H.H. Gossen and J.H. von Thunen – that economic processes were amenable to marginal techniques of analysis, i.e. the method for the determination of optimum positions through infinitesimal variations, at the margin, of specified variables; (iii) the mathematical formulation of the concept of general equilibrium – essentially a vision of the interdependence of economic phenomena and of the feedback properties of the price mechanism in pure market economies which derives from the first two books of the *Wealth of Nations* but had been, in a way, largely bypassed by the two generations of classical economists following Adam Smith.[1]

But these achievements, and the higher standards of clarity, rigour and precision in economic analysis associated with the rise of neo-classical theory, were not cost free. For they involved, among other things, a drastic simplification and homogenization of human agency in economic affairs. Accounts of individual behaviour in practical life had to be severely normalized. The new departure in economic theorizing carried with it a narrowing of the factors bearing on

choice. In particular, it entailed the ruling out of teleological accounts
of behaviour, that is, of human agency described and explained in
terms of the purposes, non-economic goals and value-judgements
(moral choices) of those who undertake them. And as a corollary of
this, there was now a marked tendency to treat human nature as a
constant over time and to assume that the individual agent's self-
interest in economic affairs was a clear, straightforward and self-
explanatory notion. The break, as I shall presently try to show, was
no less with the Millian than with the Marshallian world.

Marshall, as seen above, interpreted Mill's 'admirable' 1848
Principles – by far the most popular and authoritative treatise in the
English classical tradition – as 'the first important indication of the
new movement' in the growth of economics as a science (PEc,631–2).
This movement, held Marshall, was characterized by the fundamental revision of the Ricardian reductionist treatment of economic
behaviour and 'the growing tendency of economists to take account of
the pliability of human nature'. In a passage which brings out his
views about the impact on economics and the wider social influence of
the Millian contribution, he wrote:

Mill's followers have continued his movement away from the position taken
up by the immediate followers of Ricardo; and the human as distinguished
from the mechanical element is taking a more and more prominent place in
economics . . . A higher notion of social duty is spreading everywhere. In
Parliament, in the press and in the pulpit, the spirit of humanity speaks more
distinctly and more earnestly. Mill and the economists who have followed
him have helped onwards this general movement, and they in their turn
have been helped onwards by it. (PEc,632)[2]

Mill, indeed, had to a great extent moved away from the
behavioural assumptions underlying Benthamite hedonics and Ricardian economics. 'While minds are coarse they require coarse
stimuli, and let them have them'; but clearly, he thought, minds were
not expected to remain coarse for long, and 'the present [1848] very
early stage of human improvement', with its stress on competition
and capital accumulation at any cost, and with its tacit consensus that
'to grow as rich as possible [is] the universal object of ambition',
should not be seen as 'the most desirable lot of human kind, or
anything but the disagreeable symptoms of one of the phases of
industrial progress' (CW3,754). Mill's defence of the stationary state
in Book IV of the *Principles*, it may also be noted, tallies with his
criticism of Bentham's inability to see that a man's conception of what

is in his own interest is not, as matter of course, always equivalent to the narrowest and most selfish (or 'vulgar') sense of self-interest. 'Habitually and throughout his works', he wrote about his former mentor,

the moment he has shown that a man's selfish interest would prompt him to a particular course of action, he lays it down without further parley that the man's interest lies that way; and, by sliding insensibly from the vulgar sense of the word [interest] into the philosophical, and from the philosophical back into the vulgar, the conclusion which is always brought out is, that the man will act as the selfish interest prompts . . . [But] upon those who need to be strengthened and upheld by a really inspired moralist . . . the effect of such writings as Mr. Bentham's, if they be read and believed and their spirit imbibed, must either be hopeless despondency and gloom, or a reckless giving themselves up to a life of that miserable self-seeking, which they are taught to regard as inherent in their original and unalterable nature . . . [He] assumes that mankind are alike in all times and places, that they have the same wants and are exposed to the same evils. (CW10,14–16)

Bentham's position, held Mill, was not only theoretically mistaken – 'he supposes mankind to be swayed by only a part of the inducements which really actuate them, but of that part he imagines them to be much cooler and more thoughtful calculators than they are' (CW10,17) – but also practically mischievous, for it meant closing the door to human improvement and the utilitarian good. Thus, while acknowledging the current predisposition of the many to self-interest narrowly (or 'vulgarly') defined, Mill insisted that things could, should and indeed were already beginning to change. Not all men saw their self-interest in the same way and some would genuinely prefer 'to be Socrates dissatisfied than a pig satisfied':

There is nothing in the constitution of human nature to forbid its being so in all mankind. Until it is so, the race will never enjoy one-tenth part of the happiness which our nature is susceptible of. I regard any considerable increase of human happiness, through mere changes in outward circumstances, unaccompanied by changes in the states of the desires, as hopeless. (CW10,15)

A basically similar emphasis on the variability of the content of self-interested motivation and the perfectibility of man runs through Marshall's economic writings. He referred to ethics as the 'mistress' of economics and to 'the progress of man's nature' as 'the centre of the ultimate aim of economic studies'. He maintained that the theory of production ('efforts and activities') must have precedence over that of consumption ('wants') in economics, seeing that 'while wants are the rulers of life among the lower animals, it is to changes in the forms of efforts and activities that we must turn when in search for the keynotes of the history of mankind' (PEc,72).[3]

Throughout the *Principles*, Marshall stressed that: 'It is deliberate-ness, and not selfishness, that is the characteristic of the modern age . . . a certain independence and habit of choosing one's own course for oneself, a self-reliance, a deliberation and yet a promptness of choice and judgement, and a habit of forecasting the future and of shaping one's course with reference to distant aims' (PEc,4–5). 'This strength of the man himself', he suggested later on (in Book IV), 'this resolution, energy and self-mastery, or in short this "vigour" is the source of all progress: it shows itself in great deeds, in great thoughts and in the capacity for true religious feeling' (PEc,162). As he put it in *Industry and Trade* (1919):

The problem of social aims takes on new forms in every age: but underlying all there is the one fundamental principle, viz. that progress mainly depends on the extent to which the strongest, and not merely the highest, forces of human nature can be utilized for the increase of social good . . . For there has always been a substratum of agreement that social good lies mainly in that healthful exercise and development of faculties which yields happiness without pall, because it sustains self-respect and is sustained by hope. No utilization of waste gases in the blast furnace can compare with the triumph of making work for the public good pleasurable in itself, and of stimulating men of all classes to great endeavours by other means than that evidence of power which manifests itself by lavish expenditure.[4]

Thus, Marshall left no doubts that he regarded his own thought and teaching as a direct continuation of the Millian movement through which 'the human as distinguished from the mechanical element is taking a more and more prominent place in economics' (PEc,632). As agents become increasingly moral in ordinary economic life – more resolute, ready for motivated co-operation and more capable of positive initiative in all spheres of action – so economic science, he held, should follow suit and not only allow for ethical considerations to weigh more in the explanation of economic behaviour but, what to him was doubtless vital, it should also give positive help in the efforts of the community to think clearly and wisely about ethical problems in private (how one should live?) and public life (what makes a community just and good?).

It is not hard to see, with the benefit of hindsight, that developments since Marshall's day have remorselessly confuted his expectations about 'the growing tendency of economists to take account of the pliability of human nature' – the notion that 'the changes in human nature during the last fifty years have been so rapid as to force themselves on the attention [of economists]' (PEc,631). Mainstream economic scientists since Marshall clearly did not feel their attention drawn to any mirage of human perfectibility, just as they did not feel in any sense inclined to worship at Marshall's Mecca (evolutionary biology).

According to Jevons and standard neo-classical doctrine, the laws of pure economic theory 'are so simple in their foundation that they would apply, more or less completely, to all human beings of whom we have any knowledge . . . The theory of economy proves to be, in fact, the mechanics of utility and self-interest'. Introducing his pure theory of economics, Jevons claimed: 'Oversights may have been committed in tracing out its details, but in its main features this theory must be the true one. Its method is as sure and demonstrative as that of kinematics or statics, nay, almost as self-evident as are the elements of Euclid, when the real meaning of the formulae is fully seized'.[5]

It should however be noted that there is no essential connection between standard neo-classical theory and the psychological hedonism put forward by Bentham. For even though Jevons and Edgeworth, as seen above (chapter 3), had tended to conflate the two and to couch their propositions in the language of Benthamite utilitarianism, other leaders of the neo-classical movement, like for example the Austrians C. Menger and E. Bohm-Bawerk, had formulated their theories without resorting to Bentham's or any other psychological doctrine.

The point is well brought out by Robbins in his attempt to locate and clarify the nature of the neo-classical departure in economic analysis. 'The hedonistic trimmings of the works of Jevons and his followers were incidental to the main structure of a theory which – as the parallel development in Vienna showed – is capable of being set out and defended in absolutely non-hedonistic terms'; all that is assumed by the theory, continued Robbins, 'is that different goods have different uses and that these different uses have different significances for action, such that in a given situation one use will be preferred before another and one good before another. Why the human animal attaches particular values in this sense to particular things, is a question which we do not discuss. That is quite properly a question for psychologists or perhaps even physiologists'. Hence the conclusion that 'The economist is not concerned with ends as such': 'In pure Mechanics we explore the implication of the existence of certain given properties of bodies. In pure Economics we examine the implication of the existence of scarce means with alternative uses'.[6]

Thus, the critical move in the 'rewriting from the foundations upwards' associated with the rise of standard neo-classical theory was not its reliance on any particular psychological (hedonism) or ethical (egoism) doctrine. The crucial step here was the decision to disregard all questions concerning the origins and formation of the agent's 'tastes and preferences' – his choice of ends and the non-economic motivations of his economic activities – so as to concentrate the analytical effort on the theory of market interactions and the logic of individual behaviour regarded as a set of consistent reactions to the stimuli appropriate in an economic setting (i.e. prices). As the tastes and preferences of agents are assumed as data, and as the scarce means ('endowments') at their disposal have been exogenously given, so the pure theorist has a free hand to speculate on the coherence and the overall properties of the system produced by their mutual transactions.

The outcome is a purely atomistic conception of the economy in which the notion of rationality applies to the ways in which given 'tastes and preferences' are satisfied and the 'obstacles' to their satisfaction overcome, but not to the formation and selection of behaviour as such. As V. Pareto made clear in his *Manual of Political Economy* (1909), the entire theory rests on 'the determination of the quantities of goods which constitute combinations between which the individual is indifferent . . . the individual can disappear, provided he leaves us this photograph of his tastes . . . The theory of economic science thus acquires the rigor of rational mechanics'.[7]

So, in the event, it was the work of Marshall's own generation to 'shunt the car of Economic science' (Jevons) firmly on to a mechanical line, and, more importantly, to ensure that the attention of subsequent generations of academic economists was duly directed towards the unfolding of the newly established research programme. Marshall's vigorous attempt to take up the Millian tradition notwithstanding, the reaction against classical political economy took the form of a growing refinement and formalization of 'pure economic theory', i.e. the 'mechanics of self-interest and utility'. Moreover, a highly selective use of Marshall's works made it possible to enlist even him to the new movement. All that was needed here was to carve out from his *Principles* the easily detachable partial equilibrium analysis put forward in Book V, while turning a convenient blind eye to the remaining five books of his major theoretical work. A similar neglect awaited, of course, his important assessment of the role and limits of 'mechanical analogies' in economic theory and of the place of the famous Book V of the *Principles* in his own thinking which came out in 'Distribution and exchange' (1898), his major contribution to the *Economic Journal*.[8]

Marshall, it is true, never managed to complete his very ambitious theoretical enterprise in the province of economics: in the sixth edition of his *Principles* (1910), the words 'Vol. I' in the title-page were replaced by 'An introductory volume'. And he remarked also that he considered his treatment of the time-variable in the value theory and partial equilibrium model set forth in Book V as his signal contribution to economics. Yet – and this seems to mark him off from other highbrow neo-classical theorists – he insisted all along in stressing the shortcomings of what had been accomplished in the realm of pure theory and in drawing attention to the fact that modern market economies depended on the adequate moral underpinning for their proper functioning. Even the purely economic sphere of action was anchored on the non-economic commitments, goals and motivations of agents. As he put it in Book IV ('Agents of Production') of the *Principles*: 'The religious, the moral, the intellectual and the artistic faculties on which the progress of industry depends, are not acquired solely for the sake of the things that may be got by them; but are developed by exercise for the sake of some pleasure and the happiness which they themselves bring' (PEc,206).

Moreover, human perfectibility, though a slow process, should be taken into account. For 'though there is a kernel of man's nature that has scarcely changed, yet many elements of his character, that are most effective for economic uses, are of modern growth'; 'human nature', he stressed, 'can be modified: new ideals, new opportunities and new methods of action may, as history shows, alter it very much even in a few generations; and this change in human nature has perhaps never covered so wide an area and moved so fast as in the present generation'.[9] It was this latter belief that led Marshall to predict the 'growing tendency of economists to take account of the pliability of human nature'; but his expectations on this point turned out to be no less grossly mistaken wishful-thinking than, say, those of his (then famous) contemporary, the social philosopher H. Spencer, about the inevitable and imminent 'withering away' of the State's control over the economy in the most advanced nations of the world.

The upshot of the remarks above may be summed up as follows. With the advent of neo-classical theory (*pace* Marshall), the specialization in the analysis of economic behaviour is carried further. First, the decision is taken to ignore the origins and formation of the agent's preferences and non-economic ends; they are taken as data and everything is then built from their implications. And second, economic action itself is depurated of psychological and ethical elements, and construed as a process of attaining given ends by the selection of the 'optimal', 'most efficient' or 'rational' means available for the agent.

At the level of the individual agent, equilibrium results from the opposition between his 'tastes', which are given, and the 'obstacles' to satisfying them. The decision-process involved is typically represented as one of optimization. It involves the collecting and processing of relevant information (itself a costly process), and is carried out with a view to the selection of the course of action which will yield the highest monetary return. Hence, it involves the use of intellectual skills, that is, the search for and computation of information dispersed in the economic environment, but abstracts from other mental factors and considerations bearing on ordinary economic conduct, like for instance the sway of habit or the political and moral commitments of agents and decision-makers.

If the account above is roughly correct, then it is now possible to bring out some logical parallels and contrasts between the two approaches to human agency discussed above, viz. the 'economic man' assumed by pure economic theory and the 'man-machine' construct which (as seen in chapter 2) is associated with the rise of modern science. The subject is of course vast, and there is no space (or presumption) here to do more than to suggest a few relevant points. Although there are some superficial resemblances between the two approaches, I shall argue, it would be mistaken and misleading to press the comparison too far. The concepts in question have a different epistemological status and only the 'economic man' concept lends itself to a normative reading; it may thus be seen as a particular version of economic philosophy which, like its rivals in the field (see chapter 1), bids for power over men's beliefs and opinions.

To begin with the logical *parallels* between the 'economic man' and the 'man-machine' concepts it may be said that both belong to a mechanistic programme of enquiry. The quotations by leading economists given above, comprise a plethora of references to 'mechanics', 'mechanical sciences', 'rational mechanics', 'mechanical analogies', 'Mecanique Sociale', and so on. This is not gratuitous. Though there may be here an implicit attempt to cash in on the prestige and authority of mathematical physics, the fact remains that there is also a genuine effort by the economic theorists in question to achieve a scientific understanding of human agency and to get rid of all traces of teleological explanations and final causes in their reasonings.

The aim is to explain the behaviour of the system by the behaviour of each 'particle' (agent) in it and by their dynamic interplay. The overall result of this interplay is depicted as an ordered, self-regulated 'cosmos' (a cherished metaphor); and so far as 'particles' and 'cosmos' are concerned, safety lay in asking only 'how?', never 'why?'. To put it crudely (and paraphrasing Voltaire), agents are free to dispute about the 'good life' and the 'good society' as much as they care to, but 'these disputes are like idle table-talk: each one forgets after dinner what he has said, and goes where his interest and his taste call him'. It is no part of the pure theorist's business to enquire why each 'particle' behaves just as it supposedly does.

On the other hand, there are important *contrasts* to be made. The parallel between the two concepts only works at a fairly superficial level of analysis. First, because the behaviour of 'economic man', unlike that of the 'man-machine', is crucially dependent on mental events, that is, deliberation and the use of knowledge. The 'man-machine' doctrine writes off the causal efficacy of all mental processes: the human mind, to borrow T.H. Huxley's famous analogy, is best seen as the whistle of a steam engine, i.e. a fortuitous and irrelevant spin-off of physiological mechanism. The key tenet here is 'the principle that ideas, motives and feelings have no part in determining conduct and therefore no part in explaining it'.[10]

The contrast with 'economic man' is stark. For here the conscious values and ulterior ends of agents are not explained away as imaginary causes but simply taken as data. As Robbins has recently put it, highlighting the contrast, 'The influence of the Reformation made no change in the forces of gravity – but it certainly must have changed the demand for fish on Fridays'.[11] More importantly, even within the purely economic sphere of action thinking processes play a crucial role. Though not given to let his beliefs and opinions – those 'outstanding and disturbing forces' (Jevons) – interfere with his dealings or muddle his calculations, 'economic man' still has a mind that matters. Indeed, all his transactions in the circle of exchange are ultimately predicated on a distinctly mental and deliberative operation, viz. intelligent and conscious information-processing. A suitably trimmed mind still rules.

Second, and this is a central point of this chapter, the 'man-machine' and the 'economic man' concepts have distinct epistemological status and, for this reason, lend themselves to different conceptual uses. Both, to be sure, are the result of abstraction. But while 'economic man' has been developed by a specialized social science, with the aim of throwing light on one particular domain of economic life (as opposed to providing a full explanation of concrete behaviour), the 'man-machine' construct aims at a much wider, indeed an all-embracing or totalizing range of application. Whereas 'economic man' applies and is at its best in matters of moral *indifference* like, say, 'the response of a consumer to a rise in the price of butter relative to that of margarine', the physicalist thesis, in turn, implies the *inefficacy* of moral reasoning and of the mental as such.

As a matter of fact, the chief exponents of standard neo-classical economics, while taking full advantage of 'economic man' in their theorizing, and making sometimes overbold claims about the results achieved, were also careful to point out that other sources of knowledge needed to be tapped in order to bring pure theory closer to empirical facts and arrive at satisfactory explanations of behaviour in concrete cases. Jevons, Menger and Edgeworth all stressed the view that they were dealing with a restricted domain of human conduct in practical life – what the British had called 'calculus of utility' and Menger 'economizing behaviour'. They believed that specializing in this way was necessary because it was the best way forward, in the realm of pure theory, so as to avoid the blind alley to which Millian orthodoxy had led.

As Pareto perhaps more than any other modern theorist made clear, mathematical economics is the study of one specific type of actions, namely 'logical actions'. Logical actions are those which are:

(a) based on processes of reasoning (to rule out purely instinctive behaviour like e.g. that of bees building cells in a honey-comb in a way that turns out to maximize their capacity to store honey), and (b) those which logically or rationally link the appropriate means with the given ends (as opposed to 'non-logical actions', i.e. those originating from 'definite psychic states', 'sentiments' and 'sub-conscious feelings', and which are based not on calculation and the selection of appropriate means, but on things like custom, habit, superstitious beliefs, aesthetic values, notions of duty, and the like).

But concrete actions, held Pareto, are always synthetic. They comprise, in varying degrees, both logical and non-logical elements which can only be separated by analysis and abstraction. Hence, he concluded: 'It would not be very reasonable to claim to organize economic phenomena by the theories of pure economics alone'. And Pareto himself, it may be useful to note, impressed with the grip of 'non-logical actions' on the behaviour of agents about him, and especially with what he saw as our 'marked tendency to imagine that non-logical actions are logical', devoted a substantial amount of his own research to the study of 'non-logical actions' and the mechanisms through which agents deceive themselves and others by pretending – first and foremost to themselves – that they are carrying out purely 'logical actions'.[12]

But if the 'economic man' construct may be seen, at least on a first approach, as no more than a working hypothesis in a specialized discipline, designed to give some insight into an admittedly partial aspect of ordinary behaviour, the same cannot be said of the 'man-machine' concept. For the latter, as I shall now argue, constitutes a metaphysical standpoint, i.e. a statement about the nature of the universe (or the totality of the real) and man's place in it. According to this view, as Mill reminds us in his early *A System of Logic* (1843):

One state of mind is never really produced by another: all are produced by states of body. When one thought seems to call up another by association, it is not really a thought which recalls a thought; the association did not exist between the two thoughts, but between the two states of the brain or nerves which preceded the thoughts; one of those states recalls the other, each being attended, in its passage, by the particular mental state which is consequent upon it. (CW8,850)

Thus it would turn out that, as Huxley were to put it in his 'On the hypothesis that animals are automata and its history' (1874), 'Our mental conditions are simply the symbols in consciousness of the changes which take place automatically in the organism; [and] to take an extreme illustration, the feeling we call volition is not the cause of a voluntary act, but the symbol of that state of the brain which is the immediate cause of the act'.[13]

In this picture, although the mental states (sentiments, beliefs, goals, etc.) of the individual agent are still allowed to coexist with his bodily actions, they cannot, as matter of principle, explain them. For not only the infra-human world, the argument runs, but *homo sapiens* himself and his practical affairs must be studied *sub specie machinae* if a truly scientific understanding of man and his goings-on is ever to be had. And if it could ever be shown, to the satisfaction of all rational enquirers, that the 'man-machine' doctrine is true, then the sample of statements given in chapter 1, to the effect that 'Ideas rule the world of human affairs and its events', would be forced out of the field to join company with other long entertained myths about the causes of human behaviour now filling the pages of anthropological treatises on 'primitive mentality'. Even 'economic man', it might be said, would look embarrassingly high-minded and naive.

Of course, neither Mill nor Huxley ventured to make a conclusive verdict on this *vexata quaestio* (Mill), and it clearly remains even now an open problem. Physicalism, determinism and the 'man-machine' standpoint may be said to belong to that select class of issues which, as it has been recently remarked, are likely 'to provide philosophers with matter for argument as long as there are philosophers left to argue'. Economic philosophers and social scientists in general seem to have responded essentially along a Lockean or pragmatic line to the long-standing problems of autonomy and the role of ethical values in the age of science: 'The Question is not proper', held Locke, 'whether the Will be free, but whether a Man be free':

He that has his Chains knocked off, and the Prison-doors set open to him, is perfectly at liberty, because he may either go or stay, as he best likes; though his preference be determined to stay, by the darkness of the Night, or illness of the Weather, or want of other Lodging. He ceases not to be free; though the desire of some convenience to be had there, absolutely determines his preference, and makes him stay in his Prison.[14]

A man is free even if he chooses to stay in prison. But if his condition is such that his desire whether to stay or go has no say on this matter, then he is not free. The inner citadel ('the Will') is left intact; the real issue concerns the conditions for carrying out one's choices.

Other scientific enquirers, however, have not shrunk from attacking the inner citadel. Shifting our attention to the practical problem of the conditions for the exercise of liberty (as proposed by Locke) may be a useful tactic. But it by no means settles the formidable intellectual problem posed by the question whether man's conscious will and mental states, in their relation to observable behaviour, belong or not, as a class, to the countless number of imaginary causes exposed and exploded by the growth of science.

The issue, in fact, seems to be just as knotty and undecided today as it was in La Mettrie's time. R. Sperry – a leading American neuroscientist concerned with the question of the functional relations between ethical values and brain physiology – suggests that 'Those centermost processes of the brain with which consciousness is presumably associated are simply not understood'. As he goes on to report in *Science and Moral Priority* (1983):

Our explanatory picture for brain function is reasonably satisfactory for the sensory input pathways and the distal portion of the motor outflow. But that great in-between realm, starting at the stage where the incoming excitatory messages first reach the cortical surface of the brain, still today is very aptly referred to as the 'mysterious black box'.

And Sperry himself, for all his belief in the notion that man is metaphysically unique and 'mind moves matter in the [human] brain', is prepared to admit that, as he says, 'The more we learn about the brain and behaviour, the more deterministic, lawful, and causal it appears'. Moreover, he adds, 'the conviction held by most brain researchers – up to some 99.9 per cent of us, I suppose – [is] that conscious mental forces can be safely ignored, insofar as the objective, scientific study of the brain is concerned'.[15]

So, unlike 'economic man', the 'man-machine' conjecture aims at a full-scale reduction of the human world to its own terms of description and explanation. It is therefore utterly incompatible with the view (which is central to economic philosophy and the social sciences in general) according to which, one way or another, 'ideas and other mental entities push around the physiological and biochemical events in the brain'.

Another way to look at the proposed contrast between 'economic man' – a working hypothesis in a specialized discipline – and the 'man-machine' construct – part of a science-based metaphysical doctrine – is to point to the fact that only the former lends itself to a normative reading.

Obviously, there is no question of the individual agent approaching or failing to approach to the standards of behaviour set by the 'man-machine' concept. The question here is whether his mental states are relevant or not in accounting for his bodily actions. And the answer, accordingly, is 'yes' or 'no'. If an *experimentum crucis* could be devised, capable of satisfying even the most hard-nosed empiricist that mental states *are* relevant, 'man-machine' would fail. But if a credible account of his actions can be given, showing that his bodily movements, like the world of ordinary physical phenomena, is complete in itself or self-sufficient, and thus can be successfully predicted without any reference being made to his mental states, then 'man-machine' *may* be right. (There is no final, absolute truth in science: there could still be found a rival theory which proved at least as powerful as the 'man-machine' conjecture in terms of prediction and was also simpler, more general or less alien to human subjective experience.) What is out of the question in any case is the notion that the individual agent may live up to, or fall short of, the 'man-machine' paradigm.

Clearly, the same is not true of the 'economic man' construct. Indeed, as seen above, it is perfectly possible to argue – and many have already done so – that the interests of society as a whole are best served when agents pay no heed to what they might think are the interest of society as a whole, but mould their behaviour upon the standards of 'rational' or 'logical' conduct set by the 'economic man': 'What the rational [economic] man would do, the plain man should do . . . Where it [economic theory] does not explain, it shows men how to do better. So, whenever actual agents are found not to be as the theory implies, it is a criticism not of the theory but of the agents'.[16]

'Economic man' here becomes an ideal to be looked up to. Akin, therefore, not to the man *sub specie machinae* of modern science but to 'Socratic man' or, more precisely, to the 'ideology man' of economic philosophy (chapter 1). And so there is no more reason to complain (as the young Marx did) that: 'In the economic system, under the rule of private property, the interest which any individual has in society is in inverse proportion to the interest that society has in him'.[17] *Tout est bien*: all is for the best.

It is this last turn in the argument that clearly brings out the reason why even the most ambitious attempts to devise a 'Mecanique Sociale' analogous to the 'Mecanique Celeste' of modern science, and to gradually refine it into a credible mathematical model of our economic life, still rely on one basic exogenous, impeccably moral starting-point, viz. the initial decision of agents to get rid of their beliefs and opinions – those 'outstanding and disturbing forces' – once they enter the economic circuit and begin their mutual transactions. For a thoroughly mechanical economic cosmos, in which agents never fail to bow down to the price signals thrown off by the markets, and readily shift their endowments to assets and activities yielding higher rates of return, is in effect just as much dependent on a set of beliefs shared by the bulk of its members as a highly traditional economic system, in which religious superstition (e.g. belief in the sacredness of certain species of trees and animals, or in the depravity of money-lending at interest) impinges upon the everyday doings of the community.

The central element holding together such economic cosmos in which there is a perfect homogeneity across individual agents, so that all return the same 'logical' answer when they are given the same information, would be the agents' view that it is *right and proper* that economic transactions should not be ends in themselves, but merely instrumental roundabouts divested of any wider significance. Even trader-consumer 'pleasure-machines', the argument goes, must first think it fit to be so. And this act of choice, no matter how unreflected it actually happens to be, is determined by one's beliefs and opinions in essentially the same way as, to take an extreme case, Socrates' decisions not to use rhetoric to further his self-defence in his trial, not to bring his wife and children before the jury and not to run away from prison when the opportunity arose, but to accept his sentence and drink the hemlock 'with good humour and without the least distaste.'

This helps to see why 'economic man', unlike the 'man-machine' concept, is not inconsistent with the standpoint of economic philosophy as presented in chapter 1. It must be stressed, however, that to argue that even a wholly mechanical picture of the economy falls short of prescinding from the agents' beliefs and opinions does *not* imply (a) that the latter do in fact determine behaviour or (b) that the ideas of political and economic philosophers play a central role in the underlying belief-forming process. All that can be really said is that the mechanization of the economic picture (chapter 3 to 4) fails to disprove or rule out the claim (chapter 1) that ideas govern our socio-economic life in such a way as to make its workings fundamentally distinct from those obtaining in the non-human, thoroughly mechanical, universe (chapter 2).

The real threat to the view that there can be a line of causation leading from the agent's beliefs and goals to his behaviour, and that there exists such a thing as *acting from opinions*, seems to come from advances in the growth of knowledge about man in disciplines like molecular biology, neurobiology, psychobiology and sociobiology. No prophetic skills are needed to predict that the growth of knowledge in these areas shall increasingly undermine the gulf still separating our understanding of human and non-human actions – the 'bifurcation of nature'. But physicalism and the 'man-machine' doctrine, it should also be stressed, arise out of the human desire for an understanding of the totality of the real and the ultimate character of the world. Thus they are not scientific theories – i.e. a set of tentative hypotheses about well-defined ranges of phenomena – but rather part of a metaphysical world-outlook; for a science-based *Weltanschauung*, no matter how impeccably built out of the results which the specialized sciences present for our belief, loses nothing of its metaphysical (non-experimental) character for that.

At the same time, it seems reasonable to suggest that there is still a long way and much hard scientific labour to go before the monistic goal is finally pushed through and man's mental states can be shown to (at most) simply coexist with his actions. This feat, if ever carried through, would vindicate A.N. Whitehead's bold proposition that 'the laws of physics are the decrees of fate – [and] fate, remorseless and indifferent, urging a tragic incident to its inevitable issue, is the vision possessed by science'.[18] No *deus ex machina*, no human will could then possibly intervene in 'the remorseless working of things' presiding over that old scientific metaphor, 'the theatre of nature'. And man, like an engine tracking an absurdly crooked road, would finally resign to the Stoic reflection: 'If I do not want to go along the fated path, having become a bad man, I will go along it nevertheless'.[19]

The point of the discussion above is to draw attention to a simple fact. Economic philosophy asserts the agency of 'consciously formulated ideas acting as a driving force effecting transitions from social state to social state'.[20] But this account of events relies on a hypothetical starting-point. For if one takes the opposite view, and seriously entertains the notion that 'Properly understood, without facile evasion, a world which is eligible for scientific understanding, *ipso facto* also leaves no room for freedom, responsibility and validity of thought',[21] then it follows that, from a scientific point of view, these 'consciously formulated ideas' have no power to intervene as a force in their own right in the determination of behaviour. Physicalism, if nothing else, encourages the search for ways in which to check and qualify exaggerated claims regarding the role of philosophy ('ideas') in the processes of belief-formation and social change.

It is in fact noteworthy that such inflated claims are by no means the monopoly of economic philosophers. They are, in a way, typical of most modern philosophers concerned with the more practical aspects of human affairs. I. Berlin, for example, has argued: 'Philosophical concepts nurtured in the stillness of a professor's study could destroy a civilization'. T.M. Knox, reacting against Oxford's linguistic philosophy and its disregard of 'real life' issues, wrote: 'Common sense and the ordinary English in which it is expressed are a repository of former philosophies. A philosophy takes time to become part and parcel of the thinking of the man in the street: but it gets there eventually'. And many historians and philosophers of science appear to have adopted the view, explicitly formulated by E.A. Burtt, that 'In the last analysis it is the ultimate picture which an age forms of the nature of its world that is its most fundamental possession. It is the final controlling factor in all thinking whatever'.[22]

A further illustration of this tendency to present an over-intellectualized picture of the role of ideas as determinants of behaviour occurs in the following statement by one of the fathers and leading exponents of pragmatism, the American psychologist W. James. 'There are some people, and I am one of them', wrote James quoting with warm approval the words of a contemporaneous essayist, 'who think that the most practical and important thing about a man is still his view of the universe':

We think that for a landlady considering a lodger, it is important to know his income, but still more important to know his philosophy. We think that for a general about to fight an enemy, it is important to know the enemy's numbers, but still more important to know the enemy's philosophy. We think the question is not whether the theory of the cosmos affects matters, but whether, in the long run, anything else affects them.[23]

This statement, it can no doubt be argued, like some of those previously quoted, is not meant to be taken literally. It relies on the rhetorical device of exaggeration for effect (amplification) and deliberately caricatures the point so as to impress it more vividly on the imagination. In fact, James himself, as he goes on to consider some metaphysical problems from a pragmatic standpoint, is prepared to concede that, after all, it is only as a 'promise', as a 'doctrine of relief' in the face of a future that 'feels to us unsafe and needs some higher guarantee', that one is entitled to grant man some measure of autonomy and thus to shut out the 'paralysing ghost' of physicalism and the view that 'necessity and impossibility between them rule the destinies of the world'.

But then, it must be replied, if the aim is to raise the chances of making good this promise, surely the strategy of rhetorical exaggeration will not do. The contention here is that in order to support the view that there is such a thing as *acting from opinion*, and there exists such a thing as working and mobilizable moral resources in the economy, then the best thing to do is to try to understand more about the ways in which the 'war of ideas' is waged, beliefs and mental habits decay and return to vogue, and eventually *prima facie* find their way as independent forces into limited areas of practical life. This is no doubt a highly complex phenomenon, intricate and difficult to reconstruct even in outline, but it is surely a more promising alternative to the physicalist thesis than professions of faith in the irresistible and unacknowledged (?) sovereignty of ideas over human affairs. Those who believe in the decisive historical influence of ideas should feel compelled not to simply claim, in grandiose terms, that ideas have triumphantly (or grievously) ruled the world, but rather to spell out in more detail the processes and means through which theories and viewpoints come to shape institutions and events.

In the following chapters I shall examine some of the limits and constraints facing the individual agent as he tries (a) to form views about his private and public interests, and (b) to square his actions in accordance with the relevant practical conclusions. There are two fundamental reasons, I shall argue, why the notion that 'Ideas rule the world of human affairs and its events' must be strongly qualified:

(i) Only a limited segment of the actions carried out in practical life is in effect open to the influence of the agent's goals and values. The economic process in any complex society requires the operation of conduct-enforcing mechanisms, and this factor imposes significant constraints on the autonomy or 'freedom to do' of the bulk of its members. In the next chapter I shall try to spell out and discuss this proposition.

(ii) Rational argument and persuasion have a limited role in our belief-forming habits and processes. The beliefs and opinions that gain currency at a particular time and place, and *prima facie* determine the behaviour of agents, are not 'philosophical concepts nurtured in the stillness of a professor's study' (Berlin), nor 'a purely intellectual matter' (Mises). It is misleading to suggest that 'our present decisions are determined by what happened long ago in a remote specialty without the general public ever knowing about it', as Hayek and many others have argued. The agent's opinions of private and common interest are largely the result of his sub-rational dispositions and motivations (what Hume and Adam Smith would describe as the passions of the imagination), and it is important to distinguish between the beliefs and opinions paraded by men on the one hand and those betrayed by their actions on the other. This argument is developed and illustrated in the two last chapters of part I.

CHAPTER 5

The logic of the economic situation
Complex societies and the choice of conduct-enforcing mechanisms

The limits of economic philosophy may be classified as external and internal. In this chapter I shall discuss the nature of the *external* limits facing the individual agent as he attempts to live up to his beliefs and opinions in ordinary life. The basic proposition is that only a limited segment of our economic actions is in effect open to the influence of our goals and values. The argument here, as I will try to show, springs from the distinction between voluntary and involuntary actions. Only voluntary actions are in principle amenable to conscious control and, for this reason, susceptible of being altered by the agent's beliefs and deliberations. Involuntary actions lie outside the range of wilful and purposeful interference by those who perform them.

The best illustrations of involuntary actions are the myriad of automatic adjustments and organic processes taking place in the human body which are entirely closed to conscious volition. The wide range of bodily occurrences of this kind – from blushing, ageing and heart-beating to the restoration of the oxygen level in the blood to normal (through an increase in the rate of breathing) when the concentration of carbon dioxide in the air is raised – have been the source of wonder to biologists and disquiet to some philosophers.

'What is it that acts, operates, moves the heart, intestines, nerves?', asked the Swedish eighteenth-century naturalist C. Linnaeus: 'Nothing moves of its own accord. What is it that causes a cleansing vomiting, which produces sweat, which kindles fevers, which heals wounds? It is something in me, something extraordinary about me'.[1] But for those who held the Pythagorean view that man's soul was something divine – a fallen god imprisoned in the body ('living tomb') – there was nothing striking about the runaway body: 'Plotinus, the philosopher our contemporary', reports his disciple and biographer Porphyry in the third century AD, 'seemed ashamed of being in the body. So deeply rooted was this feeling that he could

68

never be induced to tell of his ancestry, his parentage, or his birth-place'.[2]

Locke, in his important reflection on human agency in Book II (chapter 21) of *An Essay Concerning Human Understanding* (1694), made the relevant point very clearly:

A Man's Heart beats, and the Blood circulates, which 'tis not in his Power by any Thought or Volition to stop; and therefore in respect of these Motions, where rest depends not on his choice, nor would follow the determination of his Mind, if it should preferr it, he is not a free Agent. Convulsive Motions agitate his Legs, so that though he wills it never so much, he cannot by any power of his Mind stop their Motion, (as in that odd Disease called *Chorea Sancti Viti,*) but he is perpetually dancing: He is not at Liberty in this Action, but under as much Necessity of moving, as a Stone that falls, or a Tennis-ball struck with a Racket.[3]

This is the reason why, as he goes on to conclude, voluntary action – i.e. that in which choice has a bearing – is not the opposite to necessary or causally determined, but rather to involuntary action. A paraplegic man, for instance, may voluntarily choose to sit still rather than being held upright, though he is bound by necessity to sit in his chair. The Lockean prisoner (see p. 60 above), may prefer to stay in prison even after the prison officer has set all doors open before him. The relevant question, from the viewpoint of the individual agent, is whether choice has any true bearing on action; whether he has 'the Power of doing, or forbearing to do, according as the Mind shall chuse or direct'.

Most organic and vital processes of the human body are sealed off from conscious choice. But as we gradually proceed from the inner metabolism of the organism towards the outward bodily actions of ordinary life, volition and intention begin to have their say. Breathing, for example, can already be accelerated or slowed down at will; a yawning may be called forth to convey a message; and there is a sense in which, for instance, procuring food, cooking and eating it are voluntary activities, open to the influence of the agent's opinions and deliberations, whereas digesting it is not. A hunger-strike to death is clearly conceivable. Yet, once nourishment is let (or forced) in, the body will take care of itself, no matter what the agent may think.

But of course to say that in his intercourse with external objects the agent may well enjoy a degree of autonomy does not mean that it will invariably be so. It is precisely the relative openness of conduct in such matters that renders it vulnerable to other forms of control like coercion, manipulation by stimuli-management and the 'action at a distance' of persuasive, wise words. In this chapter, I shall try to argue that the economic process in any complex society (i.e. based on an extensive division of labour between different individuals and groups of individuals) sets significant constraints on the autonomy or 'freedom to do' of the bulk of its members and thus limits, to some extent, their capability to act according to their own beliefs and opinions.

The clearest example of involuntary action in socio-economic life is labouring under straightforward slavery. Coercion into a set course of action takes the form of overt physical threat and, on occasion, an exemplary whipping. But, as the emancipated slaves of antiquity like the first-century AD Stoic Epictetus soon began to realize, the question of autonomy in economic activities is far from resolved with the abolition of compulsory labour: 'Let him who wishes to be free not wish for anything or avoid anything that depends on others; or else he is bound to be a slave'.[4] And J. Steuart, the Scottish precursor of Adam Smith, put his finger on the real nerve of the issue when, commenting on the decline of slavery as an institution, he went on to conclude: 'Men were then forced to labour, because they were slaves to others; men are now forced to labour because they are slaves of their own wants'.[5] The suspension of explicit, external means of compulsion paves the way to the emergence of no less compelling or effective conduct-enforcing mechanisms.

First and foremost among the wants and needs compelling men to labour are, no doubt, what Smith called the 'passions of the body' – those 'appetites which take their origin from a certain state of the body', and which can be functionally classified (following Aristotelian taxonomy) as the nutritive and the reproductive principles.[6] So, to say that agents are slaves of their own wants means, primarily, to say that agents are slaves of their own bodies, i.e. of the appetites which their bodies share with all other living animals and which are prerequisites for the preservation of both the individual and the species.

This, it should perhaps be noted, is the reason why the Stoic ideal of absolute self-sufficiency is bound to fail. There is no point in holding the view that the good, virtuous man will 'not fear that food will fail him or complain if it does'; for his body will not observe the logic of his orders and no amount of self-determination will be able to bring *it* to the state of proud indifference which his mind professes to enjoy. Like other moral enthusiasts, the Stoics were apt to boast of things they would probably find themselves unable to perform if and when the time for carrying them out arrived. As it has been aptly observed, 'no mind has ever been as moral as the preacher's tongue'; and Seneca's tragicomic career as Nero's tutor, senator, subject and then victim is probably a piece of biographical evidence as good as any to remind us of just how the beliefs and opinions paraded by a great Stoic moralist may have had very little to do with those betrayed by his conduct.[7] (This problem will be taken up in chapter 6.)

It is equally suggestive on this head to note that even Paley, notwithstanding all his insistence on the importance of general rules of conduct (rule-utilitarianism), thought it morally sound to abrogate *ad hoc* the rule that the private property of external goods ought to be respected, in cases where the agent's primary bodily needs are at stake. The 'right of extreme necessity' would, in his view, grant an agent with 'a right to use or destroy another's property, when it is necessary for [his] own preservation to do so'.[8] Restitution, of course, whenever feasible, should be observed.

From the viewpoint of economic action, the main implication of the existence of wants and needs which run impervious to the opinions and preferences of the agent is as follows. Securing some form of access to the things which human life cannot do without becomes compulsory; and if access to such things is for some reason hard and costly, then the greater will be the strain and risk which agents will be compelled to run or submit to in order to get them.

The surest way all those 'unhappy persons who in the great lottery of life have drawn a blank' can secure a lifeline to such things as they cannot do without, is by exchanging a portion of their actions which are open to voluntary and purposeful shaping *for* the monetary right to purchase the things they want. This, roughly speaking, is the situation facing 'a poor man seeking work, seeking leave to toil that he might be fed and sheltered'.[9] When a job is forthcoming, he hands over by contract his right to impress his beliefs and opinions upon his actions (a slice of his 'freedom to do') and receives, in exchange, the right to put his bodily appetites to rest and raise a family. Otherwise he begs or queues up for the dole or starves.

The interesting thing about the difficulty of access to the things that human life cannot do without (i.e. scarcity) is that, if it does not happen to be so, it can still be made so. Perhaps the most effective way of achieving this is by the awakening, in the agents, of a wider range of enslaving wants. On this point at least, thinkers as far apart as Malthus and Hegel were in complete agreement. 'The greatest of all difficulties in converting uncivilized and thinly peopled countries into civilized and populous ones', wrote Malthus in his *Principles*, 'is to inspire them [i.e. their inhabitants] with the wants best calculated to excite their exertions in the production of wealth'.[10] And Hegel – equally struck by the slowness with which the 'indolent' inhabitants of the New World were exploiting and peopling their continent – remarked as follows about the Jesuits' endeavour to convert the natives to European mores and habits:

When the Jesuits and the Catholic clergy proposed to accustom the Indians to European culture and manners (they have, as is well known, founded a state in Paraguay and convents in Mexico and California), they commenced a close intimacy with them, and prescribed for them the duties of the day, which, slothful though their disposition was, they complied with under the authority of the Friars. These prescripts (at midnight a bell had to remind them even of their matrimonial duties), were first, and very wisely, directed to the creation of wants – the springs of human activity generally.[11]

In effect, however, the awakening of gripping wants in line with Malthus' and Hegel's suggestion makes it difficult – and not only for the analyst, but for the agent as well – to draw a line separating the goats from the sheep. As common experience shows, the notion of true wants and needs, that is, those that cannot be dispensed with, has fluid boundaries. 'Need is considered the cause why something came to be; but in truth it is often merely an effect of what has come to be';[12] and as the regular and repeated gratification of petty wants finally transforms them into veritable needs, it becomes increasingly harder to distinguish the biological core, necessary for keeping 'mind and carcass' running fit, from all that has come to be required to make the journey worthwhile (or at least endurable). Few, however, would perhaps disagree with the rough estimation put forward in 1860 by J. Ruskin, to the effect that 'three-fourths of the demands existing in the world are romantic; founded on visions, idealisms, hopes, and affections; and the regulation of the purse is, in its essence, regulation of the imagination and the heart'.[13] What most modern economic analysts would surely quarrel with is Marshall's view that, since 'consumption is the end of production', economists have the duty of helping the community in which they live and work to think more clearly and wisely about their wants and the variety of non-economic costs involved in satisfying them.

It must also be noticed that abstaining from one's individual beliefs and inclinations, in order to spend one's working life carrying out programmed courses of action, is by no means an exclusive privilege of those agents who have drawn the Malthusian blank in terms of the financial and genetic endowments with which they have been, so to speak, 'sent off into the desert'. The unskilled industrial worker, no doubt, if he is lucky enough to find a job, or simply desperate enough to price himself into one, represents the most extreme typification of an agent's lack of autonomy with respect to his own labour-process. As F. Engels has observed, this is a problem partly rooted in modern industrial technology and the factory-system; and as such it is, as he stressed, 'independent of all social organization': 'The automatic machinery of a big factory is much more despotic than the small capitalists who employ workers ever have been. At least with regard to the hours of work one may write upon the portals of these factories: "Lasciate ogni autonomia, voi che entrate!"'[14] But in regard to this particular problem, as I shall presently argue, the unskilled industrial worker is by no means alone.

Division of labour *within* each particular workshop had meant first the resolution of the production line into a series of discrete, well-defined and sequential operations. But this had led in turn to a most remarkable unintended outcome: the gradual opening up of the labour-process to the introduction of mechanical technology and machinery. As it happened, the previous simplification of labour had in effect opened the door and then invited in, as it were, the use of machinery to replace – or, if not to replace, to modify – the participation of labour in the productive process.

Thus division of labour within the workshop implied (a) the need for external co-ordination of the simultaneous and relatively simple activities of workers participating in a given labour-process; and (b) the continuing and growing scope for further mechanization of the labour-process, through the replacement and modification of human labour by machinery. These two factors, and especially (b), are the general causes behind the situation depicted by Engels, in which the labour-journey is reduced to an abstract, passive and simple routine and work itself has been transformed into 'wage-earning activity'.(Engels, unlike Marx, did not entertain excessively high hopes as to the possibilities of changing or 'redeeming' the industrial labour process in a centrally planned economy.)[15]

When he searches for a job, the unskilled worker sets a price on himself in exchange for which he ceases to be a morally autonomous person and becomes the impersonal deliverer of an abstract function. But the fact of the matter, as I will try to show, is that in any complex society this is a practice that goes far beyond the experience of the industrial proletariat. First, because it has its counterpart in the service sector of the economy, where many categories of activity – from bank-cashier and ticket-collector to typist, taxi driver and waiter – are characterized by the fact that their logic is stable enough to allow for their eventual replacement by mechanical devices. Can there be a better proof of machine-like labour than the fact that it is (or soon shall be) replaceable by automatic machinery?

And second because, as it will be presently argued, the division of labour taking place within each particular productive unit of the economy is only one part of the story. The other part, which is in many respects more important than the first, has to do with the *social division of labour* and the resulting problem of economic co-ordination.

The general axiom here is Aristotle's notion that: 'The life of money-making is one undertaken under compulsion'. As such, once one is in it – and as he says later on, 'it is impossible, or not easy, to do noble acts without the proper equipment' – there arises a situation of compulsion, that is to say, a situation characterized by the fact that 'the moving principle is outside, being a principle in which nothing is contributed by the person who acts'.[16]

The primary job of any corporate business, as it is well known, is to make money for its stockholders. But the life of money-making has a logic of its own – as the French proverb sums it, 'L'argent n'a pas de maître'. Thus if, for example, research into the relationship between productivity and the age of employees establishes the view that it pays off to man a given industrial or managerial department only with persons under the age of, say, thirty-four, and, if a Schumpeterian 'go-getter' steps forward to successfully introduce this measure into his business, then a situation arises in which his competitors will find themselves under strong pressure to follow suit. If they allow their moral opinions and personal inclinations to interfere with their transactions in the life of money-making, and if they are allowed by shareholders to go on doing what they believe is right and proper, then they are bound not only to let down the 'rational economic man' of modern economics, but also to make less money and, if the environment is tight or the economy sluggish, eventually to go bankrupt.

Similarly, the businessman who chooses to spend on the training of the handicapped, or on the environment (even if only by abstaining from damaging it too much), or in supporting higher education and the arts, may find that he is losing ground to competitors and putting his business at risk (e.g. *via* a hostile take-over bid from a less scrupulous concern). He may also find, what is perhaps more likely, that he is putting his own career as a private executive in jeopardy and, in a way, committing professional suicide. His predicament resembles that of the Keynesian long-term investor who, by playing fair and acting on the basis of genuine long-term expectations, finds himself playing the 'fool among knaves' and is penalized for not doing like everybody else and going in for opportunist, quick results. An essentially analogous dilemma, it may be noted, permeates Machiavelli's advice to the Prince:

And the manner in which we live, and that in which we ought to live, are things so wide asunder, that he who quits the one to betake himself to the other is more likely to destroy than to save himself; since any one who would act up to a perfect standard of goodness in everything, must be ruined among so many who are not good. It is essential, therefore, for a Prince who would maintain his position, to have learned how to be other than good, and to use or not use his goodness as necessity requires.[17]

Autonomy, in this context, is a path to failure and even self-destruction. Survival exacts conformity. Public virtue is conducive to private ruin. Clearly, it might be added, the relevant question here is not Juvenal's 'Who cares for reputation if he keeps his cash?'. Rather, the question now is who can afford to care for his reputation – or to have a clear conscience – even when his job and career are seriously put at risk by it?

So the competitive process works as a conduct-enforcing mechanism which leaves little up to the good (or bad) intentions of the firm's management. True, it may prevent, to some extent, incompetence and inefficiency; but it also precludes agents acting 'by their own lights', i.e. as it seems to them that they ought to act. The point is well-captured by Marx in his discussion of the capitalist's drive for gain and private accumulation:

Only as a personification of capital is the capitalist respectable. As such, he shares with the miser an absolute drive towards self-enrichment. But what appears in the miser as the mania of an individual is in the capitalist the effect of a social mechanism in which he is merely a cog. Moreover, the development of capitalist production makes it necessary constantly to increase the capital laid out in a given industrial undertaking, and competition subordinates every individual capitalist to the immanent laws of capitalist production, as external and coercive laws.[18]

Of course, what is missing from Marx's picture is the fact that no complex society can do without some form of 'social mechanism' which co-ordinates the actions of dispersed agents by enforcing certain types of behaviour. In a centrally planned economy, it will be argued, the co-ordination is achieved by the political authorities and the institutions of command and surveillance.

As Adam Smith first realized and brilliantly pointed out in the first two books of the *Wealth of Nations*, the competitive process in a market economy generates, through its flexible price network, a complex system of feedback mechanisms responsible for the co-ordination of a great number of isolated units of production which are defined and kept apart by the fundamental fact of modern commercial society, the social division of labour. The problem of co-ordination here is essentially the problem of regulating the allocation of the productive resources of society – the control over which is dispersed among a great number of isolated agents – not in any arbitrary way, but in accordance with all the relevant and extremely diffuse and volatile information regarding (a) the costs of production (supply) and (b) the evaluation of different classes of goods by consumers (demand).

In a pure capitalist market economy the job of co-ordination is done by the price system. The mechanism of price-formation would, according to Smith's vision, work as the chain-gear through which updated economic information is processed and readily made available to producers and consumers. Thus, though all agents in the economy pursue only their selfish and private ends, by having to bow down to the changing price signals – those 'irrefutable arguments' – being sent by the markets, it happily turns out that the keener their 'dollar-hunting' (to use Mill's expression), the more they will be contributing to purposes which go far beyond their limited, self-centred perspective. In its *Wealth of Nations* impersonation, the 'invisible hand' stands for the working out of the 'unplanned plan' of commercial society and the enhancement of national prosperity across the board.[19]

The price system sets the rules which economic activities must follow in order to succeed, or at least to survive, in the market-place. The life of money-making – 'By right means if you can, but by any means make money'[20] – is undertaken under compulsion because its logic is externally set. In so far as they are working within the framework set by the market order, 'Genghis Khan and the saint' – the voracious timber-merchant and the committed conservationist – will all have to play according to a book which is not of their own making. The conduct-enforcing mechanism at work here, which originates from the primacy of the money-motive, will operate in much the same way as it does for the factory-worker who, as just seen, is bound to be dismissed from his job or even to provoke an accident in the workshop if he fails to pay heed to Engels' warning and forgets to leave his autonomy behind when he begins his working-day.

In a pure socialist planned economy, the Smithian 'unplanned plan' is replaced by an only too visible and explicit central plan. Commands, in the form of production targets and procedural norms, and the monitoring over the execution of the commands issued, are substituted for the impersonal workings of the price mechanism. The central planning committee is in the driver's seat. But this of course does not mean that it will be capable of achieving whatever it plans to; for the central committee, no matter how competent and hard-working, will face a serious problem as to how it may elicit reliable information about the changing production possibilities and consumer wants, and as to how it may handle and turn all this formidable amount of information to good account, if it were somehow made available.[21] The central issue, however, from the viewpoint of the moral autonomy yardstick, is that central planning brings no obvious improvement regarding the individual agent's capability to act 'by his own lights' in the economic sphere of action.

If he is an ordinary industrial worker, he must carry on doing factory-work and being, as it were, 'a stopgap to fill a hole in human inventiveness'. If he earns his livelihood as a local bureaucrat, he must follow the commands issued by the central authority and make sure, if he prizes his career, that they are carried out by those under his autarchy. And, if he is a top bureaucrat, he may well have a say on the commands being issued but (a) his decisions will be taken, to a considerable degree, 'in the dark' – due to the informational and computational *lacunae* underlying the decision-making process; – and (b) he will find himself unable to ensure that provincial bureaucrats will actually obey the norms and fulfil the targets set by the central committee, even though the latter may certainly punish those who venture to depart from its commands and are caught. If an agent

cannot bring himself to see that the plan is 'objectively' in his own –
and in everybody else's – best interests, he will have to co-operate and
perform his bit nevertheless. Otherwise he becomes an outcast or is
sent for psychiatric internment or starves.

Hence the *external* constraint facing the individual agent as he
attempts to live up to his beliefs and opinions in ordinary life. This
limitation of our autonomy or 'freedom to do', I suggest, offers a
fundamental reason for qualifying the economic philosophy claim
that 'Ideas rule the world of human affairs and its events' (chapter 1).

There are considerable segments of action in practical life in which
the logic of the economic situation, requiring some form of spontaneous or explicit co-ordination of a great number of dispersed and
relatively uninformed agents, is the determining factor. The individual agent's beliefs and values (his 'ideology') make little or no
difference in so far as his outward behaviour in the system is
concerned. Agents become, so to speak, trapped into courses of action
with their own logic, and their autonomy to dissent once they have
stepped onto the economic circuit is, in many cases, no greater than,
say, the freedom to choose how to digest food once it is let into the
body.

The argument, of course, must not be pushed too far. The pure
market and the pure command economy are both 'ideal types' and it
would be misleading to imagine that they do more than to capture
and highlight certain essential features of the workings of concrete
economies. The competitive process is often rather less watertight
than the concept of a pure market system would seem to suggest, and
local bureaucrats may well have a lot more room for manoeuvre than
would be the case in a strictly centralized command economy.
Indeed, no actual economy can thrive and prosper without a fresh
supply of individual initiative and mould-breaking 'creative destruction' at some point in the economic process.

Moreover, it is still open to any given society whether to economize
or not on its reliance upon conduct-enforcing mechanisms like
factory-work, market-competition or central planning. Although the
costs in terms of goods and material well-being foregone may be high,
agents may still prefer to enjoy more 'freedom to do', i.e. to consume
less with a view to minimizing the time spent doing things they would
not normally do and yet end up doing in order to acquire the goods
and services they want. To achieve this, they would have to prize their
autonomy and unlearn some wants.

But the fact remains – and the concepts of a pure market and a pure command economic system help to bring it out – that any complex society sets significant constraints on the capability of the individual agent to deviate from the behaviour prescribed by the economic situation facing him. In a famous passage of the *Wealth of Nations* Smith wrote: 'I have never known much good done by those who affected to trade for the publick good. It is an affectation, indeed, not very common among merchants, and very few words need be employed in dissuading them from it' (WN,456). The point I have tried to stress in this chapter is that, even if agents truly concerned themselves with social issues and the common good, it would not make as much difference to their economic behaviour as it might at first appear. For they would still find that, in effect, their concern turned out to be severely restricted by the existence of more or less powerful conduct-enforcing mechanisms and the need to survive or to survive in business (or in office).

The practical upshot of the argument developed in this chapter is well-conveyed by F. Knight, an early leader of the Chicago school, in 'The ethics of competition' (1923):

When we consider that productive activity takes up the larger part of the waking lives of the great mass of mankind, it is surely not to be assumed without investigation or inquiry that production is a means only, a necessary evil, a sacrifice made for the sake of some good entirely outside the production process. We are impelled to look for ends in the economic process itself, and to give thoughtful consideration to the possibilities of participation in economic activity as a sphere of self-expression and creative achievement.[22]

A similar emphasis, it may also be noted, on the need to consider the autonomy-related aspects of our economic arrangements, can be found in Mill's comments on the institution of wage-labour:

To work at the bidding and for the profit of another, without any interest in the work – the price of their labour being adjusted by hostile competition, one side demanding as much and the other paying as little as possible – is not, even when wages are high, a satisfactory state to human beings of educated intelligence, who have ceased to think themselves naturally inferior to those whom they serve. (CW3,766)

The issue, it might be thought, has a Marxist ring to it. But in fact it should be central to any serious consideration of the role of ethics in economic behaviour. It has not lost its pertinence and it seems just as relevant today – in spite of the shadow cast by mass unemployment – as it was when the remarks by Mill and Knight were made.

It remains certainly *prima facie* a matter of individual choice – and here beliefs and opinions may well matter – embarking at all on such lines of conduct whose moving principle is out of the agent's reach. As it has been observed, 'there are, if only rarely, men who would rather perish than work without any pleasure in their work'.[23] But for the great majority who would not rather perish than submit to somewhat stringent conduct-enforcing mechanisms, and who seem resigned to leave the autonomy of their working lives behind in order to be paid (and provided, of course, it is a 'decent pay'), a span of practical life will go on much the same, quite unaffected by the 'war of ideas' and the ideological storms which may agitate the intellectual minority.

CHAPTER 6

The passions of the imagination, I Hume and Adam Smith on the sub-rational determinants of belief

In the last chapter, I attempted to show how the economic process in any complex society takes its toll in terms of the individual agent's autonomy or 'freedom to do'. There is some scope for choice as regards the co-ordination system adopted and whether to economize or not on the use of conduct-enforcing mechanisms. Changes in the rules of the economic game may be thought worth having, so as to try to rule out the occurrence of certain undesirable outcomes. But in any case there will be large areas of behaviour in economic life which lie outside the sphere of 'ideas'. In these areas, the agent's beliefs and opinions turn out to be of little or no significance in so far as his outward, observable conduct in the system is concerned.

In this chapter, I shall draw attention to the existence of powerful *internal* or psychological constraints on the autonomy of the individual agent. Drawing on the philosophy of action put forward by Hume and Adam Smith, I will suggest that agents act on the basis of what they believe is in their own interest, but that this opinion of interest is largely the work of their sub-rational (meaning *non-rational* rather than *irrational*) dispositions and motivations. An important step in this argument will be the attempt to elucidate the eighteenth-century concept of passion.

The key principle here is the Humean notion that 'belief is more properly an act of the sensitive, than of the cogitative part of our natures' (THN, 183). Agents, it will be argued, are not entirely aware of the workings of their own minds or able to fully regulate them – their self-knowledge and self-command are severely limited. And these factors, I will suggest, have significant implications at the level of everyday empirical thinking and ordinary economic behaviour. This emphasis on the sub-rational input of our belief-fixation mechanisms, I shall also argue, helps to explain why Hume (as indicated in chapter 1) came to side with the 'majority view', in the

sense of seriously calling in question the role and efficacy of
philosophy as an independent variable in the processes of belief-
formation and social change.

Assuming that there is nothing fundamentally wrong with the
notion that ideas can set in motion and alter behaviour in practical
life, it is still necessary to ask: are we responsible for all our beliefs and
opinions, or is belief, essentially, something that happens to us? How
do we choose and justify to ourselves ideas which command our belief
but for which adequate grounds are lacking? And are the ideas which
seem able to affect and change social behaviour really 'sovereign
rulers', or are they, as it were, largely the 'symptoms' or 'flag-signals'
of more basic psychological forces and propensities acting in us
though not always known to ourselves?

We may begin by noting that the existence of inexpugnable beliefs
shared by a great number of agents and intellectuals did not fail to
catch the attention of the more sceptical thinkers belonging to the
eighteenth-century Enlightenment, 'an age of reason based upon
faith'.[1]

'I took care not to dispute anything he said, for there is no arguing
with an Enthusiast', remarked Voltaire on his visit to an English
Quaker. In a passage which clearly echoes Locke's attack on
'enthusiasm' (i.e. the mental habit through which 'confidence of
being right is made an argument of truth'), he continued: 'Better not
to take it into one's head to tell a lover the faults of his mistress, or a
litigant the weakness of his cause – or to talk sense to a fanatic'.[2] There
are areas of belief which turn out to be remarkably well protected
from the destructive effects of critical analysis. The thinking subject
has somehow sealed off the relevant set of beliefs – a 'fortress of
certainties' – and manages to keep them at a safe distance from any
attempt at genuine questioning or self-doubt. Religious beliefs and, as
Hume put it, 'superstition and enthusiasm, the corruptions of true
religion' (E,73), are perhaps the most visible signs suggesting the
existence of belief-forming habits and elaborate intellectual construc-
tions virtually closed to the power of otherwise persuasive arguments.

Even Hegel, it may be noted, for all his unshakeable confidence in
human reason, and his conviction that 'the Being of the universe, at
first hidden and concealed, has no power which can offer resistance to
the search for knowledge', acknowledged the fact that the human
mind can, under certain circumstances, prove peculiarly resistant to
the strictures of the 'eye of Reason': 'Religion, particularly imagina-

tive religion, cannot be torn from the whole life and heart of a people by cold syllogisms constructed in a study'.[3]

And the young Marx, in his doctoral dissertation on Greek atomism, also noticed the existence of beliefs which appear to involve more than the possibility of error and do not yield to enlightened assaults: 'Come with your gods into a country where other gods are worshipped, and you will be shown to suffer from fantasies and abstractions'. Only in the 'country of reason', he added, in the domain of critical philosophy, religious convictions had no rights of citizenship and could therefore be done away with, in so far as 'that which a particular country is for particular alien gods, the country of reason is for God in general, a region in which he ceases to exist'.[4]

But then, if we take Marx's suggestion seriously, the following question is bound to arise. Once the philosopher sets himself off, sending all 'gods' and 'God in general' into an exile from the well-demarcated and jealously guarded 'country of reason', where will he stop?

If the philosopher cultivates the skill of providing sound and valid grounds for claims to knowledge, he must of course not rest content with the exposure of the errors and illusions of past traditions, but proceed to a careful critical examination of *his own* convictions and conceptual presuppositions. The question is how far will he be able to go, before putting a more or less arbitrary stop to his search for further grounds capable of assuring all other rational enquirers about the validity of the truth-claims he has made or is about to make? How will he settle the process of self-doubt, and thus secure a 'fortress of certainties' for himself from which to wage his own expansionary offensive in the 'war of ideas'? Are economic philosophers exempted from building propositions and viewpoints upon one or more end-points, i.e. unanalysable and rather opaque premises in the chains of rational justification they offer?

The merit of scepticism is to show that if it is true, on the one hand, to say that 'Science is the great antidote to the poison of enthusiasm and superstition',[5] it is also true, on the other, that 'philosophical enthusiasm' is a no less pernicious or common poison. 'Philosophical enthusiasm' here means what might be called self-satisfied thinking or 'thought at rest'. It occurs when a thinker warms up, as it were, to his own thinking processes and is led to overlook the fact that there is an arbitrary element built into his theories – that all theoretical and practical enquiries, including of course his own, proceed from and stand upon a 'hard core' of primary beliefs whose validation is highly uncertain. 'One absurdity having been granted, the rest follows. Nothing difficult about that'.[6]

Thus, the 'philosophical enthusiast' not only closes the door to an investigation into the prejudgements underlying his own thinking, but is apt to embark on an all out campaign to make converts to his truth. As J. Swift (Adam Smith's favourite English writer) pointedly observed: 'What Man in the natural State, or Course of Thinking, did ever conceive it in his Power, to reduce the Notions of all Mankind, exactly to the same Length, and Breadth, and Heighth of his own? Yet this is the first humble and civil Design of all Innovators in the Empire of Reason'.[7] The sceptic's job is to guard against self-satisfied thinking and the 'intoxication of prosperity' in the realm of thought; to recall that 'At the foundation of well-founded belief lies belief that is not founded'.[8] 'Keep sober and remember to be sceptical' (Hume's motto).

The problem of 'philosophical enthusiasm' is of course closely related to the problem of dogmatism in theoretical and practical thinking: (a) the advancing of propositions purporting to lay open the 'ultimate secrets' of the universe and man's place in it, and (b) the formulation of moral codes, social policies and philosophical blue-prints for mankind which present themselves as truly corresponding to the dictates of 'Reason', 'Nature' or 'History'. A set of primary principles has become unavailable for further critical assessment and is now taken for granted as the only true foundation for claims to knowledge concerning what *is* and what *ought to be*. Did not Hume predict rather well some future developments in dogmatic meta-physics and moral and economic philosophy when he remarked that, notwithstanding 'frequent disappointment' and the breakdown of the Cartesian ambitious 'tree of knowledge', 'Each adventurous genius will still leap at the arduous prize, and find himself stimulated, rather than discouraged, by the failures of his predecessors, while he hopes that the glory of achieving so hard an adventure is reserved for him alone'? (1stE, 12).

Enthusiasm for science and a scientific world-outlook is one of the variants of 'philosophical enthusiasm' opposed by the eighteenth-century 'enlightened sceptics' like J. d'Alembert, P. Bayle, Hume and others. To the popular view expressed by the poet – 'Nature and Nature's laws lay hid in night; God said, "Let Newton be", and all was light' – Hume replied in a much more sober (and perhaps no less quoted) statement: 'While Newton seemed to draw off the veil from some of the mysteries of nature, he shewed at the same time the imperfections of the mechanical philosophy; and thereby restored her ultimate secrets to that obscurity in which they ever did and ever will remain'.[9] Or as he put it elsewhere: 'The most perfect philosophy of the natural kind only staves off our ignorance a little longer: as perhaps the most perfect philosophy of the moral or metaphysical kind serves only to discover larger portions of it' (1stE,31).

Even science, that 'great antidote to the poison of superstition', may become poison itself when invested with excessive authority. 'I was resolved not to be an enthusiast in philosophy, while I was blaming other enthusiasms', wrote Hume to Lord Kames on his return from the Jesuit College La Flèche (a Cartesian stronghold in Anjou, France where Descartes himself had been educated about a century earlier). And this critical stance towards 'philosophical enthusiasm', the need to 'keep sober' and to guard against an unwarranted faith in science, helps to explain why Hume came to hold the view that, as he would stress in the introduction of *A Treatise*, 'the science of man is the only solid foundation for the other sciences': 'There is no question of importance, whose decision is not compriz'd in the science of man; and there is none, which can be decided with any certainty, before we become acquainted with that science . . . Human Nature is the only science of man; and yet has been hitherto the most neglected' (THN,xvi and 273).[10]

From the viewpoint of human *action*, the sceptic enterprise runs into an interesting paradox. More than any other professional of ideas, the sceptic specializes in the scrutiny of his own beliefs and opinions. Self-doubt and the courage to attack his own convictions and their grounds are for him virtues at least as important as having the courage of one's convictions. But, if he pushes the former a little too far, he will find himself utterly unable to comply with the latter.

If he is bold and detached enough to assail and undermine the ultimate certainties on which human reasoning rests, he will then find it *ipso facto* impossible to carry out his sceptical conclusions and translate them into action in ordinary life. Scepticism turns out to be incompatible with *any* course of action in common life, and those who attempt to put it into practice are likely (if ever possible) to end up in hospitals (e.g. if one really doubts one has a body or that the external world exists) or madhouses (e.g. hesitations about the truthfulness of memory or about personal identity and the reality of the ego).

This is the practical reason why, as Hume wrote concluding Book I ('Of the Understanding') of his *Treatise*: 'A true sceptic will be diffident of his philosophical doubts, as well as of his philosophical conviction' (THN,273). The Humean sceptic ventures to go a step further than the 'merely sceptical' philosopher would go. For he devotes himself so earnestly to the critical task of testing and scanning his own beliefs and opinions – so as to expose their shaky foundations – that he ends up doubting not only his convictions, but his doubts as well. If I want (or need) to act, then I will have to (and I will) close the door on doubt. Any action and all positive enquiry negate the purely destructive, armchair mode of scepticism. One must stop somewhere. The peculiarly Humean stress on the notion that common sense, and the 'majority view', must be listened to, can be seen as following naturally from this move.

Indeed, no one seems to have lived the paradox of scepticism with more intensity and awareness than Hume. The theme is recurrent in his early and mature writings, and one of its most vivid occurrences comes up in his so-called 'philosophical testament', the posthumously published *Dialogues Concerning Natural Religion* (1779). 'In reality', urges Cleanthes, a spokesman for deism and the doctrine of design, as he turns against the scepticism hinted at by Philo,

In reality . . . it seems certain, that tho' a Man, in a Flush of Humour, after intense Reflection on the many Contradictions and Imperfections of human Reason, may entirely renounce all Belief and Opinion; it is impossible for him to persevere in his total Scepticism, or make it appear in his Conduct for a few Hours. External Objects press in upon him: Passions sollicit him: His philosophical Melancholy dissipates; and even the utmost Violence upon his own Temper will not be able, during any time, to preserve the poor Appearance of Scepticism.[11]

Hence the Pyrrhonian philosopher or radical sceptic, writes Hume,

must acknowledge, if he will acknowledge anything, that all human life must perish, were his principles universally and steadily to prevail. All discourse, all action would immediately cease; and men remain in a total lethargy, till the necessities of nature, unsatisfied, put an end to their miserable existence. It is true, so fatal an event is very little to be dreaded. Nature is always too strong for principle. And though a Pyrrhonian may throw himself and others into a momentary confusion by his profound reasonings; the first and most trivial event in life will put to flight all his doubts and scruples, and leave him in the same, in every point of action and speculation, with the philosophers of every other sect, or with those who never concerned themselves in any philosophical researches. (1stE,160)

But as the last sentence of the quotation above already indicates, the argument against scepticism has much wider implications. In effect, it calls into question the very notion that philosophy or systematic and abstract thought plays a fundamental role in belief-formation and ordinary life. The underlying principle supporting Hume's naturalist countercharge to scepticism – encapsulated in the notion that 'Nature is always too strong for principle' – is his discovery that there is a chasm between the results of philosophical reflection ('ideas') on the one hand, and everyday empirical thinking ('belief') on the other, to the effect that 'Very refin'd reflections have little or no influence upon us':

There is a great difference betwixt such opinions as we form after a calm and profound reflection, and such as we embrace by a kind of instinct or natural impulse, on account of their suitableness and conformity to the mind. If these opinions become contrary, 'tis not difficult to foresee which of them will have the advantage. As long as our attention is bent upon the subject, the philosophical and study'd principle may prevail; but the moment we relax our thoughts, nature will display herself, and draw us back to our former opinion. Nay she has sometimes such an influence, that she can stop our progress, even in the midst of our most profound reflections, and keep us from running on with all the consequences of any philosophical opinion . . . Nature is obstinate, and will not quit the field, however strongly attack'd by reason. (THN,214–5)

When he steps out of his study, notes Hume, 'the philosopher is lost in the man' and 'sinks by degrees into the Plebeian'. Whereas Marx had said of the modern industrial worker, that he 'feels himself only when he is not working, when he is working he does not feel himself',[12] we may now say of the philosopher that, if he has the strength not to halt self-doubt at some superficial and arbitrary point, then he feels himself only when he is working, when he is not working he does not feel himself.

In the light of this reasoning, it is understandable that Hume would have serious misgivings about normative moral philosophy and the view that virtue could be taught or social agents persuaded to mend their ways and live according to the dictates of duty, reason or the highest good. Theories and ideas have only a very limited influence in

the determination of man's actions. While maintaining that opinion
of interest governs human practical behaviour, he stressed that 'the
empire of philosophy extends over a few, and with regard to these too,
her authority is very weak and limited' (E,169). The philosopher
himself, as seen above, is no exception to this rule. Though he may
reap noble truths and ideals in his enquiries, and urge others (in
print) to adopt them in their lives and polity, he is nonetheless unable
to do or feel as he would:

He sees, but feels not sufficiently their truth; and is always a sublime
philosopher, when he needs not; that is, as long as nothing disturbs him, or
rouzes his affections. While others play, he wonders at their keenness and
ardour; but he no sooner puts his own at stake, than he is commonly
transported with the same passions, that he so much condemned, while he
remained a simple spectator. (E,176)

As the young Hume had put it in his letter to Lord Kames cited
above, 'How happens it, that we philosophers cannot as heartily
despise the world, as it despises us?'

  Thus, the impotency of the learned to impress their conclusions
upon their conduct and to square their actions by the results of the
enquiry undertaken suggests that the opinions and beliefs governing
behaviour have to do *not* so much with the 'reflections of philosophy',
which are 'too subtle and distant to take place in common life, or
eradicate any affection', but rather with 'the fabric and constitution
of our mind', which 'no more depends on our choice, than that of our
body' (E,168 & 172). It is therefore not surprising that Hume would
conclude – in marked contrast with the economic philosophers from
Paley to Hayek reviewed in chapter 1 – that:

Whoever considers, without prejudice, the course of human actions, will
find, that mankind are almost entirely guided by constitution and temper,
and that general maxims have little influence, but so far as they affect our
taste or sentiment. (E,169)

The yoke of spontaneous belief-forming mental habits and non-
rational custom binds together the learned and the generality of
mankind, including of course the 'philosophers themselves, who, in
all the active parts of life, are, in the main, the same with the vulgar,
and are governed by the same maxims' (1stE,106).[13] As he put it in
'Of commerce' (1752): 'When a man deliberates concerning his
conduct in any particular affair, and forms schemes in politics, trade,
oeconomy, or any business in life, he never ought to draw his

arguments too fine, or connect too long a chain of consequences together. Something is sure to happen, that will disconcert his reasoning, and produce an event different from what he expected' (E,254).

In order to highlight the sharp contrast between Hume's position on this issue and that of the 'enlightened enthusiast' of eighteenth-century thought (and after), it may be well to recall, for example, some remarks by the French 'philosophe' and revolutionary leader, Marquis de Condorcet, in his sanguine statement of the principle of human perfectibility in *Esquisse d'un Tableau Historique des Progrès de L'Esprit Humain*, published by the French government in the Third Year (1795) of the Republic:

All errors in politics and morals are based on philosophical errors and these in turn are connected with scientific errors. There is not a religious system nor a supernatural extravagance that is not founded on ignorance of the laws of nature. The inventors, the defenders of these absurdities could not foresee the successive perfection of the human mind . . . We shall point out that the principles of philosophy, the slogans of liberty, the recognition of the true rights of man and his real interests, have spread through far too great a number of nations, and now direct in each of them the opinions of far too great a number of enlightened men, for us to fear that they will ever be allowed to relapse into oblivion.[14]

Of course, no twentieth-century political or economic philosopher would now venture to make a prophecy like the one in the last sentence of this quote. What is common between Condorcet's views and those of the economic philosophers discussed in chapter 1, especially the Austrian neo-liberal school, is the strong tendency to intellectualize the origins of society's problems and to grossly enlarge the role of philosophy in the processes of belief-formation and social change – the notions that: (a) 'philosophical errors' and 'ideas' rule the world, (b) 'errors' and 'superstitions' are the result of cognitive mistakes, and (c) 'salvation' and 'cure', i.e. the adoption of their own views and opinions, 'is a purely intellectual matter'.

Consider, for example, in connection with this point, the Hayekian campaign against 'the errors of constructivism', 'the extreme rationalism of the Descartes-Hegel-Marx school', 'the progressive destruction of irreplaceable values by scientific error' or, yet, his thoroughly Condorcetian statement according to which:

If our civilization survives, which it will do only if it renounces those errors, I believe men will look back on our age as an age of superstition, chiefly connected with the names of Karl Marx and Sigmund Freud. I believe people will discover that the most widely held ideas which dominated the twentieth century, those of a planned economy with a just distribution, a freeing ourselves from repressions and conventional morals, of permissive education as a way to freedom, and the replacement of the market by a rational arrangement of a body with coercive powers, were all based on superstitions in the strict sense of the word.[15]

Statements of this nature represent the fixation of belief as a purely intellectual affair and social change as being essentially the result of 'ideological warfare'. The mistake from which these misrepresentations arise, I shall argue, is the failure to take into account the work of the 'passions' in the process of belief-formation – the Humean notion that 'The command of the mind over itself is limited, as well as its command over the body . . . Our authority over our sentiments and passions is much weaker than that over our ideas; and even the latter authority is circumscribed within very narrow boundaries' (1stE,68).

The key term used by the eighteenth-century 'enlightened sceptics' to refer to this 'species of instinct or mechanical power, that acts in us unknown to ourselves' (1stE,108), and which so powerfully constrains from below our beliefs and opinions, is the term *passion*.

'Our passions', Adam Smith was fond of saying, 'all justify themselves, that is, suggest to us opinions which justify them'.[16] Belief, according to this view, is primarily a function of what accords with the agent's sentiments and psychological needs. The determinants of our relevant beliefs and opinions are not to be sought only or chiefly in the heavenly abode of philosophy ('ideas' and 'errors'). A fundamental role is given to the part played by our sub-rational dispositions and motivations ('passions') in our belief-forming mechanisms. But what does passion mean in this context? And how does it influence the fixation of belief?

In Book II ('Of the Passions') of his *Treatise*, Hume analysed the 'different causes and effects of the calm and violent passions', trying to show, among other things, how 'the notion of duty, when opposite to the passions, is seldom able to overcome them' (THN,421). The analytical spirit of his undertaking is well conveyed by the words of the Dutch philosopher B. de Spinoza who, in the former century, had proposed to study 'human passions [humanos affectus] like love, hate, anger, envy, pride, pity, and the other feelings that agitate the mind, not as vices of human nature, but as properties which belong to it in the same way as heat, cold, storm, thunder and the like belong to the nature of the atmosphere'.[17]

While rejecting the Cartesian notion that 'the mind has absolute power over its actions', Spinoza had attempted to examine 'the nature and strength of the emotions, and the power of the mind against them for their restraint'. But, whereas he adopted a geometrical, rigidly deductive method of enquiry ('I shall consider human actions and desires in exactly the same manner, as though I were concerned with lines, planes, and solids'), Hume and Smith approached the subject in a more experimental or empirical spirit, trying to base their general conclusions on the observation of ordinary behaviour and the study of history.[18]

The general intention underlying the Humean philosophy of action is perhaps best captured by what the French seventeenth-century moralist Duc de La Rochefoucauld had said in one of his maxims, viz. that 'We are very far from realizing all that our passions make us do'. For 'Man', he held, 'often thinks he is control when he is being controlled'; and he is being controlled not because he is subject to restrictions and compulsions that are external to him (cf. chapter 5), but because his self-knowledge and self-command are severely limited: 'The passions are the only orators who always convince'.[19] As Hume were to put it: 'Nothing is more vigilant and inventive than our passions' (THN, 526). (As I shall try to show in the next chapter, both Hume and Smith were to spend no little effort in the attempt to spell out how and why all this applied to our ordinary economic behaviour.)

Of course, the term *passion* in this context must not be confused with the current popular usage of the word. *Passion*, in our late twentieth-century vocabulary, is closely associated with the (probably) early nineteenth-century and Romantic-inspired new meaning for the term, as denoting primarily fits and outbursts of feeling, violent and capricious emotional storms, and especially sexual lust.

This, however, represents already a considerable change and degeneration of its former meaning. For Hume and Smith, as indeed for the eighteenth-century Enlightenment in its variety of intellectual tendencies, *passion* still kept for the most part its classical meaning, and denoted not only the stormy or fit-like, but all the passive (same Latin root *passio*: 'to suffer') mental processes taking place in the human mind, that is to say, that which it 'suffers' or undergoes ('the horses'), as opposed to that which it does when it tries to assert itself and exercise free choice ('the rider'). The term passion refers thus, as Spinoza put it, to any 'state wherein the mind is passive'.[20] Passions, in this sense, can be calm and steady as well as violent and freakish, and not a hair's breadth less potent for that.

Adam Smith, in *Theory of Moral Sentiments*, speaks of 'the Passions which take their origin from the body' and those 'which take their origin from a particular turn of habit of the Imagination'. He concentrates the analysis markedly on the latter, and this is the reason why self-command – i.e. not yielding to fear, anger, pride, enthusiasm and so on, but also checking our tendency to incur in self-deception and misrepresent to ourselves our own conduct – turns out to be, in his moral system, the cardinal virtue that a man may possess.

To act according to the dictates of prudence, of justice, and proper beneficence, seems to have no great merit where there is no temptation to do otherwise. But to act with cool deliberation in the midst of the greatest dangers and difficulties; to observe religiously the sacred rules of justice in spite of both the greatest interests which might tempt, and the greatest injuries which might provoke us to violate them; never to suffer the benevolence of our temper to be damped or discouraged by the malignity and ingratitude of the individuals towards whom it may have been exercised; is the character of the most exalted wisdom and virtue. Self-command is not only itself a great virtue, but from it all other virtues seem to derive their principle lustre. (TMS,241; see also TMS,244–5)

The greatest artists, as Smith observed, are never fully satisfied with their own productions and accomplishments. They know they could have done better. But their situation, he noted, is still far better than the one facing men of action:

The artist sits down to his work undisturbed, at leisure, in the full possession and recollection of all his skill, experience and knowledge. The wise man must support the propriety of his own conduct in health and in sickness, in success and in disappointment, in the hour of fatigue and drowsy indolence, as well as in that of the most awakened attention. The most sudden and unexpected assaults of difficulty and distress must never surprise him. The injustice of other people must never provoke him to injustice. The violence of faction must never confound him. All the hardships and hazards of war must never either dishearten or appal him. (TMS,249)

The centrality of self-command in Smith's theory, it may be noted in passing, places it within the Aristotelian tradition in ethical thought. For as Smith himself pointed out, in his discussion of the concept of virtue in the history of ethics:

Virtue, according to Plato, might be considered as a species of science, and no man, he thought, could see clearly and demonstratively what was right and what was wrong, and not act accordingly. Passion might make us act contrary to doubtful and uncertain opinions, not to plain and evident judgements. Aristotle, on the contrary, was of opinion, that no conviction of the understanding was capable of getting the better of inveterate habits, and that good morals arose not from knowledge but from action. (TMS,272; see also TMS,237)

The human mind is apt to behave in unpredictable ways – and eventually to run badly astray – when confronted with conditions of extreme adversity or with exceptional circumstances in general. As Bacon had put it, 'a man's disposition is never well known till he be crossed': 'Prosperity doth best discover vice, but Adversity doth best discover virtue'.[21] The fluctuations of fortune have great influence over the beliefs and opinions of agents. And even the wise man, held Smith, if he is unsure about his ability to hold fast and firm to his best self, 'will avoid, as much as duty and propriety will permit, the situations for which he is not perfectly fitted' (TMS,245).

As the quotations in the last paragraphs probably make clear, Smith's stress on self-command springs from the associated view that the agent's sub-rational dispositions and motivations powerfully affect his thinking processes and behaviour. Perfect knowledge, if it is not supported by self-command, is of no avail. In effect, as I shall presently try to show, this notion that the 'passions of the imagination' play a central role in our belief-forming mechanisms, and hence in our ordinary conduct, runs a distinct thread through Smith's works as a whole:

(a) The famous 'desire to better one's condition' presiding over the *Wealth of Nations* is of course a passion; it is sustained by the appropriate set of beliefs and it belongs clearly to the realm of the imagination (this point will be taken up in chapter 7 below).

(b) Similarly, the 'love of system', argued Smith, the pleasure we take in beholding in the imagination the harmonious functioning of a 'great system of government', is often a more powerful motive to public reform than the expected utility, efficiency or social welfare resulting from it:

We take pleasure in beholding the perfection of so beautiful and grand a system, and we are uneasy till we remove any obstruction that can in the least disturb or encumber the regularity of its motions . . . If you would implant public virtue in the breast of him who seems heedless of the interest of his country, it will often be to no purpose to tell him, what superior advantages the subjects of a well-governed state enjoy . . . These consider- ations will commonly make no great impression. You will be more likely to persuade, if you describe the great system of public police which procures this advantages, if you explain the connexions and dependencies of its several parts, their mutual subordination to one another, and their general subserviency to the happiness of the society; if you show how this system might be introduced into his own country, what it is that hinders it from taking place there at present, how these obstructions might be removed, and all the several wheels of the machine of government be made to move with more harmony and smoothness, without grating upon one another, or mutually retarding one another's motions. It is scarce possible that a man should listen to a discourse of this kind, and not feel himself animated to some degree of public spirit. He will, at least for the moment, feel some desire to remove those obstructions, and to put into motion so beautiful and so orderly a machine. (TMS,185–6)

(c) Hot-headed reformers and revolutionaries, in their turn, by mixing the 'spirit of system' with that 'public spirit which is founded upon the love of humanity', are apt to end up inflaming their views 'even to the madness of fanaticism'. They are frequently carried away by their own zeal to bring about change and of course 'entertain no doubt of the immense superiority of their own judgement':

They often propose, upon this account, to new-model the constitution, and to alter, in some of its most essential parts, that system of government under which the subjects of a great empire have enjoyed, perhaps, peace, security, and even glory, during the course of several centuries together. The great body of the [discontented] party are commonly intoxicated with the imaginary beauty of this ideal system, of which they have no experience, but which has been represented to them in all the most dazzling colours in which the eloquence of their leaders could paint it. Those leaders themselves, though they originally may have meant nothing but their own aggrandise- ment, become many of them in time the dupes of their own sophistry, and are as eager for this great reformation as the weakest and foolishest of their followers . . . The man of system . . . is apt to be very wise in his own conceit; and he is often so enamoured with the supposed beauty of his own ideal plan of government, that he cannot suffer the smallest deviation from any part of it. (TMS,232–4)

It is consistent with this view (as it will be seen in part II below) that economic philosophers may find it difficult to secure a proper understanding of their messages, and indeed, as it has been rightly observed, 'many of the earliest admirers of the *Wealth of Nations* were driven by the very "spirit of system" that its author had disavowed'.[22]

(d) As a former teacher of rhetoric himself, Smith was unusually aware of the extent to which persuasion is a function not only of the content of what is being said, but also of the speaker's ability to address the imagination and sentiments of his audience or, as it were, to play behind the audience's back and subtly win over its sympathy and trust. 'The desire of being believed, the desire of persuading, of leading and directing other people, seems to be one of the strongest of all our natural desires. It is, perhaps, the instinct upon which is founded the faculty of speech, the characteristical faculty of human nature' (TMS,336). Further, it may be added, since this 'natural desire' is not primarily about imparting knowledge to hearers, but about the production of conviction regardless of strict veracity, it gives great importance to rhetoric, i.e. the art of making out a case even when, as so often in the discussion of public affairs, we can prove but a very small part of the arguments and facts.[23] For 'the natural disposition', held Smith, 'is always to believe': 'The man scarce lives who is not more credulous than he ought to be' (TMS,335-6).

(e) Finally, in his important essay on the psychology of scientific endeavour, illustrated by the history of astronomy, Smith attempted to explain the scientific enterprise itself by bringing in three connected and all-too-human passions that would tend, first to disturb, and then to restore, peace of mind in moments of idle contemplation – the sentiments of Surprise, Wonder and Admiration. Thus, according to Smith's view, utilitarian and rational considerations would have played a very limited and secondary role in the origin and growth of modern science. It is noteworthy that 'curiosity' and 'love of truth' – those 'first sources of all our enquiries' so analogous to 'hunting' – are the last 'passions' discussed by Hume in Book II of the *Treatise*.[24] Both Hume (cf. THN,271) and Smith never tired to point out 'how easily the learned give up the evidence of their senses to preserve the coherence of the ideas of their imagination' (EPS,77).

The most crucial analytical implication of this view stressing the primacy of the passions in ordinary thinking and the fixation of belief is that it throws light on the ways in which opinions of private and common interest are formed.

It would be a cross mistake to equate this notion of passion – denoting all passive, largely unconscious mental processes in our mind's life – with that of self-interest used by modern pure economic theory, or with that of class-interest operated by most Ricardian and Marxist theorists. For the fact is that both, the atomized and the class-structured versions of human self-interest in economic affairs, beg the whole question which is central to an understanding of the possible relations between morality and practical life, viz. how agents come to form an opinion of their own self-interest and how they may change it or even fail badly to act on it. In effect, enthusiasm for money-making (that 'somewhat disgusting morbidity' which Keynes once proposed to 'hand over with a shudder to the specialists in mental disease'[25]), just as much as enthusiasm for, say, egalitarianism, are but indications that passions have been awakened, and that some of the possible objects of human interest have been invested with sufficient value to entice the agents concerned from other possible objects of human interest like, say, the preservation of the habitable earth and of excellence in the arts from both kinds of enthusiasm respectively.

The primacy of the passions in general, and especially of the 'mental passions', with regard to the individual agent's perceptions of interest, is perhaps best brought out by Hume in his appendix on self-love in the second *Enquiry*. Because of its importance for an understanding of the role of the passions in the process of belief-formation and for much of the discussion in the next chapter, it is perhaps well to quote this passage at length:

There are bodily wants or appetites acknowledged by every one, which necessarily precede all sensual enjoyment, and carry us directly to seek possession of the object. Thus, hunger and thirst have eating and drinking for their end; and from the gratification of these primary appetites arises a pleasure, which may become the object of another species of desire or inclination that is secondary and interested. In the same manner there are mental passions by which we are impelled immediately to seek particular objects, such as fame or power, or vengeance without any regard to interest; and when these objects are attained a pleasing enjoyment ensues, as the consequence of our indulged affections. Nature must, by the internal frame and constitution of the mind, give an original propensity to fame, ere we can reap any pleasure from that acquisition, or pursue it from motives of self-love, and a desire of happiness. If I have no vanity, I take no delight in praise: if I be void of ambition, power gives me no enjoyment: if I be not angry, the punishment of an adversary is totally indifferent to me. In all these cases there is a passion which points immediately to the object, and constitutes it our good or happiness; as there are other secondary passions which afterwards arise and pursue it as part of our happiness, when once it is constituted such by our original affections. Were there no appetite of any kind antecendent to self-love, that propensity could scarcely ever exert itself; because we should, in that case, have felt few and slender pains or pleasures, and have little misery or happiness to avoid or to pursue. (2ndE,301–2)

As this passage probably makes clear, there is no real contradiction between the agent's passions and interests. Self-interest, abstractly considered, moves nothing. Pleasure and enjoyment, which are the direct objects of interested behaviour, are derivative and secondary *vis-à-vis* the agent's passions. The content of particular representations of individual interest is given independently by the passions, in particular those which, as Smith put it, 'take their origin from a particular turn of habit of the imagination'. And pre-eminent among the 'mental passions', as it will be argued in the next chapter, is the desire for sympathy, i.e. the respect, approval and admiration of other men: 'Whatever other passions we may be actuated by; pride, ambition, avarice, curiosity, revenge or lust; the soul and animating principle of them all is sympathy; nor wou'd they have any force, were we to abstract entirely from the thoughts and sentiments of others' (THN,363).

Morality and general rules of conduct, according to this view, exist and are necessary not in spite of the passions, but precisely because they exist and are extremely powerful (though not absolute) determinants of practical conduct. The efficacy of the passions arises largely from their role in the process of opinion-formation, and their ability to engage, for their own purposes, the fixation of belief. This is the mechanism referred to by Smith when he observed that our passions tend to justify themselves or, as he put it, 'suggest to us opinions which justify them'. It is by bringing to light the operations of the mind itself, and the ways in which it seizes on beliefs and opinions with varying degrees of confidence and tenacity, that moral philosophy may be of help in the pursuit of self-command and individual autonomy.

So, by referring the formation of opinions concerning individual self-interest to the machinery of sub-rational (as distinct from irrational) dispositions and motivations, the 'enlightened sceptics' found a *via media* between two extremes. On the one hand, the interests pursued by agents in ordinary life are not given once and for all, that is, equated with some monovalue (e.g. individual pecuniary gain or the material advantage of the class) which rules out from the start any possibility that other values may come to bear on economic behaviour. But on the other, opinions of interest are seen as not wholly malleable, that is, amenable to the fancy of agents or the 'cold syllogisms' conjured up by philosophers in their studies.

The fixation of the relevant beliefs, in this view, is not a 'purely intellectual matter' or the result of 'philosophical error'. Agents act on what they have come to regard as being their interests but, and this is the crucial point, the way in which they come to perceive such interests as their own is not the high road of rational calculation, conscious thinking and deliberation, nor the careful reading of the 'classics' (or the fashionable) in moral, political and economic philosophy; rather, it is the work of the passions, that is, those sub-rational sentiments, emotions and desires which alone are capable of bestowing value on any object and thus raise men from rest (or the abyss of self-doubt) into action and all the beliefs and opinions that go with it.

CHAPTER 7

The passions of the imagination, II
Hume and Adam Smith on the psychology of the economic agent

In the last chapter, I examined the concept of passion in the thought of Hume and Adam Smith and suggested that it plays a central role in their analyses of belief-formation processes and human agency in general. This claim, it should be said, is by no means meant to imply that Hume and Smith were in perfect agreement in everything they wrote or that there are no important contrasts to be drawn between the views and positions held by the two friends. Rather, the claim being made is that both shared some fundamental notions about the workings of the human mind, and especially about the ways in which our behaviour and the underlying belief-forming mental habits are affected by sub-rational factors.

In the present chapter I will take up the argument advanced in chapter 6. I shall try to focus more narrowly on the economic psychology put forward by the two leaders of the Scottish Enlightenment, in order to spell out how the passions work at the level of the ordinary actions of agents in earning a livelihood and pushing their way in the world. As in the former chapter, the aim here is to cover ground which may seem as common to Hume, Smith and other 'enlightened sceptics', but not to those 'enlightened enthusiasts' of the eighteenth century and after who make 'philosophical errors' and 'superstitions' the root causes of whatever they think is wrong in human affairs and thus end up trying 'to reduce the notions of all mankind exactly to the same length, and breadth and height as their own'.

Earlier (chapter 5) I referred to what Smith called the 'passions of the body', i.e. those appetites which arise from the need to preserve the individual and perpetuate the species. These are the prime movers of man's economic efforts: 'our passions are the only causes of labour' (E,261). But as society grows more complex, and moves from a system of subsistence based on hunting and pasturage to one based on farming and commerce,[1] the 'mental passions' – i.e. 'those which take their origin from a particular habit of the imagination' – gain a much more prominent role as motive powers in the supply of labour and economic effort. A fine illustration of the way in which these 'mental passions' crystallize into opinion of interest and powerfully affect economic behaviour is Smith's discussion of the motivational set associated with the individual agent's intense interest and assiduity in the pursuit of material wealth – the famous desire to better one's condition which is held responsible for 'opulence' and the economic growth of nations.

Following Hume's classification in the *Treatise*, there are three classes of goods which may be pursued by agents and become the objects of their self-interested activities: (i) 'the internal satisfaction of our mind' (goods of the mind), (ii) 'the external advantages of our body', like e.g. enjoying good health, sex and good looks (goods of the body), and (iii) 'the enjoyment of such possessions as we have acquir'd by our industry and good fortune' (external goods) (THN,487). The Smithian theory, as it will be seen, is an attempt to account for the relative primacy of (iii) in modern commercial society, and to show how even (i) and (ii) are made, to some extent, dependent on the agent's success in securing (iii).

The central question, as formulated by Smith in the *Theory of Moral Sentiments*, concerns the nature of economic ambition and the causes underlying our desire for external goods. 'For to what purpose', asks the author of the *Wealth of Nations*,

is all the toil and bustle of this world? what is the end of avarice and ambition, of the pursuit of wealth, of power, and preheminence? Is it to supply the necessities of nature? The wages of the meanest labourer can supply them. We see that they afford him food and clothing, the comfort of a house, and of a family. If we examined his oeconomy with rigour, we should find that he spends a great part of them upon conveniencies, which may be regarded as superfluities, and that, upon extraordinary occasions, he can give something even to vanity and distinction. What then is the cause of our aversion to his situation, and why should those who have been educated in the higher ranks of life, regard it as worse than death, to be reduced to live, even without labour, upon the same simple fare with him, to dwell under the same lowly roof, and to be clothed in the same humble attire? Do they imagine that their stomach is better, or their sleep sounder in a palace than in a cottage? The contrary has been so often observed, and, indeed, is so very obvious, though it had never been observed, that there is nobody ignorant of it. From whence, then, arises that emulation which runs through all the different ranks of men, and what are the advantages which we propose by

that great purpose of human life which we call bettering our condition?
(TMS,50)

In his economic treatise, it is true, Smith studiously avoided giving
a clear, frank and straightforward answer to these questions. He
preferred to stress, instead, the consequences of this 'emulation which
runs through all the different ranks of men', and particularly how
'The natural effort of every individual to better his own condition,
when suffered to exert itself with freedom and security, is so powerful
a principle, that it is alone, and without any assistance, not only
capable of carrying on the society to wealth and prosperity, but of
surmounting a hundred impertinent obstructions with which the folly
of human laws too often incumbers its operations' (WN,540). The
desire of a great number of agents to better their economic position in
relation to others is taken as given. Growth and prosperity, it is
suggested, will not fail to win the day, and the good health of the
thriving 'political body' will not be arrested, in spite 'not only of the
disease, but of the absurd prescriptions of the doctor' (WN,343; cf.
WN,673–4 where Smith uses this notion to criticize the rigidity and
doctrinaire purism of the physiocrats).

But all we can learn, in the *Wealth of Nations*, about the character of
this all-powerful desire to better one's condition and its roots in
human psychology is that: 'An augmentation of fortune is the means
by which the greater part of men propose and wish to better their
condition. It is the means the most vulgar and the most obvious; and
the most likely way of augmenting their fortune, is to save and
accumulate some part of what they acquire, either regularly or
annually, or upon some extraordinary occasions' (WN,341–2). The
most *vulgar* and the most *obvious*: but why? This gives no more than a
very faint hint of the discussion Smith himself had been prepared to
undertake elsewhere. For in the *Theory of Moral Sentiments* he did not
shy away from raising and answering the question, and he made no
secrets of his reasons for thinking that the ruling desire in a flourishing
commercial society is indeed the most obvious and vulgar.

How, then, did Smith account for 'that emulation which runs
through all the different ranks of men'? And what would be, in his
view, the real 'advantages which we propose by that great purpose of
human life which we call bettering our condition'?

To be observed, to be attended to, to be taken notice of with sympathy,
complacency, and approbation, are all the advantages which we can
propose to derive from it. It is the vanity, not the ease, or the pleasure, which

interest us. But vanity is always founded upon the belief of our being the object of attention and approbation. The rich man glories in his riches, because he feels that they naturally draw upon him the attention of the world, and that mankind are disposed to go along with him in all those agreeable emotions with which the advantages of his situation so readily inspire him. At the thought of this, his heart seems to swell and dilate itself within him, and he is fonder of his wealth, upon this account, than for all the other advantages it procures him. The poor man, on the contrary, is ashamed of his poverty. He feels that it either places him out of the sight of mankind, or, that if they take any notice of him, they have, however, scarce any fellow-feeling with the misery and distress which he suffers. (TMS,50)[2]

Thus it is 'vanity' which most of all exemplifies the control of the agent's behaviour by sub-rational desires.

At heart every individual wishes to be esteemed, i.e. to secure for himself the good sentiments and favourable disposition of those about him. Men are vain but do not like being regarded – or to imagine themselves – as such. Hence they spontaneously tend (a) to overlook the fact that it is vanity which gives the impetus to their desire to succeed in the market-place, and (b) to disguise their sub-rational motivation with rational vestments of one sort or another. That the anxious, restless agent who has come within the circle of material ambition should represent himself as pursuing nothing but the direct utility and security afforded by his acquisitions is not in the least surprising. No one is more illusion-prone, that is, apt to a partial and interested account of his own conduct than he who is engaged in the pursuit of what makes the whole difference in the world to him. But the moral philosopher, trained in observing things with ice-cold detachment, must try to pull off the veil of self-deception.

Smith's observation, it may be noted, was not new. The late-seventeenth century French philosopher, N. Malebranche, for example, had already made clear that people are generally even more interested in appearing to others to be rich, learned and powerful than in really being so. As he put in *De la Recherche de la Verité* (1712):

Everything that gives us a certain elevation over others by making us more perfect, such as science and virtue, or else by giving us a certain authority over them by making us more powerful, such as honours and riches, seems to make us to some extent independent. All those below us revere and fear us; they are always prepared to do what pleases us for our preservation, and they dare not harm us or resist our desires . . . The reputation of being rich, learned, and virtuous produces in the imagination of those around us, or who concern us most closely, dispositions that are very advantageous to us. It prostrates them at our feet; it excites them in our favour; it inspires in them all the impulses that tend to the preservation of our being, and to the increase of our grandeur. Therefore, men preserve their reputation as a good that they need in order to live comfortably in the world.[3]

Smith's approach, however, differed from that of Malebranche and other eighteenth-century philosophers in that he paid more attention to the economic aspects of distinct esteem-acquisition mechanisms. He noticed in particular how, in a commercial society, the link between income and property on the one hand, and respect and approbation on the other, generates a powerful incentive, at the level of the individual agent, to economic endeavour and efficiency. The demand for esteem, in this context, would lead agents to apply their talents and give their best efforts to the task of improving their own economic position in relation to others; and this, as already seen, would lead to prosperity across the board. Further, as I shall presently argue, Smith advanced a general theory of human motivation in which the vanity-based pursuit of external goods is a particular and morally tolerable – even if obvious, vulgar and, for most agents, self-defeating – instance of a much wider genus.

What is it then that, in Smith's theory, 'gives to prosperity all its dazzling splendour'? What makes wealth and the possession of external goods 'the object of envy, and compensates, in the opinion of mankind, all that toil, all that anxiety, all those mortifications which must be undergone in the pursuit of it'? Moreover, the passion spent and (maybe) some results achieved, what then compensates 'all that leisure, all that ease, all that careless security, which are forfeited for ever by the acquisition'? (TMS,51).

The answer, according to Smith, is the following. There is probably no more powerful passion derived from the imagination than the desire to command the affection, respect and admiration of other men. Conversely, nothing seems to be more feared than the indifference and the sneer on the face of those among whom one was raised up and educated. We have a deeply rooted need to think well of ourselves and to believe we are well thought of by those whose opinions carry weight with us. We need, at least from time to time, 'to prop our tottering judgement on the correspondent approbation of mankind' (2ndE,276), that is, to confirm our own self-esteem by some indication that we are esteemed by those who are not so partial to us as we are to ourselves.

And even though 'to be overlooked, and to be disapproved of, are things entirely different', Smith argued, 'yet as obscurity covers us from the daylight of honour and approbation, to feel that we are taken no notice of, necessarily damps the most agreeable hope, and disappoints the most ardent desire, of human nature' (TMS,51). When they strive for success in the market-place, agents are in effect trying to cope with and partially quench this most potent and entrenched passion of the imagination:

We desire both to be respectable and to be respected. We dread both to be contemptible and to be contemned. But, upon coming into the world, we soon find that wisdom and virtue are by no means the sole objects of respect; nor vice and folly, of contempt. We frequently see the respectful attentions of the world more strongly directed towards the rich and the great, than towards the wise and the virtuous. We see frequently the vices and follies of the powerful much less despised than the poverty and weakness of the innocent. To deserve, to acquire, and to enjoy the respect and admiration of mankind, are the great objects of ambition and emulation. Two different roads are presented to us, equally leading to the attainment of this so much desired object; the one, by the study of wisdom and the practice of virtue; the other, by the acquisition of wealth and greatness. Two different characters are presented to our emulation; the one, of proud ambition and ostentatious avidity; the other, of humble modesty and equitable justice . . . They are the wise and the virtuous chiefly, a select, though, I am afraid, but a small party, who are the real and steady admirers of wisdom and virtue. The great mob of mankind are the admirers and worshippers, and, what may seem more extraordinary, most frequently the desinterested admirers and worshippers, of wealth and greatness. (TMS,62)

Thus in order to better his condition and raise himself up from the crowd, so as to secure its esteem, the agent pursues the objects esteemed by the crowd and in this way becomes one with it. He pursues wealth (or power), seeing that wealth is what everyone respects and admires, and the wealthy man the one all tend to sympathize with: 'In equal degrees of merit there is scarce any man who does not respect more the rich and great, than the poor and the humble' (TMS,62). It is not hard to see why Smith referred to 'an augmentation of fortune' as the most 'obvious' and 'vulgar' means of bettering our condition.

This would explain also why we tend, quite unknowingly and not only in the literal sense, to 'make parade of our riches, and conceal our poverty' (TMS,50): 'With the greater part of the rich people, the chief enjoyment of riches consists in the parade of riches, which in their eyes is never so compleat as when they appear to possess those decisive marks of opulence which nobody can possess but themselves' (WN, 190). Equally, it helps to see why resigning oneself to a menial job is bound to be much harder if it has to be in one's own home town, under the eyes of those whose opinions count most. While he stays in his country village, further argued Smith, 'a man of low condition' still has to act under the restraint of 'what is called a character to lose':

But as soon as he comes into a great city, he is sunk in obscurity and darkness. His conduct is observed and attended to by nobody, and he is therefore very likely to neglect it himself, and to abandon himself to every sort of low profligacy and vice. He never emerges so effectually from this obscurity, his conduct never excites so much the attention of respectable society, as by his becoming the member of a small religious sect. (WN, 795)

As the quotations above probably make clear, the two cardinal principles underlying Smith's account of ordinary behaviour are the desire for esteem ('love of Praise') and the fear of disapprobation ('dread of Blame'). 'Nature, when she formed man for society, endowed him with an original desire to please, and an original aversion to offend his brethren. She taught him to feel pleasure in their favourable, and pain in their unfavourable regard. She rendered their approbation most flattering and most agreeable to him for its own sake; and their disapprobation most mortifying and most offensive' (TMS, 116). This, it should be noted, closely corresponds to Hume's remarks in the *Treatise*, stressing the notion that 'We can form no wish, which has not a reference to society':

Whatever other passions we may be actuated by; pride, ambition, avarice, curiosity, revenge or lust; the soul or animating principle of them all is sympathy; nor wou'd they have any force, were we to abstract entirely from the thoughts and sentiments of others. Let all the powers and elements of nature conspire to serve and obey one man: Let the sun rise and set at his command: The sea and rivers roll as he pleases . . . He will still be miserable, till you give him some one person at least, with whom he may share his happiness, and whose esteem and friendship he may enjoy. (THN, 363)[4]

The minds of men are mirrors to one another, not only because they reflect each others emotions, but also because those rays of passions, sentiments and opinions may be often reverberated, and may decay away by insensible degrees. Thus the pleasure, which a rich man receives from his possessions, being thrown upon the beholder, causes a pleasure and esteem; which sentiment again, being perceiv'd and sympathiz'd with, encrease the pleasure of the possessor; and being once more reflected, become a new foundation for pleasure and esteem in the beholder. (THN, 365)

Whereas in standard utilitarian doctrine, as it is well known, 'Nature has placed mankind under the governance of two sovereign masters, pain and pleasure',[5] in the Humean and Smithian account it is not utility or pleasure, but rather the imagination, that is, sympathy and esteem, which have been given sovereign powers over man. 'Vanity' – and not the 'belly' – rules mankind. As Smith clearly put it: 'It is not ease or pleasure, but always honour, of one kind or another, though frequently an honour very ill understood, that the ambitious man really pursues'. (TMS,65) And, as he would also stress, vanity should not be condemned *tout court*. Self-love may be a virtuous motive of action (cf. his criticism of Mandeville in chapter 3 above), and 'the love of just fame, of true glory, even for its own sake, and independent of any advantage which we can derive from it, is not unworthy even of a wise man' (TMS,117). In Hume's words: 'To love the glory of virtuous deeds is a sure proof of the love of virtue' (E,86).

The task of education – and in particular of 'domestic education' (TMS,222) – is to direct vanity, as far as possible, to the proper objects of esteem and admiration, that is, to goals and activities which are praiseworthy (e.g. benevolence or keeping a cool head 'amidst the turbulence and disorder of faction'), as opposed to those which, though highly regarded and worshipped by the many, are far from admirable (e.g. parading the 'frivolous ornaments of dress and equipage' or the 'frivolous accomplishments of ordinary behaviour'). It follows from this reasoning that, whatever the verdict of the markets and of 'the great mob of mankind', 'To a real wise man the judicious and well-weighed approbation of a single wise man, gives more heartfelt satisfaction than all the noisy applauses of ten thousand ignorant though enthusiastic admirers' (TMS,253).

So there is no necessary reason why wealth – the possession of external goods – should be singled out as the object capable of transforming its owner into a respectable or admirable agent. Smith himself, in line with the Socratic and humanist tradition in moral philosophy, saw in this 'the corruption of our moral sentiments'. And this not only because he held virtue and wisdom as deserving more esteem than the 'mere trinkets of frivolous utility' worshipped by 'the great mob of mankind', but also because he felt clearly uneasy at the prospect that: 'A stranger to human nature, who saw the indifference of men about the misery of their inferiors, and the regret and indignation which they feel for the misfortunes and sufferings of those above them, would be apt to imagine, that pain must be more agonizing, and the convulsions of death more terrible to persons of higher rank, than to those of meaner stations' (TMS,52).

Desire, it is true, breeds desirability, i.e. a highly favourable *opinion* of the thing desired. The Smithian mob has a strong 'disposition to admire, and consequently to imitate, the rich and the great' (TMS,64). But the desired (e.g. the honour commanded by external goods) must not be made the cause of, or confused with, the desirable; it should not be allowed to determine our beliefs and value-judgements. We ought to strive for an impartial and objective consideration of those things that command our esteem and aversion. When we fail to do so, we are likely to fall prey to wrong-headed moral reasoning and indulge, maybe unawares, in one of the commonest sources of moral error.

Moreover, given that the external goods sought after by agents are in effect 'positional goods' – and thus are of necessity scarce and lose their 'dazzling splendour' once possessed by the many[6] – most contenders are bound to have incurred in self-deception when they anticipated that wealth would finally bring home the distinction and charm of the emulated few. Indeed, the greater part of men, as Smith notes in the *Wealth of Nations*, have an unwarranted and 'absurd presumption' about their own abilities and chances of success in life (cf. WN,124), or as Hume put it: 'Men have, in general, a much greater propensity to overvalue than undervalue themselves, notwithstanding the opinion of Aristotle' (2ndE,264).

Yet, at least the unintended consequences of this system of illusions and frustration were happily for the best. In a typical eighteenth-century argumentative manoeuvre, Smith at last turns the tables and argues that, if 'Nature is always too strong for principle' (Hume), it is none the less too strong as well for man's ordinary myopia and lack of principles. 'Nature' steps in to deceive man, even to the point of rescuing him from his own folly and stupidity. All in all, he argues, striking now the topos characteristic of the *Wealth of Nations*:

It is well that nature imposes upon us in this manner. It is this deception which rouses and keeps in continual motion the industry of mankind. It is this which first prompted them to cultivate the ground, to build houses, to found cities and commonwealths, and to invent and improve all the sciences and arts, which ennoble and embellish human life; which have entirely changed the whole face of the globe, have turned the rude forests of nature into agreeable and fertile plains, and made the trackless and barren ocean a new fund of subsistence, and the great high road of communication to the different nations of the earth. (TMS,183)[7]

In the Smithian world, one might say, as in Montaigne's, people struggle to be worse than they can![8] And it is not only the economic system that works, through the 'invisible hand', behind the backs of the participants. The individual participants themselves are being carried away – and to a very considerable extent – by motives and belief-forming mechanisms that work, as it were, behind the backs of their own minds.

But still, one is tempted to ask, from whence this transformation of external goods into an object of passion and privileged lever to general esteem and respectability? What makes it possible for positional goods to become the source of 'honour' and spontaneous approbation, and for the affluent agent to become, in the eyes of the many, the *good* agent? How is one to explain the fact that the 'fureur de se distinguer' (Rousseau) and 'pour obtenir dans l'esprit des autres une place honorable' (Malebranche) finds expression in the pursuit of private material gain? Is this something liable to change by the power of ideas to transform human conduct?

The first point to be considered in answering these questions is the reason why material acquisition seems to have precedence over other values, even after the wants of that 'slowly moving tortoise', the body, have been adequately cared for. As it has been observed, when the body has been satisfied the mind is in principle free and 'apt to wander further, to range over the fields of science, or sport in the regions of the imagination, to fancy that it has "shuffled off this mortal coil", and is seeking its kindred element'.[9] But the jump, even when it is seriously attempted, often turns out to be much harder than it would at first appear. Why has the possession of *external goods* rather than, say, the pursuit of intellectual improvement and excellence in the arts (goods of the mind), or physical beauty and athletic skills (goods of the body), become the prime object of emulation and envy in social life?

'The affair', replies Malthus in the *First Essay*, 'is not an affair of reasoning, but of experience'. Even if one accepts the view that the internal satisfaction of our minds in intellectual pursuits is preferable to the Benthamite enjoyment of external goods (and also less destructive of the natural environment), or, yet, that there is good reason to agree with the Stoic slave Epictetus that 'even if you are not yet a Socrates, still you ought to live as one who wishes to be a Socrates'; even so, asks Malthus, 'how am I to communicate this truth to a person who has scarcely ever felt intellectual pleasure. I may as well attempt to explain the nature and beauty of colours to a blind man'. There can be no genuine volition, except of those things which are somehow already known.

Indeed Rev. Malthus, the curate of Albury (Surrey), appears to speak here out of his own professional experience, and visibly takes a much less confident view on the issue than his former mentor, Paley, who had felt no doubt he could dispel the lure of the pleasures of sense by showing their transitory and deceptive character *vis-à-vis* the pleasures of intellect. 'If I am ever so laborious, patient, and clear, and have the most repeated opportunities of expostulation', reported Malthus, 'any real progress toward the accomplishment of my purpose seems absolutely hopeless':

All that I can say is, that the wisest and best men in all ages had agreed in giving the preference, very greatly, to the pleasures of intellect; and that my own experience completely confirmed the truth of their decisions; that I had found sensual pleasures vain, transient, and continually attended with tedium and disgust; but that intellectual pleasures appeared to me ever fresh and young, filled up all my hours satisfactorily, gave a new zest to life, and diffused a lasting serenity over my mind. If he believe me it can only be from respect and veneration for my authority; it is credulity, and not conviction. I have not said anything, nor can any thing be said of a nature to produce real conviction. The affair is not an affair of reasoning, but of experience.[10]

The principle underlying Malthus' reasoning on what has been more recently called the 'obscurantism of pleasure',[11] is the one brought out by Hume in his discussion of the influence of the imagination on the passions in Book II of the *Treatise*, viz. the notion according to which: 'Any pleasure, with which we are acquainted, affects us more than any other, which we own to be superior, but of whose nature we are wholly ignorant' (THN,424).

This factor – i.e. our strong tendency to let the memory of past, already experienced pleasures, to determine our current value-judgements and conduct – is of course one of the major sources of inertia in human behaviour and of stability in socio-economic affairs. It helps to understand the reason why, for example, 'a trivial good may, from certain circumstances, produce a desire superior to what arises from the greatest and most valuable enjoyment' (THN,416). And it is perhaps interesting to note how, nearly two centuries later, its importance for the understanding of the mind at work would be stressed in very forceful terms by the father of psychoanalysis:

'Whoever understands the human mind knows that hardly anything is harder for a man than to give up a pleasure which he has once experienced'.[12] Moreover, it is through the action of this principle that the 'obscurantism of pleasure' depicted by Malthus tends to perpetuate itself, while expostulations like Paley's and those of so many others in the history of ethics and economics are likely to go on falling on deaf ears.

In the light of this factor one can also understand why the shortening of the working day did not lead, as Marx rather naively anticipated, to the general pursuit of 'higher activities' (e.g. enjoying Plato and Goethe) during the 'free time' now available to workers. The fallacy here springs directly from the unwarranted assumption that the Aristotelian view – 'When pressing needs are satisfied, man turns to the general and more elevated'[13] – would apply *ipso facto* to the generality of men and women in modern industrial societies. We may also recall here the similarity between the Marxist picture of 'socialist man' in the 'realm of freedom' and the Godwinian conviction that, as though it were a matter of course, 'The more men are raised above poverty and a life of expedients, the more decency will prevail in their conduct, and sobriety in their sentiments'.[14]

Yet, if Smith is correct in saying that the pleasure and ease afforded by external goods are only the supposed motives prompting agents to the life of vigorous money-making, and that vanity is in fact the passion which rouses them so to act, it is still necessary to ask how is it possible at all that the possession of material goods can become the cause of sentiments like vanity and its reverse in the many, envy. Malthus' argument may well explain the basic reason why the possession of external goods is the prime object of emulation and desire in social life – the pleasure and worth of other goods, and especially of the more refined goods of the mind, are largely closed (or insipid) to the great majority of agents. But it does not account for the reason why it can be so in the first place. What kind of relation obtains between an agent and his external goods that somehow makes it possible that they should enhance his self-esteem and give rise to pride in him and admiration in the beholder?

In Book II of his *Treatise*, and especially in the second part of his little-known 'A dissertation on the passions' (1757), Hume tackled and tried to answer this question.

Every valuable quality of the mind, whether of the imagination, judgement, memory or disposition; wit, good sense, learning, courage, justice, integrity;

all these are the causes of pride; and their opposites of humility. Nor are these passions confin'd to the mind, but extend their view to the body likewise. A man may be proud of his beauty, strength, agility, good mien, address in dancing, riding, fencing, and of his dexterity in any manual business or manufacture. But this is not all. The passions looking farther, comprehend whatever objects are in the least ally'd or related to us. Our country, family, children, relations, riches, houses, gardens, horses, dogs, cloaths; any of these may become a cause either of pride or of humility. (THN,279)

These are thoroughly customary mental habits. And the human mind is so used to them that it tends to slip into the illusion that they are obvious or known simply because they are familiar and, as with the notion of causality, the nearest at hand. 'We found vanity upon houses, gardens, equipage, and other external objects, as well as upon personal merit and accomplishments; and tho' these external advantages be in themselves widely distant from thought or a person, yet they considerably influence even a passion, which is directed to that as its ultimate object' (THN,303). But what grants that it can be so, that external objects can boost one's self-esteem and manage to secure the largely disinterested deference and goodwill of the many?

The key to this riddle, suggests Hume, is to be found in the *relation of property* – a mental and essentially non-rational belief-forming habit or associative mechanism:

This happens when external objects acquire any particular relation to ourselves, and are associated or connected with us. A beautiful fish in the ocean, a well-proportioned animal in a forest, and indeed, any thing, which neither belong nor is related to us, has no manner of influence on our vanity, whatever extraordinary qualities it may be endowed with, and whatever degree of surprise and admiration it may naturally occasion. It must be someway associated with us, in order to touch our pride. Its idea must hang, in a manner, upon that of ourselves, and the transition from one to the other must be easy and natural.[15]

The distinctive feature of the relation of property is that it brings the agent and the external good so close to each other that it allows for an overlapping between the self of the proprietor and the object under his right. 'The imagination passes naturally and easily from the consideration of a field to that of the person to whom it belongs', 'the mention of the property naturally carries our thought to the proprietor, and of the proprietor to the property' (THN,310): this smooth transition lends plausibility to feelings of pride and self-esteem on account of the external goods possessed. 'Property therefore', concludes Hume, 'is a species of causation': 'It enables the person to produce alterations on the object, and it supposes that his condition is improved or altered by it. It is indeed the relation the most interesting of any, and occurs the most frequently to the mind'.[16]

Further, it is possible to add, the chances of completely doing away with this firmly rooted 'species of causation' are perhaps as good as the chances of really dissuading agents from the prejudice of the imagination with respect to the value of distinct kinds of pleasure, so as to dispel that 'obscurantism of pleasure' which moral philosophers have observed and condemned with varying degrees of vehemence – but little or no success – since the days of Socrates and Critias, Lucretius and Memmius, Seneca and Nero. Yet, it does not seem unreasonable to expect that a greater awareness of this peculiar 'species of causation', and of the attendant prejudice of the imagination through which 'we naturally esteem and respect the rich, even before we discover in them any favourable disposition towards us' (THN,361), may help curb at least some of the more aberrant attempts to smuggle in claims of moral or intellectual goodness derived from nothing more than the exercise of political power or the ownership of positional goods.

As Hume (and Smith) observed, 'There are few persons, that are satisfy'd with their own character, or genius, or fortune, who are not desirous of shewing themselves to the world, and of acquiring the love and approbation of mankind. Now 'tis evident, that the very same qualities and circumstances, which are the causes of pride and self-esteem, are also the causes of vanity or the desire of reputation; and that we always put to view those particulars with which in ourselves we are best satisfy'd' (THN,331-2). There is no necessary or inescapable reason, it is true, why 'fortune' – as opposed to 'character' and 'genius' – should be the common currency on which the esteem-acquisition game is run. But to imagine that socialism (i.e. abolishing the private property of the means of production), or that any kind of philosophical or political *coup*, will by itself entail the abolition of the Humean relation of property with regard to external goods is, according to this view, just another comfortable illusion, originated from an overestimation of the area of rationality in the workings of the human mind.

The upshot of the discussion above is that the problem of individual autonomy deserves a more careful consideration. The 'free time' demanded by Marx – 'Economy of time, to this all economy ultimately reduces itself'[17] – is an important social goal (chapter 5).

But it is by no means the final word on this issue. For, as I have tried to argue, no amount of 'freedom to do' or opportunities for a 'good life' can bring greater autonomy if it is not accompanied by the quest for self-knowledge (knowledge of the things that command our esteem and approbation) and self-command (living up to one's views and opinions).

The process of belief-formation – as Hume, Smith and Malthus have stressed – is itself subject to powerful sub-rational undercurrents. The relation between our conscious beliefs and our ordinary conduct is apt to be rather less straightforward than it might at first appear. If the 'enlightened sceptics' are right, then the task of actively revising and changing our belief-forming habits turns out to be much more difficult and, when successful, hard to fix, than many social theorists would make us think. And as Keynes, among others, has pointed out, our worst difficulties often begin precisely when we are able to do as we like: 'To those who sweat for their daily bread leisure is a longed-for sweet – until they get it'.[18]

Marshall once suggested that, although a government could order a good edition of Shakespeare's works to be printed, still it could not get them written.[19] We may now add that it could not get them read or enjoyed by the people as well; for even though there is a lot governments can do to improve popular education and to help tackle the incalculable waste due to the 'obscurantism of pleasure' depicted by Malthus, it is beyond their power to rule out by decree mental habits which appear to be firmly rooted in the machinery of our sub-rational emotions and propensities.

Literacy and conventional schooling – the 'teaching of the alphabet to all people' which Carlyle had demanded in *Chartism*[20] – have enabled the great majority of men and women, including much of the Third World, to read. But this has also brought to light the fact that 'the teaching of all men to read' is by no means enough to enable people to enjoy and appreciate literature and the arts in their 'free time'. For they may well choose Benthamite 'push-pin' (or the so-called 'dirt and trash' of modern mass culture), while letting the Millian 'arts and sciences of music and poetry' waste away untouched and unknown.

Just as primitive communities may have suffered from cold and hypothermia on the sites of what now are coal-mines, so, it might be argued, we starve and live longish and cosy (but still brutish) lives, and destroy our natural environment more than it would be otherwise necessary, because we are unable to put our spiritual and aesthetic capabilities to good account. 'Our age may talk about economy but it is in fact a squanderer: it squanders the most precious thing there is, the spirit'.[21] A century and a half after its formulation, the Millian ideal of a stationary state still reads like 'a lyric cry in the midst of business'.

So if it is true, on the one hand, that (a) moral and aesthetic education are still much needed, so as to help enhance people's capabilities for making the most of existing cultural and environmental resources, it seems equally true, on the other, that (b) only the individual agent knows what his needs are, and thus there is no way in which an external authority can enforce the enjoyment of 'great art' or suppress the demand for 'dirt and trash'. While vulgar economic laissez-faire gives great emphasis to (b), but fails even to address the problem posed by (a), twentieth-century experiments in socialism have tended to give some scope to the implementation of (a) and to demonstrate the dangers of overlooking (b), that is, the fact that there is no such thing as a 'dictatorship over needs' or enforced capabilities. The problems of economic initiative and the efficient use of existing resources can only be genuinely solved from below.

Conclusion to part I

So, the message of the eighteenth-century 'enlightened sceptics' is clear: 'nothing tends more to disturb our understanding, and precipitate us into any opinions, however unreasonable, than their connection with passion' (THN,321). Or, as the poet finely put it: 'Are passions, then, the pagans of the soul? Reason alone baptized?'[1]

The study of man, according to this view, yields the conclusion that, although human nature is essentially uniform 'in all nations and ages' and stable 'in its principles and operations' (1stE,83), man's beliefs and opinions tend to be rather more volatile. As Hume observed: 'Man is a very variable being, and susceptible of many different opinions, principles, and rules of conduct. What may be true, while he adheres to one way of thinking, will be found false, when he has embraced an opposite set of manners and opinions' (E,255–6).

The whole argument (chapters 6 and 7) is aptly summarized by Malthus' assertion that 'The voluntary actions of men may originate in their opinions: but these opinions will be very differently modified in creatures compounded of a rational faculty and corporeal propensities, from what they would be in beings wholly intellectual'. The individual economic agent is best seen as a 'compound being': 'A truth may be brought home to his conviction as a rational being, though he may determine to act contrary to it, as a compound being'.[2] Thus he lacks the 'rationality' and regularity of the 'pleasure-machine' presupposed by standard neo-classical economics, and yet he is not as 'perfectible' and malleable to moral and scientific education as suggested by the Millian-Marshallian school (chapters 3 and 4).

This conveys the second fundamental reason why the view that 'Ideas rule the world of human affairs and its events' must be qualified. Just as there are areas of *action* in practical life where the logic of the economic situation rather than the beliefs and opinions of agents determines conduct (chapter 5), so there are areas of *belief* which are relatively closed to agents' voluntary choice, and which powerfully affect their behaviour as producers, consumers and decision-makers (chapters 6 and 7).

Economic philosophers from Paley to Hayek (chapter 1), have been inclined to make persuasion and the 'war of ideas' – their own art – the controlling forces in human affairs. Economic philosophers, it is said, are the unacknowledged legislators of the world. But this claim, I have tried to argue, though it should not be summarily dismissed as a relic of pre-scientific views about the human mind (chapters 2 and 4), is none the less a serious misconception of events – it overlooks the part played by sub-rational factors in ordinary thinking, exaggerates the influence of ideas in practical behaviour, neglects the logic of the economic situation in complex societies and is based on an over-intellectualized account of the role of political and economic philosophy in the processes of belief-formation and social change. 'Generally speaking, the errors in religion are dangerous; those in philosophy only ridiculous' (THN,272).

If this is true, then it turns out that what agents *make* of the ideas philosophers put up for sale is immensely more important than the ideas themselves. Pushing the point a little further it would be possible to say, as a concluding remark, that the true victims of the 'war of ideas' are therefore not the agents – who merely lay hold of the ideas that happen to suit them – but rather the philosophers, whose ideas shall very likely be put to uses they did not foresee, and so help bring about consequences they did not intend and perhaps would not desire to produce.

In part II, I shall try to bring out, examine and illustrate the role of the passions of the imagination in (a) the intergenerational transmission and (b) the interpersonal communication of abstract systems of political and economic thought.

PART II

Patterns of misunderstanding

In part I (chapters 6 and 7) it was suggested that the passions of the imagination play a central role in the processes of belief-formation and social change. In part II, I shall try to follow up this line of argument by focusing on the ways in which the non-rational input of our belief-fixation mechanisms may affect the transmission and reception of abstract systems of economic and political thought. Whereas part I dealt primarily with the issue of the determinants of opinions of self-interest and common good shaping the behaviour of large numbers of agents, part II deals with problems bearing on the commerce between minds and our capacity for misunderstanding other people's ideas.

The general axiom in this domain is the Lockean notion (discussed in chapter 15 below) that readers, no less than authors, are fallible subjects: 'Though every thing said in the Text be infallibly true, yet the Reader may be, nay cannot chuse but be very fallible in the understanding of it'. We have to understand what is said or written before we can disagree or agree with it. But understanding, it will be argued, admits of degrees. As it is known, readings of the same message or body of text often fail to agree and not all understanding-claims can be simultaneously held true. The history of ideas as an intellectual enterprise, I will suggest in chapter 8, may be seen as a never-ending struggle to 'put the record straight', that is, to bring to light, spell out and ward off the occurrence of misapprehensions in particular intellectual exchanges.

The main object in part II has been to construct a *taxonomy of misunderstandings* – to map out, describe and analyse some of the most frequent modes or patterns of misunderstanding in the history of ideas, with special reference to the history of economic and political thought. So, no particular case of misunderstanding in intellectual exchanges has been reconstructed in great historical detail, since the basic concern throughout has been rather to identify and examine possible pitfalls awaiting attempts to grasp thoughts and conclusions reached by minds distinct from one's own (chapters 8 to 12). Particular attention, however, has been given to the veritable maze of misunderstanding-claims clustering around Malthus' population theory (chapter 13). In addition, I shall also have the occasion to enquire into the origins of the Humean-Smithian theory of belief-formation in the history of British philosophy (chapter 11).

It should also be noted that, even though I have used the term a lot, I have not attempted anywhere to give a formal definition of misunderstanding. I have relied, instead, on the ordinary use of the term in common speech and in intellectual history, as denoting the spontaneous misapprehension or misinterpretation of someone else's ideas (i.e. 'pure misunderstanding') rather than their deliberate misreporting to a third party ('misrepresentation'). Pure misunderstanding, in this sense, is a solo affair between the thinking subject and the message or text before him. Misrepresentations can be – and perhaps often are – perpetrated, but one can only 'suffer' or become the victim of pure misunderstanding. (If I don't believe that I've understood something, then I can be sure that I've not misunderstood it, but if I think that I've truly grasped and 'seen through' the text under scrutiny, then I may have fallen prey to some form of misunderstanding.)

The central argument in part II is the view that receivers, and not authors, set and vary the meaning of what is being said. The specific interpretation a given message or text receives will depend, as a rule, not only on the author's intention and clarity but also, and to a large degree, on the perceived exigencies of practical life (the 'problems of the age') and the particular interests, goals and concerns of its individual users.

The basic contention is that the relative neglect of the problem of misunderstanding and of the sources of distortion bearing on the commerce between minds is a further fundamental reason why economic and political philosophers have persistently overestimated the power of ideas to transform human conduct and institutions. As I shall try to argue, the widely held notion that 'Ideas rule the world of human affairs and its events' makes excessive and unwarrantable demands as regards both the transparency and the transmissibility of highly abstract systems of thought. Chapters 14 and 15 and the conclusion to part II are devoted to this point.

Socrates. You know, Phaedrus, that's the strange thing about writing, which makes it truly analogous to painting. The painter's products stand before us as though they were alive: but if you question them, they maintain a most majestic silence. It is the same with written words: they seem to talk to you as though they were intelligent, but if you ask them anything about what they say, from a desire to be instructed, they go on telling you just the same thing for ever. And once a thing is put in writing, the composition, whatever it may be, drifts all over the place, getting into the hands not only of those who understand it, but equally of those who have no business with it; it doesn't know how to address the right people, and not address the wrong. And when it is ill-treated and unfairly abused it always needs its parent to come to its help, being unable to defend or help itself.

Plato's *Phaedrus*, 275d–e

CHAPTER 8

Understanding misunderstandings
The intergenerational transmission of ideas and the time-factor

'I know I meant just what you explain, but I did not explain my own meaning so well as you. You understand me as well as I do myself, but you express me better than I could express myself. Pray accept the sincerest acknowledgements'.[1] Thus wrote the eighteenth-century English poet A. Pope in a letter to his future literary executor and editor, the theologian W. Warburton, thanking him for the publication of an exegetic defence of the *Essay on Man*.

The poet's remark bears a certain analogy with the compliment Adam Smith is reported to have once paid to William Pitt, the young prime minister who was by then supposedly 'reforming the national finances with the *Wealth of Nations* in his hand'.[2] One evening in 1787, having just dined with Pitt at the house of a common Scottish friend in London and learned from the prime minister himself how effusively he supported the views put forward in the *Wealth of Nations*, Smith observed to Henry Addington (another guest at the dinner-party): 'What an extraordinary man Pitt is – he makes me understand my own ideas better than before'.[3]

But although superficially resembling the poet's enthusiastic reply to the man who unlocked the true meaning of his work, Smith's aside on his first meeting with the younger Pitt is, to say the least, highly ambiguous. For bearing in mind Smith's persistent scepticism about the power of moral philosophy and social theory to effectively change the course of human affairs; his attack on the 'spirit of system' (as seen in chapter 6 above); his criticism of the French physiocrats for their tendency to always appeal to government direct intervention on behalf of 'the exact regimen of perfect liberty and perfect justice' (see WN,674) and his well-known description of the professional politician, also in Book IV of the *Wealth of Nations*, as 'that insidious and crafty animal, vulgarly called a statesman or politician, whose councils are directed by the momentary fluctuation of affairs'

(WN,468); than it is indeed very likely that his tribute to Pitt was in fact shot through with irony.

W. Bagehot, it is true, in his 1861 portrait of the younger Pitt, depicted him as being no ordinary, thoughtless administrator, but a 'man of ideas' – 'the ideal type of the relation between ideas and acts'. 'He was the first great English statesman', wrote Bagehot, 'who read, understood, and valued the *Wealth of Nations*'.[4] Smith himself, however, as just seen, had gone even further and said that the young prime minister had helped him to understand his own ideas 'better than before'. But if that had been in fact the case, it can now be argued, it may be that this was not so much because Pitt had taught Smith anything he did not know about his own economic theory, but rather because he had unwittingly made the philosopher more aware of the uses to which his ideas could lend themselves when assimilated into party politics. This – and not the prime minister's supposed analytical sharpness as a reader of the famous treatise – would have instructed Smith about his own thinking. Ironists pose as unknowing.

But whatever the proper interpretation of this curious episode, the truth of the matter is that no single theory – and the abstract ideas of economists and political philosophers especially so – gains access to the public debate safe and proof against misunderstanding, distortion or downright propagandistic abuse. No set of ideas or economic theory, no matter how clear and technically refined, is hijack-proof. There exists no built-in device to forestall or prevent their eventual misuse and perversion in the political process. Like the morphological traits of a biological species or the technical capabilities of a human community, ideas may find themselves put to uses and contributing to effects which were no part of the designs (or lack of designs) of the original authors. Attempts to move even the surface of one's readers' minds in the desired direction may go badly astray.

In what follows, I shall assume that the domain of misunderstanding is the *interpersonal transmission of ideas through language*. Misunderstandings, in this sense, take place not in the 'commerce of the mind with things' but in the commerce between minds. It involves some failure in the transmission of thought or, more drastically, communication breakdowns. Claims and counter-claims involving one or more types of misunderstanding are not hard to find. They comprise not only (a) the countless claims suggesting the direct misapprehension or misinterpretation of a given text or speech-act, but also claims concerning (b) questions of priority (like missing the originality or path-breaking character of a work), (c) neglected sources (revealing connections and connotations which would otherwise remain inaccessible), (d) non-transparency of isolated texts (the ideas of an author should be seen in relation to his evolution and wider intellectual enterprise), (e) underrated influence (failure to see the true impact of an author or work on subsequent developments), and so on.

The ubiquity of misunderstandings in the history of ideas needs no pleading. As the American intellectual historian A.O. Lovejoy has pointed out,

The history of philosophy and of all phases of man's reflection *is*, in great part, a history of confusions of ideas . . . The adequate record of even the confusions of our forebears may help, not only to clarify those confusions, but to engender a salutary doubt whether we are wholly immune from different but equally great confusions. For though we have more empirical information at our disposal, we have not different or better minds.

Similarly, the French historian of ideas A. Koyré remarks that 'philosophers . . . seldom, if ever, convince each other, and a discussion between two philosophers resembles as often as not a "dialogue de sourds"'. Indeed, as Locke had already noticed about intellectual exchanges and controversies: 'Comments beget Comments, and Explications make new matter for Explications . . . doth it not often happen, that a Man of an ordinary Capacity, very well understands a Text, or a Law, that he reads, till he consults an Expositor, or goes to Council; who by that time he hath done explaining them, makes the Words signifie either nothing at all, or what he pleases'.[5]

It would perhaps be no exaggeration to say that the history of ideas as practised within any ordinary academic discipline, and as a discipline in its own right, hinges on the problem of misunderstanding. It owes its existence to the existence of this problem, and it thrives on it. For if the works of any previous or living author were somehow ambiguity-proof, and their meaning and significance perfectly transparent (whatever that may be), then the whole business of writing on them and offering new readings, clues and interpretations would be not only patently idle but hardly conceivable.

But if it is true, as appears to be the case, that misunderstanding-claims (in one or more of the senses listed above) nearly always supply the plot for concrete studies in the history of ideas, and that this problem seems to be its central, unifying concern, then how are we to account for such widespread occurrence of failures in the transmission of thought? What after all makes the transmission of ideas such a minefield of unintended results? Are authors necessarily the best authorities on their own work? Do misunderstandings fall into classes, or are they individual, singular occurrences about which nothing useful can be said in a more general and abstract way? And supposing one were to define particular patterns or modes of misunderstanding in intellectual exchanges, what sort of criterion could one use in order to achieve this?

Now, the reasons underlying and accounting for the occurrence of concrete cases of misunderstanding in the history of ideas are obviously too varied to be encompassed by any single or small set of explanatory hypotheses. The *why* of failed communications is probably no less diversified than their *how*, that is, the particular configuration they may assume in any given intellectual exchange. Yet, as I shall presently try to argue, it may be possible to produce a taxonomy of misunderstandings. The aim is to identify and illustrate at least some of the more basic patterns of misunderstanding in the history of ideas – patterns which seem to recur with remarkable frequency in intellectual exchanges. To support this claim, I will draw in particular (but not exclusively) on the wealth of empirical data supplied by the history of economic thought.

In the remainder of this chapter, I shall try to examine how the temporal element – the time-factor – involved in the intergenerational transmission of ideas accounts for the occurrence of a significant class of misunderstandings. Then I shall proceed (chapters 9 to 13) to consider in more detail sources of misunderstanding which are independent of the time-factor and may prevent (or render more difficult) the adequate transmission of ideas between contemporaneous minds. Finally, in the two last chapters of part II an attempt will be made to apply the results and conclusions of the previous discussion to a critical assessment of the role of political and economic philosophy in the processes of belief-formation and social change.

The time-factor intervenes in three basic ways. To begin with, terms undergo variations of meaning and, as a consequence, the ideas they embody acquire new and often unexpected connotations. It is surely no coincidence that a number of intellectual historians have found it necessary to devote a great deal of time and effort in the attempt to recover, analyse and draw attention to what has been called the 'semantic biography' of words or 'philosophical semantics'. As Lovejoy has pointed out,

A term, a phrase, a formula, which gains currency or acceptance because one of its meanings, or of the thoughts which it suggests, is congenial to the prevalent beliefs, the standards of value, the tastes of a certain age, may help to alter beliefs, standards of value, and tastes, because other meanings or suggested implications, not clearly distinguished by those who employ it, gradually become the dominant elements of its signification.[6]

Not unlike coins and paper money, words and concepts suffer a continuous variation in their purchasing power, even though their face-values remain unaltered since their dropping (dead-born or otherwise) from the press. And the philologist's word of caution – 'with every piece of knowledge one has to stumble over dead, petrified words, and one will sooner break a leg than a word'[7] – applies to the historian of ideas just as much as it does to the latter-day economist or political philosopher studying the work of his predecessors and tracing out the genealogy of his own theories and views.

No student of eighteenth-century texts, for example, can fail to notice the striking frequency with which certain particular words like 'Nature' or 'Passion' tend to occur in a great variety of contexts. As B. Willey observes in his work on the concept and usage of 'Nature' in the thought of that period, whereas nowadays the reader of such texts finds himself bewildered by the multiplicity and ambiguity of meanings associated with this and a few other terms, it is plausible to assume that it must have been different for an eighteenth-century readership.[8] For them, it was rather the clarity and authority of these words that went, so to speak, without saying. And authors felt themselves free to cash in on this tacit agreement, rarely, if ever, pausing to consider why their purchasing power in terms of persuasion was so high.

Words which used to 'work' and presumably excite the imagination of those to whom they were addressed, now look insipid and fail to do so. Thus wholesale changes of currency or denomination – spontaneous 'monetary reforms' – are also possible, if rare, events in the 'semantic biography' of languages. If it is true, as it has been said, that 'The greatest men always are attached to their century by some weakness', then we may also say that it is precisely their attachment to terms, phrases and linguistic formulae *peculiar to their age* which has been, in many cases, the cause of their weakness – and of our difficulties in not misunderstanding them.

It is of course only too easy for a less cautious reader at a later date to read meanings of his liking into such power-bringing words and concepts, creating thereby a noble and soothing pedigree for his own beliefs and opinions. He manages to keep off any trace of 'semantic discomfort' in his readings and hence, to use C.S. Lewis' striking formulation in *Studies in Words*, 'the difficulty of "making sense" out of a strange phrase will seldom be for him insuperable. Where the duller reader simply does not understand, he misunderstands – triumphantly, brilliantly'.[9] For the student of the classics in the history of science and philosophy, the wider lesson is well conveyed by Kuhn's recommendation that: 'When reading the works of an important thinker, look first for the apparent absurdities in the text and ask yourself how a sensible person could have written them. When you find an answer . . . when those passages make sense, then you may find that more central passages, ones you previously thought you understood, have changed their meaning'.[10]

Another and related reason why ideas may elude the intentions of their creators has to do with the fact that no author is able to predict or control the uses to which his work will be put once it becomes public. This will apply *a fortiori* after his death. For no writer on human affairs can possibly foresee and forestall the relations obtaining between his own work on the one hand, and the concrete problems brought about by the future course of events on the other. His ideas, when they do not fall into oblivion, are therefore bound to take on new meanings and a significance that go beyond what he had originally intended.

As it has been perspicuously observed, 'One reason why authors become dated, even though they once amounted to something, is that their writings, when reinforced by their contemporary setting, speak strongly to men, whereas without this reinforcement their works die, as if bereft of the illumination that gave them their colour'. The contemporary setting here comprises not only (i) a set of linguistic conventions but also (ii) the intellectual and (iii) the practical contexts which authors must (to some extent) take for granted in their attempts to move other minds in the desired direction. 'At present', stresses L. Wittgenstein, 'we are combating a trend. But this trend will die out, superseded by others, and then the way we are arguing against it will no longer be understood; people will not see why all this needed saying'.[11] However, it can be argued, it may still be the case that people will see and supply other, rather different reasons why all this once needed saying. Hence the way we are at present arguing will be more than simply no longer understood – it will be misunderstood.

The mechanism at work in this case is the exact converse of the one suggested by the notion of a writing being deprived of its 'true colour' due to the passing away of the setting which formerly illuminated it. For nothing rules out the possibility that works generally regarded as long dead and buried suddenly find themselves resuscitated. Thus, they come to 'speak strongly' to some men once more, reinforced by a problem-situation – a 'posthumous setting' – which vaguely resembles the one faced by their authors in the first place. These writings are, therefore, not so much deprived of that context which once gave them their 'colour', as they are, on the contrary, seen through a frame which gives them an entirely new and often misleading meaning and significance. They regain their appeal and even their 'colour', though the latter may of course have little in common with the original one.

The history of ideas provides a wealth of illustrations of misunderstandings of this class. Consider the two following examples. When, for instance, (a) Hayek takes up the Popperian offensive stance (as set forth in *The Open Society and Its Enemies*) and goes on to accuse Hegel of being, as he puts it, 'that ultra-rationalist who has become the fountain head of most modern irrationalism and totalitarianism', or when, for that matter, (b) G. Lukács states to his own satisfaction (in an 1955 article called 'On the responsibility of intellectuals'), that 'one cannot find in Hitler one word which had not already been stated by Nietzsche or Bergson, Spengler or Ortega y Gasset "on high level"', they are both arguing that the words and arguments of the philosophers in question spoke strongly to some men in situations they could not have foreseen and that they did so in ways that led, somehow, to tragic events.[12]

Of course neither Hayek nor Lukács did bother to ask whether each of the named philosophers would have also approved of the ways in which their ideas were 'revived' by future generations, or how far their views had been grossly misinterpreted and perverted in the process. For the fact is that their teachings were (and still are) used by purveyors of many sharply conflicting codes and causes, and as E. Cassirer rightly stressed with respect to the 'Pyrrhic victory' of Hegelianism in his *The Myth of the State*: 'Different schools and parties all appeal to Hegel's authority but, at the same time, they give entirely different and incompatible interpretations of his fundamental principles'.[13] The very notion that every philosophy belongs to its age, and is biassed by the limitations of its own time, is a key *leitmotiv* of Hegel's thought. To blame him (or those referred to by

Lukács) for what was made of his philosophy by future generations, is no better than blaming A. Nobel for the use of dynamite in warfare or G. Mendel for the genetic experiments carried out in Auschwitz.

Thus it is obviously not necessary to endorse the sweeping accusations put forward by Hayek and Lukács in examples (a) and (b) above to see that the general problem they allude to is real and relevant to the history of ideas. A statement and defence of, say, 'As much (or as little) State as possible *here and now*', will continue to do its 'work' in the future, when the problems are different, the information available is greater and even when, perhaps, the author of the defence in question would not think it to be the case to exhaust his powers of persuasion and eloquence on behalf of the chosen cause.

The printed text is made of 'dead, petrified words' – it can only repeat itself and is unable to help itself. Hence authors are denied the chance to learn. There is no conceivable 'posthumous setting' capable of making them decide to change their professed beliefs and opinions. But those who come to read and study them, in contrast, are alive and always somehow pressed by practical and personal concerns, from the desire to do good and to help solve the problems of the age, to the individual search for power, security and success. The spontaneous tendency is to scan and discover in old texts ideas which happen to be of interest or simply fashionable now. Readers (good and bad) have the final say on what survives from the past, and how.

To sum up, the reading of modern meanings into old, highly figurative and indeterminate terms on the one hand, and the recycling of texts to suit the demands of another setting and 'form of life' on the other, are both mechanisms resulting from the time-factor which affects the intergenerational transmission of surviving ideas. The linguistic, intellectual and practical contexts which authors take for granted as they address their contemporaries on some topic of more or less general concern are not readily available – and in some cases they are hardly recoverable at all – for readers of a generation sharing a somewhat distinct currency of immediate understanding and facing a new set of problems and prospects.

Popular and long-cherished legends in the history of economics, like for instance the picture of Adam Smith as the 'sunny optimist' advocating unbridled laissez-faire and preaching 'Enrichissez-vous!', or of Malthus (to give an example which shall be discussed in detail in chapter 13 below) as the 'gloomy doom-prophet' who set out to deny the possibility of tackling malnutrition and mass-poverty, can perhaps be seen as owing their existence, at least in part, to an overlooking of the problems bearing on the transmission of ideas through time.

As Robbins pointed out in his study of British nineteenth-century economic thought,

It is no exaggeration to say that it is impossible to understand the evolution and the meaning of Western liberal civilization without some understanding of Classical Political Economy. But, for all this, it is very little understood. It is true that as a result of the labours of a few outstanding scholars . . . many parts of this subject have been better surveyed and analysed than ever before. But the main body of contemporary opinion [1952] shows little awareness of this . . . Indeed, the position is much worse than this. Popular writing in this connexion is far below the zero of knowledge or common decency. On this plane, not only is any real knowledge of the Classical writers non-existent but, further, their place has been taken by a set of mythological figures, passing by the same names, but not infrequently invested with attitudes almost the exact reverse of those which the originals adopted. These dummies are very malignant creatures indeed.[14]

It would be wrong to claim, I think, that the situation depicted by Robbins has changed for the better in the mean time. To study the *fortuna* of the great works in the history of economics is to be constantly reminded of the notion that: 'It is the fate of knowledge to begin as heresy and end as superstition'. As G. Stigler has recently commented, reflecting on his lifelong experience as an intellectual historian and teacher of the history of economics at Chicago University:

The writings of economists long departed allow a degree of detachment for a reader that is probably impossible to achieve with living authors. One surprising feature taught by intellectual history is the persistence of uncertainty over what a person really meant. One might think that intellectual competence and goodwill are all that are required to understand what a scholar intends to say, but the study of any important scholar of the past will show this belief to be most naive . . . Scholars have a strong penchant for referring to their intellectual ancestors, whether favorably or unfavorably, and usually whether they have read the works of these ancestors or not . . . Jacob Viner, whose vast and honest erudition has long been my despair, once told me that the average modern reference to the classical economists is so vulgarly ignorant as not to deserve notice, let alone refutation.[15]

Historians of ideas are familiar with backward-looking habits of mind being vitiated by the desire to reconstruct all past thought in a 'rational' way, that is, as though it were a poorer, still naive version of what is now canonical. Misunderstandings are often the result of the anachronistic fallacy – the tendency to reduce past developments in the realm of abstract thought to the status of a 'spurious present'.[16]

But it would not perhaps be too rash to suggest also that one of the chief sources of distortion accounting for that gallery of 'mythological figures' referred to by Robbins and Stigler is related to the very transformation of certain works into so-called 'classics'. It is with good reason that the 'classics' in the history of political and economic thought have been compared to 'aristocrats and royals', seeing that many people feel they need merely to learn their titles in order to claim close acquaintance with them. In a passage from his *Manual* which brings together many of the themes and threads running through the present work, Pareto brought this very problem to the fore:

The economic and social theories used by those who take part in the social struggle ought to be judged not for their objective value but primarily for their effectiveness in arousing emotions. The scientific refutation of them which can be made is useless, however correct it may be objectively. That is not all. When it is useful to them, men can believe a theory of which they know nothing more than its name. This is a phenomenon common to all religions. The majority of Marxian socialists have not read the works of Marx. In some particular cases there is definite proof of this. For example, before these works had been translated into French and Italian, the French and Italian socialists who did not know German certainly could not have read them. The last parts of Marx's *Capital* were translated into French at the time when Marxism began to decline in France. All the scientific debates for or against free trade have had no, or only a trivial, influence on the practice of free trade or protection.[17]

Thus, what was once 'heresy' may end up as the banner of prejudiced orthodoxy and dogmatism; securing no doubt the glory of the name that goes with it, but at the cost of distorting, sometimes beyond recognition, all it was meant to stand for. Has it not been said, with a healthy dose of realism, that 'Fame, after all, is only the quintessence of all the misunderstandings that collect around a name'?

CHAPTER 9

Contracts and traps
Bacon's contract of error and the notion of pure misunderstanding

The time-factor in the appropriation of works and intellectual traditions is not, certainly, the only reason why ideas may elude their original spokesmen and eventually thwart the intentions of those who did their best to make them public. The commerce between minds belonging to the same generation is also liable to go astray, giving rise to peculiar outcomes ('externalities') in the transmission of ideas. As it will be seen in this chapter, the 'entropy of information' – the tendency of messages to gradually lose their original content and dissipate as they are transmitted from one person to the next – has been the subject of detailed research in modern experimental psychology.

As Francis Bacon had already noticed early in the seventeenth century (his own experience as an author no doubt contributing to the conclusion), 'it is not a thing so easy as is conceived to convey the conceit of one man's mind into the mind of another without loss or mistaking, specially in notions new and differing from those that are received'.[1] The transmission of ideas through language is usually accompanied by a certain loss or dissipation of the information they contain. In a very few cases (e.g. in the example which opens chapter 8), it is true, authors do come to believe that the content of their work has been enhanced, even in their own eyes, by a particularly careful and empathetic reader. Indeed, as F. Nietzsche reminds us: 'Good readers continually improve a book and good opponents clarify it'.[2] But all indications however, as it will be presently seen, are that such cases are in effect extremely rare exceptions.

Bacon's direct observation about the frequency of 'loss or mistaking' in the transmission of ideas has been amply corroborated by findings in modern psychology. Experimental research on this subject, carried out by the English psychologist F.C. Bartlett, has supplied a great deal of interesting evidence on the extent to which the degradation and dissipation ('entropy') of information in the process of exchange is in fact the statistically predominant outcome.

Bartlett applied the 'method of serial reproduction' to study the combined changes produced by the sequential transmission of a given message through a chain of serially linked individuals. The extensive and controlled testing which was carried out involved the oral reproduction, in separate experiments, of folk-stories, argumentative prose passages and descriptive material, and the results obtained revealed just how marked is the tendency for messages to change and dissipate as they move along down the chain. To avoid any unintentional and further illustration of Bartlett's conclusion, it may be wise to quote his own words:

> It is now perfectly clear that serial reproduction [of messages] normally brings about startling and radical alterations in the material dealt with. Epithets are changed into their opposites; incidents and events are transposed; names and numbers rarely survive intact for more than a few reproductions; opinions and conclusions are reversed – nearly every possible variation seems as if it can take place, even in a relatively short series. At the same time, the subjects may be very well satisfied with their efforts, believing themselves to have passed on all important features with little or no change, and merely, perhaps, to have omitted unessential matters.

Moreover, as Bartlett himself carefully points out, these results still probably underestimate the extent of the loss and mistaking which takes place in ordinary life transactions. 'A subject who takes part in an experiment is, as rule, more careful than usual, and hence we may reasonably suppose that the changes effected by Serial Reproduction in the course of the social intercourse of daily life will probably occur yet more easily and be yet more striking than those which have been illustrated in the present tests'.[3]

Evidence from practical life – and in particular from the 'dialogue de sourds' of so many controversies in philosophy, economics and politics – comes from a variety of sources. Thus Locke, writing at the close of the seventeenth century in a memorandum on the misuse of language in public debate and the 'affected obscurity' of philosophers, observed: 'You will I think agree with me that there is nothing wherein men more mistake themselves and mislead others than in writing and reading of books [but] whether the writers mislead the readers or *vice versa* I will not examine: so it is they both seem willing to deceive and be deceived'. In Book III (chapters 9–11) of his *Essay Concerning Human Understanding*, Locke expanded on this problem and argued that most intellectual disputes he had come across were found, upon closer examination, to be in effect just verbal:

I am apt to imagine, that were the imperfections of Language, as the Instrument of Knowledge, more thoroughly weighed, a great many of the Controversies that make such a noise in the World, would of themselves cease; and the way to Knowledge, and, perhaps, Peace too, lie a great deal opener than it does . . . The multiplication and obstinacy of Disputes, which has so laid waste the intellectual World, is owing to nothing more, than to this ill use of Words. For though it be generally believed, that there is great diversity of Opinions in the Volumes and Variety of Controversies, the World is distracted with; yet the most I can find, that the contending learned Men of different Parties do, in their Arguings with one another, is, that they speak different Languages.[4]

A similar line of reasoning, we may note, would lead Carlyle to an even more radical conclusion. For since, as he argued, 'no man at bottom means injustice' and 'it is always for some obscure distorted image of a right that he contends', then it would follow that, as he put it, 'all battle is misunderstanding: did the parties know one another, the battle would cease'.[5] Of course, we need not go all the way with this radical and absolute claim to appreciate the pertinency of the Lockean, more factual standpoint. At the same time, it should not go unnoticed that agreement, concord and peace, as Locke himself did not fail to observe, are just as much liable to misunderstanding as controversy, dispute and battle. For men may (and often do) think they agree with one another when, in effect, it turns out that this was not the case, and the agreement had been based on nothing more than an equivocal understanding or superficial linguistic resemblances.

It is interesting to note that in *The Advancement of Learning* Bacon had already tackled the problem of misunderstanding as a combination of deceiving and self-deception. Indeed, he offered a memorable description of how the attempt to transmit thought and ideas slips, on many occasions, into what he termed 'a kind of contract of error between the deliverer and the receiver'. With a keen eye to the institutional pressures normally bearing on the actors involved in the organized supply and demand of knowledge (formal teaching), Bacon maintained that the widespread occurrence of such 'contracts' resulted from the fact that, as he wrote,

he that delivereth knowledge, desireth to deliver it in such form as may be best believed, and not as may be best examined; and he that receiveth knowledge, desireth rather present satisfaction, than expectant inquiry; and so rather not to doubt, than not to err: glory making the author not lay open his weakness, and sloth making the disciple not to know his strength.[6]

As a result of this process, not only the progress of knowledge would suffer, and both parties in the contract enjoy an illusory and highly misleading partnership, but also, as Bacon remarks elsewhere, a situation would eventually arise in which 'the lectures and other exercises are so managed that the last thing anyone would be likely to entertain is an unfamiliar thought. Anyone who allows himself freedom of inquiry or independence of judgement promptly finds himself isolated'.[7]

The 'contract of error' type of exchange depicted by Bacon springs from the fact that both parties in it have failed to put their cognitive interests first. The deliverer, it is clear, seeks out chiefly to keep intact his authority and to foster his own reputation. He attempts to achieve this by parading a barrage of 'certainties', and thus hides from the receivers (and even from himself *in extremis*) whatever may harm his 'discoveries' and standing. He obviously neglects, therefore, the Socratic lesson – 'in philosophical discussions he who is worsted gains more in proportion as he learns more'; and he is not bothered by the fear that 'trying to impress' is likely to backfire if, as it has been said, 'nothing is so unimpressive as behaviour designed to impress'.[8]

The receiver, in turn, is a tacit accomplice in this contract. Indeed, he makes himself an easy prey. For he takes a rather passive attitude in the exchange – 'we are lazier in mind than in body', as La Rochefoucauld reminds us – and in this way he not only spares the required effort to understand, but falls in line with what has been more recently described as 'the ineradicable tendency of the great majority of men to repeat the opinions of those few who have taken the trouble to think'.[9]

Thus, in the Baconian 'contract of error' each actor is trying to deceive the other and, in the process, they both undergo some form of self-deception. The deliverer by trusting that his reputation is sound if only the world at large bows down to it – in a mild version of the view according to which 'successful crime is virtue'. And the receiver by assenting to statements and opinions which, though he has not understood, he pretends (or believes) he has, simply because he is able to reproduce them on demand.

The point however is that the Baconian 'contract of error', as I shall now try to show, is still an impure or mixed form of misunderstanding. The reason why it is not pure misunderstanding is the fact that there is at play here an element of *deliberate misleading*. We assume that the deliverer of the message presumably knows best, although he refuses to convey this knowledge to the receiver. What he does, in fact, is to misreport his own thinking in order to manipulate the situation, build on the credulity of his audience and in this way best to secure the hearers' admiration. But this element of manipulation and deliberate misleading is, I think, best captured *not* by the notion of misunderstanding, but by that of *misrepresentation*. A close analogy here is the case of the reader/author who knowingly distorts and misreports his opponent's ideas so as to, for example, present his own theory in a more favourable light or simply to score an easy and triumphant victory.

The pure and most interesting forms of misunderstanding, as I shall argue, do not require the deliverer's intentional ploy to misguide or misinform the receiver. They are best seen, therefore, as analogous not to 'contracts', but rather to undesigned and camouflaged 'traps'.

Entrapment is by nature smooth and easy. The actors are not pursuing ends other than the growth of knowledge or the passionate search after truth. The *receiver* now comes to the fore. He sincerely believes he understands the message before him, when in fact he does not: he has fallen into a trap of his own making. If he suspects he has fallen into one, he may search for an exit (e.g. further study or an alternative reading and interpretation coupled with the more or less temporary suspension of belief). He avoids the trap of misunderstanding. But if, on the contrary, the receiver, having fallen prey to some form of misunderstanding, fails to identify what has happened, then he will not search for an exit. His (mistaken) confidence in his ability to decode and grasp adequately the message being conveyed makes him unable to help himself. There is no ploy, malice or dark intention to outshine. It is simply a case of pure misunderstanding.

Not surprisingly, it has been precisely those authors who have dared to entertain and voice 'unfamiliar thoughts' who seem to have met with the greatest difficulties in putting their messages across. Indeed, as I shall try to illustrate below, unprecedented amounts of pure misunderstanding, disputations at cross-purposes and unintended results appear to have been generated in the struggle, by relatively few highly influential authors, to undermine and replace some of the then current beliefs and habitual modes of thought. Some of these authors – and not all of them in economics – were sincerely surprised to find that only a very few accounts of their work were genuinely related to the original statement.

Consider first, for example, the following reply by Darwin to a suggestion made by A.R. Wallace, the English co-discoverer of the theory of evolution by natural selection. Writing to Darwin in 1866, seven years after the publication of *On the Origin of Species*, Wallace first reported his own experience of having been 'repeatedly struck by the utter inability of numbers of intelligent persons to see clearly, or at all, the self-acting and necessary effects of Natural Selection'. He then went on to suggest that a few specific terminological alterations – centrally the substitution of 'survival of the fittest' (H. Spencer's coinage) for the expression 'natural selection' in several instances of the latter – could be of great help not so much in securing a wider assent to the theory, as in preventing it being 'so much misrepresented and misunderstood'.

In his reply, Darwin acknowledged at once 'the advantages of Spencer's excellent expression' (and in the fifth edition (1869) 'survival of the fittest' made its debut in the pages of the *Origin*), but then proceeded to sound a more sceptical note:

I doubt whether the use of any term would have made the subject intelligible to some minds, clear as it is to others; for do we not see even to the present day Malthus on Population absurdly misunderstood? This reflection about Malthus often comforted me when I have been vexed at this misstatement of my views.[10]

Darwin's answer to Wallace reaffirmed points he had made six years earlier, when the publication of the first reviews of the *Origin* were in effect just beginning to bring home to him how the work was liable to 'misapprehension and misrepresentation'. 'I hope to God you will be more successful than I have been in making people understand your meaning', he wrote to his friend and early supporter, the botanist J.D. Hooker, while enquiring about his colleague's work in progress: 'I am inclined to give up the attempt as hopeless. Those who do not understand, it seems, cannot be made to understand'. And a day later, in a letter of 6 June 1860 to the geologist C. Lyell, Darwin returned to the problem he was facing and remarked: 'By the way what a discouraging example Malthus is, to show during what long years the plainest case may be misrepresented and misunderstood . . .

I am beginning to despair of ever making the majority understand my notions'.[11]

The issue at stake in these letters, it must be stressed, has to do not with the validity of this or another scientific theory, but rather with the sometimes formidable obstacles preventing the adequate, barely accurate grasping of particular conjectures and lines of thought. And Darwin's two references, in this context, to the problems besetting the reception of Malthus' theory – a source of discouragement in 1860 but of comfort six years later – are to the point. As I shall try to suggest in chapter 13, there is probably no exaggeration in the words of his first biographer, J. Bonar, when he claimed for Malthus the title of 'best abused man of his age'.[12]

What is interesting here is that, in Malthus' case perhaps no less than in Darwin's, we seem to face, as a rule, situations of pure, genuine misunderstanding. For in contrast with the Baconian 'contract of error', the failed exchanges in these cases may be seen as bringing together a *deliverer* who is only too ready to admit to, and to present openly, difficulties in his arguments, with *receivers* who, far from retreating to a silent and dubious acquiescence, actively misapprehend the object of their censure or praise. In the following chapters I shall attempt to analyse in more detail the mechanisms involved in cases of pure misunderstanding. Chapter 10 deals with issues regarding the *emission* of thought and the involuntary misuse of language ('supply-side'), while chapters 11 and 12 are devoted to a discussion of issues bearing on the *reception* of abstract thought and the problem of theoretical *akrasia* ('demand-side').

On the misuse of language
Ordinary language, formalism and the false-security pitfall

Lack of clarity and the involuntary misuse of language are the first obvious candidates to account for the pure (or 'trap-like') misunderstanding of a set of propositions. It is not necessary to go all the way with more extreme versions of recent linguistic philosophy – 'I really do think with my pen, because my head often knows nothing about what my hand is writing' – to see the point of what Bacon had already noticed when he remarked that: 'Although we think we govern our words, and prescribe it well "to speak as the common people do, to think as wise men do", yet certain it is that words, as a Tartar's bow, do shoot back upon the understanding of the wisest, and mightily entangle and pervert the judgement'.[1]

'It is impossible to *do* one thing only', it is often said. But it is equally impossible to *say* one thing only. Language speaks – and not always in the exact direction intended by the speaker. The amount of information carried by words and syntax far exceeds what any writer can be aware of. Darwin, for instance, in his already cited reply to Wallace, also acknowledged how he had unwittingly slipped into using the expression 'natural selection' in two quite different senses in the text of the *Origin* – as denoting a process and the outcome of the process – and added: 'but my blunder has done no harm, for I do not believe that any one, excepting you, has ever observed it'. Here again, it may be noted, a reader has been able to see things that even 'the wisest' had missed. There is no reason to doubt the author's sincere acknowledgement of the event.

Language is a tremendously powerful and cost-effective aid to man's practical life. As Adam Smith pointed out in his beautiful 'Dissertation on the origin of languages' (1761), ordinary language as we know it must have arisen and developed very gradually, as the spontaneous result of the repeated efforts of prehistoric men in their 'endeavour to make their mutual wants intelligible to each other'. For the invention, held Smith, 'even of the simplest nouns adjective [e.g. green] must have required more metaphysics than we are apt to imagine', and 'Number', he went on, always stressing the spontaneous and pre-eminently social character of language as an institution, 'considered in general, without any relation to any particular set of objects numbered, is one of the most abstract and metaphysical ideas, which the mind of man is capable of forming'.[2] Thus, when we learn to speak we inherit, largely unaware and paying only a residual learning-cost, more 'metaphysics' and abstract mental labour – i.e. the results of classing, arranging, comparing, and so on – than an isolated individual could ever dream or hope to perform in his own lifetime.

But ordinary language, powerful, expedient and resourceful as it is, is still a human institution, that is, fallible and occasionally unreliable. It opens limitless possibilities for human thought and expression. Yet it is also a minefield of unintended results.

'A clumsy man always produces a result he does not intend'. What Hegel wrote about 'uneducated workers' in general, the poet F. Holderlin (his former colleague in the theology seminar at the State University of Tubingen and close friend) said of himself: 'Much though I wish to, never I strike the right measure'.[3] But for Adam Smith and others, recognizing and facing this was in fact the very hallmark of the good professional. 'In all the liberal and ingenious arts', he wrote in the *Theory of Moral Sentiments*, comparing excellence in ordinary behaviour and in the professions, 'in painting, in poetry, in music, in eloquence, in philosophy, the great artist feels always the real imperfection of his own best works . . . It is the inferior artist only who is ever perfectly satisfied with his own performances' (TMS,248). So, unintended results in the use of language are, to a greater or less extent, inevitable. Admission of imperfection is largely a matter of the degree of care, attention and effort one has put into it (the poet being less satisfied with his own artefact than, say, the journalist with his), and of the capacity for self-criticism which, as Smith taught, marks off the progressive from the stagnant practitioner in any field.

It is interesting to note that Hegel himself – who according to many suffered from 'affected obscurity' even (or especially) in his most thought-out philosophical writings – was also willing to admit to his own shortcomings in this area. After struggling with the tortured syntax of his philosophy, Goethe famously declared: 'I am still puzzled, but on a higher level'. But in a letter of 1807 to a German classical scholar who had written to him complaining about the deep obscurity and lack of 'physical form' of his just published *Phenomenology of Mind*, Hegel observed: 'I wish I could have complied with your wish for greater clarity and comprehensibility; but this is precisely the aspect which is most difficult to attain and constitutes the mark of perfection, assuming that the content is solid, too'.[4] He maintained further, in self-defence, that philosophical argument or 'abstract material' did not allow for the same clarity of presentation which more ordinary speech – to say e.g. 'that the Prince passes through here today or that His Majesty has hunted wild boar', as he illustrated – readily allows for.

It might however be argued, against this view, that whatever has been said can be made, in due course, equally clear. There should be no necessary trade-off between clarity and profundity. For obscurity fails to achieve even superficial understanding, though it would seem to achieve a great deal more. 'Those who know that they are profound', it has been perceptively said, 'strive for clarity; those who would like to seem profound to the crowd strive for obscurity'. And as Nietzsche pointed out elsewhere, probably having Hegel and 'the bad style peculiar to him' in mind, 'Every profound thinker is more afraid of being understood than of being misunderstood'.[5] (As Hume once put it to a correspondent who had misunderstood his discussion of causality in Book I of the *Treatise*: 'Where a man of Sense mistakes my Meaning, I own I am angry. But it is only at myself: For having exprest my Meaning so ill as to have given Occasion to the Mistake'.)[6]

But whatever the validity of the view according to which whatever has been said can be made equally clear, it is doubtless the case that it is *easier* to be clear about certain things than about others. So, for example, it is easier to report an isolated fact or accident (e.g. the reading of high radiation levels near a nuclear power plant), than to spell out its relations or lack of relations with other facts and accidents (say, other nuclear mishaps or the historical relations between science and technology), or, what is undoubtedly much harder than both, to be clear and persuasive in the attempt to endow the isolated fact with special value and meaning in the context of a total conceptual framework like 'Nature', 'World History' or indeed any from a wide range of revealed, intuited and science-based *Weltanschauuungen*.

There are, of course, many different levels of understanding. Misunderstandings take place at all levels. I misunderstand my baby's moan and feed him instead of changing his soiled nappy, just as I may badly (though unknowingly) misconstrue, say, as malice-ridden, self-serving and self-congratulatory, Hegel's saying that 'A great man condemns other men to explicate him'.[7] *Ceteris paribus*, however, the following conclusion can be said to follow from the point made in the preceding paragraph. The risk of pure misunderstanding correlates positively with the level of generality and abstraction of one's good- and truth-claims.

On the other hand, it must be observed that attempts to overcome the vagueness of ordinary language by setting up new and tailor-made technical terms, interposing rigid definitions and carrying as far as possible the formalism of the presentation are likely to run into fresh problems of their own. Even clarity and precision, I shall now argue, may be bought at too high cost.

It may be useful to bring in at this juncture Marshall's considered remarks, in Books I and II of his *Principles*, on the difficulties of popular and technical economic terminology, and the reasons he offers for never straying too far from 'the familiar terms of everyday life' and from 'language that is intelligible to the general public' (PEc,43) – in effect, the Baconian recommendation (quoted above) 'to think as wise man do' but 'speak as the common people do'.

Marshall, it is true, wished to be read by leaders of opinion in the business, trade-union, press and government circles. His aim was not only to instruct but also to persuade them. Plain English was, therefore, his best ally. But there were other reasons for trying to avoid an excessive reliance on formalism and the use of technicalities in the transmission of economic ideas. Unlike other pioneers of the neo-classical movement, Marshall was well aware of how misunderstanding-prone were attempts to rely on highly technical jargon in economics and the social sciences in general, and he drew attention to one of its less obvious modes of occurrence – the 'false-security' type of misunderstanding.

The use of mathematics in economic science, argued Marshall, 'is helpful by giving command over a marvellously terse and exact language for expressing clearly some general relations and some short processes of economic reasoning; which can indeed be expressed in ordinary language, but not with equal sharpness of outline' (PEc,644). Yet, as he stressed in Book II and examined in Appendices C ('The scope and method of economics') and D ('Uses of abstract reasoning in economics') of the *Principles*, the temptation of following the example of the physical sciences and setting up a closed-circuit game run on esoteric terms and mathematical syntax should be resisted on two main gounds.

First, because allowing this to happen would lead to the complete severing of the discipline from decision-makers and the general public and, by the same token, encourage endless 'playful excursions' which, as he put it, 'might conceivably be of interest to beings who had no economic problems at all like our own' (PEc,644). This is the problem of irrelevancy which Keynes believed was plaguing academic economics in the inter-war period and which many others believe has plagued it ever since.[8] (Bacon, it may be worth noting, in his struggle against the scholastic practices permeating the sciences of his age, had spoken of their spinning of 'laborious webs of learning . . . admirable for the fineness of thread and work, but of no substance or profit'; similarly Locke, pointing to the barrenness of much 'Subtlety' and 'Acuteness' in the 'learned Men of the World', observed how some of these scholars had found it 'a good Expedient to cover their Ignorance with a curious and unexplicable Web of perplexed Words, and procure to themselves the admiration of others, by unintelligible Terms, the apter to produce wonder, because they could not be understood: whilst it appears in all History, that these profound Doctors were no wiser, nor more useful than their Neighbours; and brought but small advantage to humane Life, or the Societies, wherein they lived'.)[9]

Second, Marshall held that introducing a rigid terminology and carrying formalism too far would lead to fresh problems of communication *within* the academic community. So, referring to 'the most formal writers on economic science', he rightly indicated how 'the bold and rigid definitions, with which their expositions of the science begin, lull the reader into a false security'. The unintended effect of this excessive reliance on formalism, he went on to argue, is that the student frequently 'ascribes to what he reads a meaning different from that which the writers had in their own minds; and perhaps misrepresents them and accuses them of folly of which they had not been guilty' (PEc,43).

Thus, throughout the *Principles*, and in his discussion of the use of analogies borrowed from modern science in economic analysis, Marshall stressed how misunderstanding-prone were all attempts 'to draw broad, hard and fast lines of division, and to formulate definite propositions with regard to differences between things which nature has not separated by any such lines' (PEc,44). In a letter of 1901 he would repeat – though now using unusually rash language – the point about the use of mathematics in economics often turning out to be sterile and misleading:

In my view every economic fact, whether or not it is of such a nature as to be expressed in numbers, stands in relation as cause and effect to many other facts: and since it *never* happens that all of them can be expressed in numbers, the application of exact mathematical methods to those which can is nearly always waste of time, while in the large majority of cases it is positively misleading; and the world would have been further on its way forward if the work had never been done at all.

And in a further letter on this topic, written five years later, he went on to relate his own set of rules for the use of mathematics and formalism in economic analysis:

(1) Use mathematics as a shorthand language, rather than as an engine of inquiry. (2) Keep to them till you have done. (3) Translate into English. (4) Then illustrate by examples that are important in real life. (5) Burn the mathematics. (6) If you can't succeed in 4, burn 3. This last I did often.[10]

Clarity and precision are not enough. Marshall's warning points to an interesting and easy-to-enter type of pure misunderstanding – the inadvertent transmission of a 'false security' to readers through the use of highly formalized and self-vindicating models of the economy. It would be hard to tell how far many post-war writers of economic textbooks are not themselves rather victims – as distinct from conscious perpetrators – of the false-security type of misunderstanding depicted by Marshall. But few of those who are acquainted with the response of undergraduates to such textbooks would perhaps disagree with the view that they quite often lull the students into a false sense of security about economics, and that this is an outcome to which they very easily lend themselves.

Indeed, few of those who later claimed to have followed the Marshallian synthesis of neo-classical economics appear to have grasped the importance of this point, not only for the proper understanding of the partial equilibrium construct in Book V of the *Principles*, but also for the fruitful use of the art of model-building in economic analysis. Marshall's most gifted student (J.M. Keynes), however, provided a suitable follow-up to his master's advice by his decisions: (a) to expose conventional academic economics as 'Candide-like gardening' or 'an edifice of pure crystal', and (b) to

side, instead, with those among the less prestigious economists who, as
he put it in the *General Theory*, 'have preferred to see truth obscurely
and imperfectly rather than to maintain error, reached indeed with
clearness and consistency and by easy logic, but on hypotheses
inappropriate to the facts'.[11]

But obviously striving 'to speak as common men do' – so as to avoid
the Marshallian false-security pitfall – cannot by itself prevent other
modes of misunderstanding from taking place. And as it has been
recently pointed out about attempts to convey economic reasoning in
'spoken language', rather than formally and with the aid of
mathematical notation, 'The drawback of this approach to communicating with one's readers can be seen from the fact that nearly fifty
years after the publication of Keynes' *General Theory* economists are
still debating what Keynes really meant'.[12] A fate, one could add,
from which no other 'classic' in the history of economics, from Smith,
Ricardo and Marx to Marshall and even Arrow-Debreu has so far
managed to escape.

Commenting about recent developments in economics and the
impact of the Arrow-Debreu mathematical formulation of general
equilibrium theory, F. Hahn observes:

It was almost inevitable that when these results surfaced in the textbooks, and
rumours about them reached practical men, they were thoroughly misunderstood . . . General misunderstanding of Arrow and Debreu's work is
illustrated amply by what is called the 'new macroeconomics', mainly
propagated in the United States.

The misconception at issue here can be seen as a close variation of the
false-security pitfall. The main difference is that in this case, as Hahn
goes on to explain, the receivers do not accuse the abstract theorists of
follies of which they are in fact not guilty. Rather, they read into the
theory follies which are not there, and build upon them. So, what
started off as a rigorous, but hypothetical and highly abstract,
'thought experiment' about the workings and properties of a *pure*
market economy, is mistaken for an account of the 'real world' and a
'true model' of a particular, concrete economy. 'Economists of this
persuasion', concludes Hahn, 'take the theory to be descriptive and do
not understand its *Gedanken-Experiment* nature. Others – radical
economists for instance – make the same mistake'.[13] More than thirty
years after the mathematical formulation of general equilibrium

theory, economists are still debating what Arrow-Debreu's work really meant.

Pure mathematics deals with clear-cut, definite and abstract relations and yields necessary truths. But economic science deals with an empirically given set of facts and relations – it never goes beyond the realm of the probable and it can only yield contingent truths. When the sense of certainty and security afforded by the manipulation of mathematical axioms and techniques contaminates our truth-claims about empirical economic phenomena we are mistaking the abstract for the concrete. Marshall, as seen above, was aware of this seductive intellectual trap – the so-called 'fallacy of misplaced concreteness'. And this led him, in turn, to a much more careful use of mathematical tools and notation in economics. Like Malthus before, and Keynes after him, he did not wish to lull readers into an illusory sense of security about what had been achieved.

Now, if linguistic factors were chiefly to blame for the persistent misunderstandings associated with theories like Keynes' on the level of employment, Malthus' on population or Darwin's on the origin of species, then it would obviously be their excessive reliance on ordinary language – as opposed to a potentially misleading rigidity or formalism in the presentation – that should be singled out for inspection. The precise meaning and the relative pros and cons of expressions like 'natural selection', 'survival of the fittest', 'struggle for existence', 'liquidity trap' and a few others are still the subject of much learned controversy, and the very fact that these three authors were prepared to make extensive terminological alterations as their works went through new editions testifies to their recognition that there was scope for greater clarity and precision in the statement of their views. Keynes, for example, wrote in 1937: 'If the simple basic ideas can become familiar and acceptable, time and experience and the collaboration of a number of minds will discover the best way of expressing them'.[14]

The simple fact, however, is that books such as Malthus' *Essay* and Darwin's *Origin*, whatever their stylistic and terminological shortcomings (e.g. all the personifications of 'Nature' in both), surely do not deserve to rank high in terms of the linguistic demands they make on readers. Goethe's cool and non-committal reaction to Hegel would be out of place here. Indeed, it seems fairly safe to say that the great majority of their contemporary readers, misguided or not, felt confident that they were really coming to grips with the 'real thing' rather than misunderstanding it. Their many critics rarely, if ever, suspected that they were perhaps falling prey to some form of *ignoratio elenchi* or multiplying 'refutations' that failed to come near the theses, questions and standards of the presumed victim.

On the other hand support, no less than censure, presupposes commitment, i.e. a positive claim regarding the possession of some degree of understanding of the object of assent. And for many of Malthus' and Darwin's contemporaries, it was rather the simplicity and cogency of their theories that stood out. T.H. Huxley, for instance, on first reading the *Origin* famously confessed: 'How extremely stupid not to have thought of that!' And Darwin himself, reading Malthus's *Essay* nearly thirty years before his remark to Wallace on the work being until then often 'absurdly misunderstood', was struck by the forcefulness of the argument and the 'energetic language' of the book; in one of his working notebooks – actually in the same entry for 28 September 1838 where the original sketch of his theory of evolution occurs – he jotted down: 'yet until the one sentence of Malthus no one clearly perceived the great check among men [i.e. the positive check of famine]'.[15]

Malthus indeed, if anything, may be said to have tried a bit too hard, especially in the more polemical first *Essay* (1798), to make things easier for his readers by addressing his views (as Bagehot put it) 'to men who understand a simple and striking exaggeration far more easily than a full and accurate truth'. But in the second (1803) and subsequent editions of his work, he spared no pains in the attempt to clothe with historical evidence and empirical detail his 'simple and striking' model; in the process, he also struck out from the 1798 essay the theodicy which concluded the original work, and which he never retracted. His laborious attempt to produce better evidence for, and to improve the presentation of his theory, would prompt Marshall to praise the 1803 version of the *Essay* as 'one of the most crushing answers that patient and hard-working science has ever given to the reckless assertion of its adversaries'.[16] (Yet, as I shall try to show in chapter 13 below, the misunderstanding of the *Essay* kept apace; moreover, there is some indication to suggest that Malthus himself was far from satisfied with the ways in which his own supporters were interpreting and putting to use his views.)

The crux of the matter, however, is that whatever the inadequacies of the linguistic equipment deployed, the fact is that no amount of verbal looseness, tortured syntax and foggy arguing can by itself explain the peculiar ability of certain contributions to knowledge to attract misguided cross-fire. This is what calls for some explanation.

There may be unfortunately a grain of truth in the view that 'One takes an obscure and inexplicable thing more seriously than a clear and explicable one'.[17] Here lies, perhaps, the seed of many misunderstandings. But the fact remains that a hopelessly unintelligible work can only 'fall dead-born from the press'. It is hard to conceive of obscurity, blundering and bad style, or an undue and misleading formalism, as being *per se* passports to a leading role in public or academic debate. The spark needs the opposing stone – it is lit by impact. Some nerve must be touched if the text is somehow going to 'speak strongly to men' and command their fire. In the two following chapters, I shall consider some problems bearing on the reception ('demand') of political, economic and scientific ideas.

CHAPTER 11

Errors and illusions
Francis Bacon on the sub-rational determinants of belief

Lack of clarity and the involuntary misuse of language work as two powerful catalysts of pure misunderstanding. Like the use of needlessly technical language, they are well-trodden routes to unintended results in the transmission of messages. But there are, no doubt, many more. An instructive collection of language-related problems in the transmission of knowledge has been given by K. Arrow:

Every piece of information can be regarded as transmitted in a code and can only be used if decoded. In the first instance, a language itself is a code, and the sheer difficulty of translation perhaps can be underestimated. (The inability of English-speaking economists to learn from their French, German, and Italian colleagues is notorious.) There are problems in non-verbal forms of communication. When the British in World War II supplied us [Americans] with the plans for the jet engine, it took ten months to redraw them to conform to American usage. More subtly, as several gifted observers of the educational scene have observed, there are class and racial differences in the meaning of words, not so much in the literal denotation, but in the connotations and associations, and in the significance of non-verbal behaviour. In the complicated interplay of messages between teacher and student, the unreliabilities of communication can lead to extreme inefficiencies.[1]

But the crucial point, however, is that, although language-related problems may facilitate the process of pure misunderstanding, they cannot explain it. No degree of obscurity and looseness, and no amount of linguistic blunders in a message, can by themselves 'condemn other men to explicate it' or command the fire – misguided or otherwise – of any army of receivers. Attempted refutations, assent and criticism in general predicate positive understanding. And it is this claim to understanding which, when it happens to be unfounded, pulls the trigger of the involuntary mental phenomenon I have been calling pure misunderstanding. Only the reader is able to close a deal with the author's offer, although the latter may of course greatly facilitate and even pave the way for a corrupt transaction.

Hence there are good reasons to suppose that Darwin was pointing in the right direction when, in his 1866 reply to Wallace (see p. 138 above), he doubted 'whether the use of any term would have made the subject intelligible to some minds, clear as it is to others', hinting thus at the possibility that there might be something else to it, rather than linguistic inaccuracies, to account for the maze of misunderstandings that has clustered – and keeps propagating – round works like Malthus' and his own.

It would no doubt be wrong to presume, as already argued, that a single and all-compassing explanatory hypothesis could be framed, which was capable of covering somehow all or most relevant cases of misunderstanding. Each individual case must always be examined in its own right, and it is reasonable to expect that the minutiae of failed exchanges are unique for each particular instance of those innumerable cases in which a reader's response fails to satisfy the author that his message has been even barely comprehended. There is, however, one important general consideration which may help to spell out the workings of many unintended results in the transmission of ideas and thus to account (with other factors) for many observable anomalies in the commerce between minds. The reasoning springs from the distinction between two types of beliefs, viz. *errors* and *illusions*.[2] And, as I shall try to show in the second half of this chapter, the argument is fundamentally consistent with a central tenet of the Baconian logic.

An *error* is not the same thing as an illusion. Errors may be hard to spot, but once they have been exposed it is easy, simple and even pleasant to get rid of them. Shame and embarrassment are the predominant feelings they bring about. Unlike illusions, errors do not overlap with self-image of the thinking subject.

So when, for example, Malthus asserts (in the first *Essay*) that 'no move towards the extinction of the passion between the sexes has taken place in the *five or six thousand years* that the world has existed', or when, for that matter, Marx writes in a footnote to the first volume of *Capital*, that 'although Malthus was a parson of the Church of England he *had taken the monastic vow of celibacy* . . . this circumstance favourably distinguishes Malthus from other Protestant parsons, who have flung off the Catholic requirement of the celibacy of the priesthood',[3] they are both committing very palpable mistakes. There is little room for doubt that they would have been only too glad if they had been given the chance to correct their views in the light of more reliable information regarding the age of the Earth and Malthus' progeny. Both are in error.

Errors, of course, need not be minor and inconsequential or always malign. Some errors – e.g. failure to detect poisonous food – carry the death penalty with them. But if, say, I misread my watch and miss my flight to Rio, it may still be the case that I am not worse-off on account of my slip, as it turns out later that the plane was hijacked to Tripoli by terrorists. Errors belong with our surface, easily disposable beliefs.

But *illusions*, unlike errors, are extremely difficult to part with. The distinctive feature of illusions is that they have deeper roots in our mind's life. Their degree of entrenchment within our belief-systems is significantly stronger than is the case with errors and more ordinary beliefs; for they not only spring from and are sustained by our sub-rational psychological dispositions, but they are, for this same reason, much more resilient under challenge and harder to dispose of. The distinguishing mark of illusory beliefs is not, therefore, that they are more or less false than other beliefs but, what is critical, that they accord in a non-trivial sense with the will and wishes of their propounders.

Consider for instance the two following statements. First, the one by Adam Smith in *Theory of Moral Sentiments*: 'Take the whole earth at an average, for one man who suffers pain or misery, you will find twenty in prosperity and joy, or at least in tolerable circumstances'. Hence, why 'rather weep with the one than rejoice with the twenty'? Or yet, just to shift sharply the angle of projection, consider now Hegel's conclusion in his course on *The Philosophy of History* to the effect that even though 'the History of the World is not the theatre of happiness' (since 'periods of happiness are blank pages in it'), still there is a 'cunning of reason' to be found at work here and, all things considered, 'the real world is as it ought to be', that is to say, 'God governs the world, and the actual working of his government – the carrying out of his plan – is the History of the World'.[4]

In both cases, it seems fairly safe to say, the part played by the authors' wishes in determining belief is decisive. There is a noticeable element of feeling *for* the view advanced which is absent in cases where the thinker's will is fundamentally neutral ('cold') as to assenting or not to a given proposition. For, in the passages quoted, Smith and Hegel state and uphold beliefs which are intimately bound up with their own distinctive characters as philosophers. To revise or displace them would imply putting their own identities at risk. The combination between *self* and *belief* has a 'chemical' or 'nuclear' cohesion which is missing in the case of one's errors.

There is no trouble in imagining errors being corrected, say, Marx getting Malthus' three children right or Malthus giving up his belief in the scriptural age of the Earth. But is it at all possible to conceive an Adam Smith given to pity and lamenting about the wretchedness of the universe, or arguing (as Mill would do criticizing Bentham) that 'the race will never enjoy one-tenth part of the happiness which our nature is susceptible of' until we mend our ways and see where our true interests really lie. Or yet, a Hegelian who has come to believe that 'World History', all considered, is just what it would appear to be, that is, a Schopenhauerian clash of 'morbid cravings' and the 'battleground of tormented and agonized beings who continue to exist only by each devouring the other'?

Thus, although it is difficult to conceive what kind of empirical evidence or argument could have truly convinced Smith or Hegel to the contrary in the examples given, it seems quite certain that, if for some odd reason, this had come to happen, then the conversion processes would have been far from smooth or painless. The doctrinal repercussions would have been overwhelming. A major plank of their belief-systems would have to be replaced at sea, with the ship letting in lots of water and running badly off course. But as the replacement and repair costs are felt to rise, I shall argue, so the preventive 'safety measures' deployed by the thinking subject tend to become more elaborate. A much greater care will be taken not to allow threatening blows (i.e. adverse-looking facts or thoughts) coming anywhere too near. The point about illusions is not that they are false or irrefutable, even if, for obvious reasons, they tend to be out of the reach of argument. What makes them special *vis-à-vis* other classes of belief is the fact that doing away with them is an extremely costly and unpleasant affair.

The proposed distinction between errors and illusions can be traced back to and seen as consistent with Bacon's analysis of the Idols of the Tribe (*Idola tribus*) in the first book of the *Novum Organum* (1620). Unlike the other three 'idols' or classes of factors in the human mind which beset cognition and act as obstacles to the growth of knowledge – the Idols of the Cave (the bias peculiar to individuals and their locality), of the Theatre (the dogmas of philosophy), and of the

Market-Place (language-related problems) – the Idols of the Tribe are not the result of nurture. They are not acquired through intercourse with other men and the particular environment in which one's thinking takes place; rather, they are (and hence their name) 'inherent in human nature, and the very tribe or race of man'.

Spelling out the ways in which the Idols of the Tribe come to bear on the human understanding, persistently biassing and twisting its workings in specific directions, Bacon observed: 'The human understanding resembles not a *dry light*, but admits a tincture of the will and passions, which generate their own system accordingly: for man always believes more readily that which he prefers'. As he put it in the corresponding passage in *The Advancement of Learning*, after dealing with the 'equivocation or ambiguity of words and phrases' (Idols of the Market-Place):

But lastly, there is yet a much more important and profound kind of fallacies in the mind of man, which I find not observed or inquired at all, and think good to place here, as that which of all others appertaineth most to rectify judgement: the force whereof is such, as it doth not dazzle or snare the understanding in some particulars, but doth more generally and inwardly infect and corrupt the state thereof. For the mind of man is far from the nature of a clear and equal glass, wherein the beams of things should reflect according to their true incidence; nay, it is rather like an enchanted glass, full of superstition and imposture, if it be not delivered and reduced.

So, sub-rational dispositions are, according to this view, among the determinant factors in the fixation of belief. And any man, if he allows himself a minimum of self-enquiry, can realize that (as Bacon put it), 'his feelings imbue and corrupt his understanding in innumerable and sometimes imperceptible ways':

The human understanding when it has once adopted an opinion (either as being the received opinion or as being agreeable to itself) draws all things else to support and agree with it. And though there be a greater number and weight of instances to be found on the other side, yet these it either neglects and despises, or else by some distinction sets aside and rejects, in order that by this great and pernicious predetermination the authority of its former conclusions may remain inviolate . . . it is the peculiar and perpetual error of the human intellect to be more moved and excited by affirmatives than by negatives.[5]

Illusions, as defined above, owe their existence to this psychological mechanism described by Bacon as pertaining to the Idols of the Tribe in his doctrine of the Four Idols.

Now, the central point I wish to make in this chapter is that positive contributions to knowledge do not always take the form of (i) the exposing and displacing of errors, that is, beliefs which are relatively easy to dispose of. This history of ideas displays, every now and then, the emergence of (ii) works which strike – or at least are felt by many to strike – on firmly rooted illusions, i.e. those beliefs and opinions which exert some command upon our feelings and appear to enhance the desirability of life and living for those who embrace them. Events of class (i) bring few or no problems, it is the occurrence of (ii) that deserves to be examined in more depth.

As regards the logic of pure misunderstandings in the history of ideas, it follows from this reasoning that the fact that some particular theories and lines of thought turn out to be peculiarly liable to being misunderstood can be explained as resulting, to some degree, from their meeting not mere errors at the receiving end of the exchange, but beliefs which grow out of our passions (illusions). A question, therefore, not so much of 'the ease with which we can believe what meets our wishes',[6] but rather, if this hypothesis is correct, of the ease with which we spontaneously *misapprehend* what does not meet our wishes.

Scientists, of course, are professionally committed to controlling their own mind's functioning, so as to try and make their understanding of phenomena resemble as far as possible the *dry light* – immune to one's will and affections – depicted by Bacon. 'The kernel of the scientific outlook', wrote B. Russell in truly Baconian spirit, 'is the refusal to regard our own desires, tastes and interests as affording a key to the understanding of the world'.[7] But obviously living up to this principle of intellectual conduct is a far more demanding and tricky affair than decreeing and recommending it to others. And Bacon himself, it must be stressed, never suggested that the Idols of the Tribe could be eradicated from the human mind or that the intellectual knowledge of their *modi operandi* would by itself constitute a sufficient safeguard for the thinking subject: 'It must be confessed that it is not possible to divorce ourselves from these fallacies and false appearances, because they are inseparable from our nature and condition of life; so yet nevertheless the caution of them . . . doth extremely import the true conduct of human judgement'.[8] Moreover, it must also be noted, the conditions under which we form and fix beliefs in ordinary practical life are clearly distinct from those normally prevailing in the relatively secluded world of the study, the library and the laboratory.

The most habitual way through which the sub-rational dispositions of the human mind act as disturbing forces in the workings of the understanding is probably by shifting our attention *away* from what might undermine or threaten settled beliefs. The underlying mechanism may be described as follows.

The human mind operates under a very powerful attention-constraint. For it is (a) unable to fix its attention on more than one object at a time, and (b) the harder it tries to focus on a single, well-defined point, the more it finds itself *ipso facto* compelled to assume away and filter out from its field of attention. There are of course many ways to deal with the attention-constraint. Properly controlled, used and trimmed it yields formidable scientific abstractions, but left to run its own course in ordinary life it operates as a smoothly running device for the protection of our current beliefs.

This barrier, which works by securing the persistent deflexion of attention from what might threaten the survival of illusory beliefs, is what J. Viner has described as that 'tough shell' with which the human mind has been endowed, 'so that it resists stubbornly the undermining of its inherited beliefs by the progressive accumulation of scientific knowledge'. For 'if we are prudent', argued Viner against the view that 'the feelings and beliefs of the mass of mankind' are increasingly tutored by packed-down science, 'we should perhaps guard against overestimating the power of astronomical knowledge over man's minds and behaviour'.[9] But as it will be shown next, other illustrations may be drawn from more down-to-earth disciplines.

As it has been suggested by the American logician C.S. Peirce, many times the 'tough shell' is quite deliberately put up by the thinking subject in order to keep out of reach all that might cause a change in his opinions. Peirce has called this popular method of fixing belief the 'method of tenacity', and he has given an apt illustration (apparently drawn from his own circle) of its *modus operandi* in ordinary life. 'This simple and direct method', he wrote, 'is really pursued by many men':

I remember once being entreated not to read a certain newspaper lest it might change my opinion upon free-trade. 'Lest I might be entrapped by its fallacies and misstatements' was the form of expression. 'You are not', my friend said, 'a special student of political economy. You might, therefore, easily be deceived by fallacious arguments upon the subject. You might, then, if you read this paper, be led to believe in protection. But you admit that free-trade is the true doctrine; and you do not wish to believe what is not true'. I have often [concluded Peirce] known this system to be deliberately adopted.[10]

Thus, one clings tenaciously to believing just what one believes and manages to keep at a fairly safe distance whatever feels like threatening its survival.

It must also be said that the frame of mind which is best conducive to the adoption of the 'method of tenacity' has no ideological motherland. It travels freely between the east–west and the north–south divides.

Among more recent developments in economics one can clearly discern such frame of mind in statements like the following: (a) Hayek's suggestion that, since it is sometimes difficult to spell out convincingly all the unforeseen costs of specific government measures interfering with the free market system, so: 'A successful defence of freedom must therefore be dogmatic and make no concessions to expediency, even where it is not possible to show that, besides the known beneficial effects, some particular harmful result would also follow from its infringement'; and (b) G. Myrdal's equally dogmatic and revealing statement (in a 1951 article called 'The trend towards economic planning') to the effect that 'there exists no alternative to economic planning': 'There is, therefore, no case to be made for or against economic planning, for or against free enterprise or free trade. Ever more State intervention and economic planning is part of the historical trends . . . In reality, it was never, and is certainly not now, a choice. It is a destiny. We will have to do the best with the world we have'.[11]

What is common to (a) and (b) is the strong *a priori* commitment to the blocking of any serious doubts regarding core beliefs (illusions) in their economic thinking, viz: Hayek's belief in the goodness of the 'spontaneous order' of the market mechanism and Myrdal's in the 'historical inevitability' of socialism. Can there be any meaningful argument between upholders of (a) and (b)? Between a man who is ready and willing to 'be dogmatic' whenever his rational ammunition has run out, and another who is intimately sure and convinced that there is in fact no 'real choice' between what he and his opponents hold to be true? Without belabouring the point, I would suggest that believers in (a) and (b) simply could not think more highly of their own convictions and that this frame of mind is thoroughly inimical to the spirit of scientific enquiry.

So, there are cases in which the refusal to face and meet challenges to one's beliefs is quite deliberate. The ensuing 'protective blindness' is thus largely self-imposed – a relatively simple (if no less intractable)problem from a logical point of view. For the 'method of tenacity', by ensuring that the receiver will not even get in touch with what might cause him to change or abandon his relevant beliefs, thereby precludes also all possibility of pure misunderstanding. But that, however, is not all. A much more insidious, hard to detect and for this reason effective mechanism conditioning the process of belief-formation has to do with the forces which operate, as it were, behind the back of our minds, filtering out unwanted facts and thoughts.

The 'tough shell', in this latter case, is not deliberately set up by the agent – it grows spontaneously in his mind. And, as it is apt to escape detection, so it can best perform its mission, that is, the turning of one's attention away from whatever might undermine core beliefs or be conducive to those uneasy mental states called uncertainty and doubt. That even the relatively insulated province of pure scientific research is not free from the operations of this sub-rational mechanism can be best seen by reference to what Darwin observed in his *Autobiography* concerning his methodological 'golden rule'. Describing his research leading to the *Origin*, Darwin relates how he had 'during many years followed a golden rule', viz:

> That whenever a published fact, a new observation or thought came across me, which was opposed to my general results, to make a memorandum of it without fail and at once; for I had found by experience that such facts and thoughts were far more apt to escape from the memory than favourable ones.[12]

As this 'golden rule' makes clear, the prevailing tendency of Darwin's memory was to vitiate, in undesirable ways, his relations with the attention-constraint. And it did so not in any arbitrary or erratic way, but according to a criterion of its own and in line with what the Baconian Idols of the Tribe would predict – the supression of evidence and arguments so as to protect the relevant beliefs.

Thus, whereas Peirce's ostrich-like friend recommended nothing short of burying one's head in order to best enjoy one's beliefs, Darwin had to conduct a struggle precisely in the opposite direction: he forced himself to see and give due weight to facts and thoughts that failed to concur with the inclination of his will and wishes. This is a struggle against self-deception and it begins of course with the recognition of just how difficult it is not to deceive oneself.

His 'golden rule', we may note, falls in neatly with the philosopher's word of caution to his former pupil: 'You can't think decently if you don't want to hurt yourself'. As Bacon himself had asked, in his essay 'Of truth' (1625), 'Doth any man doubt, that if there were taken out of men's minds vain opinions, flattering hopes, false valuations, imaginations as one would, and the like, but it would leave the minds of a number of men poor shrunken things, full of melancholy and indisposition, and unpleasing to themselves?'[13] In the following chapter I will examine how the non-rational factors conditioning the fixation of belief – Bacon's Idols of the Tribe – may affect the transmission and reception of thought in the history of ideas.

CHAPTER 12

The protection of belief
Pure misunderstanding as the result of theoretical akrasia

The method of tenacity described by Peirce and the propensity to self-deception reported (and diligently resisted) by Darwin are both ways to keep our relevant beliefs safe from the brunt of unfavourable or just unfavourable-looking matter. Their common denominator is the notion of avoidance. In the one case this is achieved by the methodical looking away from what might damage the soothing illusion at issue, and in the other by our spontaneous tendency to skip from, undervalue and erase from the field of awareness facts and thoughts which prove uncomfortable to dwell upon. Both mechanisms bring out the involvement of the thinking subject's desires and emotions in the process of belief-formation – they show how this interference may affect the workings of the understanding and hence impair cognition.

These mechanisms for the protection of belief can be seen as instances of what has been recently described, in more general terms, as the phenomenon of 'theoretical *akrasia*': 'We notice or allege a case of theoretical *akrasia* whenever we speak of refusing to see, of not wanting to know, and in at least some of the cases where we accuse someone of self-deception, or of living in a fool's paradise'.[1] The term *akrasia* here, it may be noted, is borrowed from Aristotle's ethics, where it is used to refer to the failure, by an individual agent, to act in line with his own opinion about what he should do when the time to act comes. Typically, practical *akrasia* results from the fact that, in the heat of the action, the agent's sub-rational dispositions or passions override his other considerations, leading him to do or refrain from doing things he knows, and otherwise believes, he should not do. Hence the conclusion (cf. Adam Smith's account in TMS,272 cited in chapter 6 above) that intelligence is not a sufficient safeguard for a man, and that virtue has to do not so much with knowledge of the good but with action.

Theoretical akrasia takes place in the realm of intellectual conduct.

Here, it is one's logical rather than one's ethical resources that collapse. The agent's will and emotions gain the upper hand in the process of belief-formation, leading him to believe things he would not believe if he were able to apply and make use of the logical rules he otherwise adheres to. So, for example: 'A woman may "hope against hope" that her child will recover from leukaemia or poliomyelitis when there is no ground for optimism, and when she knows that there is no such ground'; similarly, there is the case in which a man's 'desire for victory or for security in a cherished conviction blinds him to the truth that his mind would grasp if it were not for the intervention of his will'. It is this last type of occurrence, as I will try to suggest in this chapter, that may be seen as relevant to the study of the history of ideas and the problem of pure misunderstanding.

A fine illustration of theoretical *akrasia*, which is in many ways analagous to the 'desire for victory and security' case just cited, is given by Dostoyevsky in his study of gambling in *The Gambler*. Consider first the question which the gambler puts to himself when, away from the roulette and in the quiet of his room, he asked: 'Is it really impossible to touch gambling without immediately becoming infected with superstition?' The casino, it might be said, stood for Dostoyevsky's gambler as a veritable 'temple' of theoretical *akrasia*, for, though he was not normally given to superstitious habits of thought, he found superstition 'infecting' his mind when he set about gambling. He depicted his own predicament as follows:

Yes, sometimes the wildest notion, the most apparently impossible idea, takes such a firm hold of the mind that at length it is taken for something realizable. More than that: if the idea coincides with a strong and passionate desire, it may sometimes be accepted as something predestined, inevitable, foreordained, something that cannot but exist or happen!

So, although he was able to see, describe and even look down on what he felt and thought when he touched gambling, it was beyond his power to prevent it from recurring when he was at play. As Dostoyevsky himself were to put it elsewhere, describing what he called 'the primordial law of human nature': 'He who makes up his mind to believe in something, can't be stopped'.[2]

Underlying the proposed application of the notion of *akrasia* to the analysis of belief-formation is the Baconian view that the human understanding is no *dry light*. Bacon had seen that intimate certainties ('faith') and jealously guarded convictions often betray one's weak spots, that is, a paucity of logical and rational grounds for the beliefs and opinions at stake. The conclusion he drew from this notion was the important rule that 'whatever one's mind seizes and dwells upon with peculiar satisfaction is to be held in suspicion'.[3] In Hume's words: 'All doctrines are to be suspected, which are favoured by our passions' (E,598). And it is perhaps noteworthy that the same early Greek philosopher (Heraclitus) who inspired Bacon's image of the 'dry light', by remarking that 'The dry light is the wisest soul', left also another fragment to the effect that 'It is pleasure to souls to become moist'.[4]

Now, the central contention here is: there is an important class of pure misunderstandings which has some form of theoretical *akrasia* as its root cause. The protection of the relevant belief is achieved not by (a) the familiar ('ostrich-like') avoidance of what might threaten it, nor by (b) a quasi-subliminal forgetting of unfavourable facts and thoughts. Rather, the protection is achieved via (c) the positive distortion of the threatening argument or conjecture, so as to neutralize its destructive power. Thus, the relatively passive strategies of refusing to see and not wanting to know give way, now, to the much more intrusive exercise of raiding well into the enemy's lines and disfiguring his thought into a suitable, more manageable adversary. If this is the case, then misunderstanding can be seen as a form of theoretical *akrasia*.

Like in other cases of pure misunderstanding, the distortion and misapprehension involved in such cases are not intentional. For only in so far as they are spontaneous occurrences – that is, events that happen to the thinking subject, as opposed to what he can choose and deliberate upon – are they capable of functioning effectively as barriers for the safeguard and sealing off of beliefs. Misunderstanding 'works' here only in so far as it is 'trap-like', that is, in so far as the distortion and misapprehension at issue remain concealed *qua* misunderstanding from the agent who undergoes it. It is an important feature of the logic of misunderstandings that they cannot be reconstructed once they have been detected and disclosed.

Thus, I may contrive and strive to misreport someone else's ideas in order to score an easy victory or to foster some laudable, overriding cause. By doing so, and if I succeed in my design, I perpetrate an act of misrepresentation. But I cannot deceive myself in the same way; for I know better, and I cannot bring myself to really believe in what I know is a misrepresentation of my own making. It is only if I believe that I have truly grasped my opponent's main arguments, and that I am indeed facing and confronting *them* rather than a 'man of straw' of my own convenience, that I will find myself able to secure reassurance in my conviction – the pleasurable feeling that my relevant beliefs have survived the 'test' and stand now as firm as ever. This, I argue, is the abstract mode of a significant class of pure misunderstandings in the history of ideas.

There is no reason, for instance, to suppose that Darwin, assessing the reception and impact of his theory of evolution, expressed an unduly generous opinion about those who made public their reading of his work. He wrote: 'I have almost always been treated honestly by my reviewers, passing over those without scientific knowledge as not worthy of notice. My views have often been grossly misrepresented, bitterly opposed and ridiculed, but this has been generally done, as I believe, in good faith'.[5] It is precisely this element of 'good faith', that is, of lack of malice and dishonest intentions in the act of misapprehending (and hence misrepresenting) someone else's ideas, which allows one to speak of genuine misunderstanding. Besides, as I have tried to suggest, only the latter is able to function effectively as a defence mechanism for the protection of the receivers' relevant beliefs. It is the confident, though mistaken, conviction that one has really grasped the deliverer's message, and thus is coming to grips with the 'real thing', which allows misunderstanding to work as a protective mechanism in this sense, on a level with the more familiar ones of biased forgetting and the method of tenacity.

Distortions and misapprehensions due to theoretical *akrasia* in the business of reading are liable to occur whenever the reader's will and sub-rational propensities amount to high obstacles against an adequate understanding of the text. As the argument set forth in the former chapter should help to make clear, the likelihood of this outcome is bound to increase as one gradually approaches beliefs on issues which are very close to the receiver's heart and self-image or, more generally, on which he happens to have strong views.

A strong-willed, committed and upwardly mobile politician, for example, is not at all likely to achieve a satisfactory use of his capacity for understanding when he attempts to grasp and fully appreciate the point of arguments and evidence that run against the very foundations of the beliefs which have hitherto formed the basis of his career. He cannot afford to allow the seeds of doubt into his 'ideology' and so risk his professional prospects, reputation and perhaps even his identity in the exercise. Of course, such a partisan mind will normally try and avoid all serious immersion in the opponent's thought, making a virtue out of what Locke once depicted as 'the habit of conversing but with one sort of men and of reading but one sort of books'. Indeed, we may even find that he will eventually confess (after Popper's remark on his approach to the arch-enemy (Hegel) of his 'open society'): 'I neither could nor wished to spend unlimited time upon deep researches into the history of a philosopher whose work I abhor'.[6]

But if this mind is, for some odd reason, led into the other camp, to probe into the enemy's lines and then to give a judgement of their soundness, then the likelihood of misunderstanding is high. As Montaigne once observed, 'To an Atheist all writings make for Atheism'.[7] Deeply committed minds will always manage to find, somehow, just what they had set out to find. How many *ists* and *isms* of the recent ideological past, we may ask, could not suitably replace 'atheist' and 'atheism' in this striking formula?

Similarly, a thinker who has come to believe with, say, Hegel, that 'The account of the creation given in Genesis is still the best, in so far as it says quite simply that the plants, the animals, and man were brought forward on separate days', and that hence 'Man has not formed himself out of the animal, nor the animal out of the plant', may find it hard to give a sympathetic hearing to, and fully take in, an evolutionist (or emanationist) account of species which happens to strike at a central pillar of his philosophical edifice. It is indeed highly suggestive that Hegel himself, though well acquainted with the geological evidence and fossil material then available, preferred still to believe (as one of his modern commentators points out) 'that the organic forms found in early geological strata never really lived: they are merely paintings or sculptures of the living, imitations and anticipations of organic forms, but produced by forces that were inorganic'.[8] Thus a potentially devastating line of thought, suggesting the possibility of the biological extinction of species and of man's animal descent, was 'defused' (misunderstood) by Hegel and forcefully assimilated into his gigantic philosophy of nature.

It would not perhaps be too rash to suggest that, at least as far as scientific detachment is concerned, Hegel's reading of geological books stood on a level with Pitt's reading of the *Wealth of Nations* (as seen in the beginning of chapter 8 above). Both, it could be argued, provide clear illustrations of the common belief-formation mechanism stressed by Adam Smith, according to which 'Our passions all justify themselves, that is, suggest to us opinions which justify them'. As Hume put it, 'A coward, whose fears are easily awaken'd, readily assents to every account of danger he meets with; as a person of a sorrowful and melancholy disposition is very credulous of every thing, that nourishes his prevailing passion' (THN, 120). A significant subset of such self-reinforcing beliefs and opinions, I have been suggesting, is constituted by the spontaneous misunderstanding of thoughts and conclusions reached by minds distinct from one's own.

Works conveying so-called 'unpleasant truths', 'disheartening reflections' and the like are of course privileged targets for misunderstandings due to some form of theoretical *akrasia*. A Devil's Chaplain, who is out to tempt readers to 'take, pluck, and eat of that forbidden fruit of the Tree of Knowledge', may find it hard to secure a hearing for his gospel. But he may find it even harder to get his message across and properly digested, when the fruits he has to offer suggest no glad tidings but appear, on the contrary, sad, bitter and repulsive.

Darwin, in an often-quoted letter of 1856 to J.D. Hooker, recalled and applied to himself the Devil's Chaplain metaphor: 'What a book a Devil's Chaplain might write on the clumsy, wasteful, blundering, low, and horribly cruel works of nature!' What is little known, however, is that the title of Devil's Chaplain had been formerly given by the Church authorities to an ex-clergyman, Rev. R. Taylor, as an attempt to curse and cast a spell on the preacher who was found guilty of blasphemy and later sentenced to two years imprisonment on account of two sermons delivered in 1831. In 1829, when the 'Devil's Chaplain' (Rev. Taylor) paid a visit to the city of Cambridge in order to preach and challenge orthodox Christianity, Darwin was an undergraduate at Christ's College carrying out his father's wish and preparing to take up a career in the Church of England.[9] Three decades later he would strike a fatal and 'devilish' (as the cited letter to Hooker implies) blow against the eighteenth-century belief in a divine Nature – the much cherished notion that *Natura Codex est Dei*.

Darwin's self-portrait as a 'book-writing Devil's Chaplain' can be seen as affording a further glimpse into his own struggle to recognize and weigh things against the inclination of his will. As the young Darwin himself had jotted down in one of his working notebooks: 'Belief allied to instinct'. He had been led to this conclusion, it appears, by observing how well-founded arguments often failed to really convince those to whom they were addressed, and who would even seem to assent to them. Recalling his time as an undergraduate at Christ's, he wrote: 'It never struck me how illogical it was to say that I believed in what I could not understand and what is in fact unintelligible'.[10]

Misunderstanding, it can now be argued, the dextrous though not wilful twisting and defusing of adverse-looking facts and ideas, is one of the roads through which 'instinct' (or 'passion') reasserts its sway upon belief. 'I plainly perceive', remarked Montaigne, 'we lend nothing unto devotion but the offices that flatter our passions';[11] but it may just as well be the case, it is now suggested, that we are apt to misunderstand what seems to negate or mortify them.

This analysis, if accurate, throws some light on Darwin's answer to Wallace suggesting that the great problems of intelligibility faced by their theory ran deeper than they might at first appear. It helps also to make some sense, I hope, of his repeated suggestions that these problems were in a fundamental way analogous to those still besetting Malthus' work. As Keynes has graphically remarked: 'Before the eighteenth century mankind entertained no false hopes. To lay the illusions which grew popular at that age's latter end, Malthus disclosed a Devil'.[12] Illusions, however, die hard, and devils elicit strange reactions. Not surprisingly, several responses to the 'written spectre' raised by Malthus afford unexceptionable illustrations of misunderstanding via theoretical *akrasia*. Moreover, it is possible to show that this affected not only many of his intellectual antagonists but, as Malthus himself indicated, even some of those who believed themselves champions of the Malthusian creed. Chapter 13 is an attempt to substantiate this claim.

On misunderstanding Malthus
The reception of the Essay on Population: critics and supporters

It is perhaps not surprising to find that nearly all nineteenth-century romantic critics of political economy should have honoured Malthus with the cream of their virulence and indignation. Ruskin, echoing and distilling Carlyle's reaction against 'Paralytic Radicalism' and the 'Benthamee-Malthusian dismal science', wrote that 'In all the ranges of human thought I know none so melancholy as the speculations of political economists on the population question'. He had singled out political economy for attack because he believed that 'nothing in history had ever been so disgraceful to human intellect as the acceptance among us of the common doctrines of political economy as a science'.

Like most of his early and mid-nineteenth-century romantic partners, Ruskin felt that 'gloom and misanthropy have become the characteristics of the age in which we live', and that the Malthusian 'doctrine of despair', which had 'cast a slur upon the face of nature', was largely to blame. In a letter of 1871, Ruskin put his finger on what he believed was the real nerve of his mental dejection; his words, it may be noted, closely resemble those of Darwin's book-writing Devil's Chaplain: 'Of all things that oppress me, this sense of the evil working of nature herself – my disgust at her barbarity – clumsiness – darkness – bitter mocking of herself – is the most desolating'.[1]

As I shall try to show in this chapter, the Malthusian 'evil nature' struck at the root of the romantic movement. Malthus had proposed to invert the order of reasoning and to face some rather unpleasant facts. As he put it in the first *Essay*, he had tried to 'reason from nature up to God, and not presume to reason from God to nature'.[2] But his doctrine, the romantics felt, was in effect a 'monstrous practical sophism'. 'I solemnly declare', said Coleridge epitomizing the romantic point of view on Malthus' theory, 'that I do not believe that all the heresies and sects and factions which the ignorance and the weakness and the wickedness of man have ever given birth to, were altogether so disgraceful to man as a Christian, a philosopher, a statesman, or citizen, as this abominable tenet'.[3]

As they felt strongly, so did they read and write. And few of them had the candour to acknowledge – as the American romantic, R.W. Emerson, would eventually do – that 'we shall never *understand* political economy until some poet shall teach it in songs, and he will not teach Malthusianism'. Most of them, on the contrary, were pretty sure they had not only mastered Malthus' thought, but also that they could look down on it as amounting to little more than 'childish Blunders' and 'Verbiage and senseless Repetition', as Coleridge scribbled in the margins of his heavily annotated copy of the second (1803) edition of the 'infamous' *Essay*.[4]

W. Hazlitt and Coleridge's Pantisocratic friend, R. Southey, were to express their anger and lack of condescension in public and at greater length. 'I confess', wrote Hazlitt, 'I do feel some degree of disgust and indignation rising within me, when I see a man of Mr Malthus' character and calling standing forward as the accuser of those "who have none to help them", as the high-priest of "pride and covetousness", forming selfishness into a regular code, with its codicils, institutes and glosses annexed, trying to muffle up the hand of charity in the fetters of the law, to suppress "the compunctious visitings of nature", to make men ashamed of compassion and good-nature as folly and weakness'. And referring elsewhere to Malthus' attempt to show the unfeasibility of the Godwinian ideal of a perfectly 'rational society', Hazlitt did not hesitate to conclude: 'A more complete piece of wrong-headedness, a more strange perversion of reason, could hardly be devised by the wit of man'.[5]

Similarly Southey, making use of Coleridge's notes on Malthus in a long review of the 1803 *Essay*, dismissed the work as vacuous, illogical and (to use Hazlitt's expression) permeated by 'sinister and servile purposes'. 'By these miserable sophisms', he wrote, 'Mr Malthus has obtained the high reputation which he at present enjoys; his book having become the political bible of the rich, the selfish, and the sensual'. A decade later, Southey would go as far as to suggest that, of all things: 'A writer ought to possess a more logical mind than Mr Malthus has been gifted with.' Moreover, he then added, 'A book necessarily leading to such topics of discussion as Mr Malthus' ought not to have been written in English', seeing that 'the main point upon which his argument turns, and the necessity of vice for the preservation of good order, were not subjects to be sent into circulation libraries and book-societies, and to be canvassed at tea-tables'.[6] The poet P. Shelley, writing in 1818, would follow suit and inveigh against 'sophism like those of Mr Malthus, calculated to lull the oppressors of mankind into a security of everlasting triumph'.[7]

The charges brought against Malthus by his romantic critics were manifold. They included those of (a) plagiarism, (b) vacuity, (c) illogicality, (d) a partisan and reactionary character, (e) being cruel to the poor, (f) debauched and (g) debasing to mankind. But none of these seems to have been so common and central to the romantic case as the charge of (h) fatalism: the view that Malthus' work had led to a widespread complacency about poverty and social deprivation by destroying all hope that economic reform might improve the material condition of the poor. His doctrine, the argument ran, was 'dreary, stolid, dismal' – 'without hope for this world or the next' (Carlyle) – or as Coleridge put it, summing up his understanding of Malthus' theory, 'we are on the brink of ruin from the excess of population, and he who would prevent the poor from rotting away in disease, misery, and wickedness, is an enemy to his country!'[8]

But this, as I try to show later on in this chapter, was not the interpretation that the author himself would have expected to follow from his text. Indeed, it seems to be an interpretation based on a severe misapprehension of what Malthus had set out to do. The underlying logical pattern of the misunderstanding at issue here was the romantics' tendency to read Malthus' descriptions and explanations in the *Essay* as if they were attempts not to bring out the nature and causes of certain events, but rather to legitimize and perpetuate – or even to commend – a given state of affairs. But to read fatalism into his population theory was interpretation, not text. It clearly was not, on the one hand, Malthus' own reading of his scientific work; in his *Principles*, for example, he advocated a more empirical and pragmatic approach to economics, rejecting the Ricardian approach and making clear that, as he put it, 'it is impossible for a government strictly to let things take their natural course'.[9] And it was not, on the other, what less emotional readers of his work, like for instance J.S. Mill and other utilitarian reformers, as it will be seen below, were able to make of his legacy.

Malthus' *Essay*, it has been aptly observed, 'is a study of the nature and causes rather of the poverty than of the wealth of nations'. As a recent commentator has described it, the bulk of the 1803 and subsequent editions of the work consisted of 'a catalogue of details of bestial life, sickness, weakness, poor food, lack of ability to care for young, scant resources, famine, infanticide, war, massacre, plunder, slavery, cold, hunger, disease, epidemics, plague, and abortion'.[10] But Malthus did not 'shut out' the possibility of economic progress and an overall improvement in well-being. True, he had argued (against Ricardo) that 'the progress of society consists of irregular movements', and he had also maintained (against Godwin, Condorcet and 'enlightened enthusiasts' in general) that 'nothing is so easy as to find fault with human institutions, nothing so difficult as to suggest adequate practical improvements'.[11] (As Lenin were to put it not long after the Russian Revolution, 'it is much easier to seize power in a revolutionary epoch than to know how to use this power properly'.)

But Malthus' romantic readers, it appears, could not bear such reality. 'Whatever our own Despondence may whisper', reported Coleridge, 'or the reputed Masters of Political Economy may have seemed to demonstrate, neither by the fears and scruples of the one, or by the confident affirmations of the other, dare we be deterred. They must both be false if the Prophet is true. We will still in the power of that faith which can hope even against hope continue to sow beside all waters'.[12] Indeed, it would be hard to improve on this assertion as an unwitting acknowledgement of theoretical *akrasia*.

It was left to Thomas de Quincey to point out, regarding Malthus' romantic critics and referring in particular to his own friend Coleridge, that 'they seem to have been somewhat captious, and in a thick mist as to the true meaning and tendency of the [Malthusian] doctrine'. 'Indeed', he went on to say, 'I question whether any man amongst them could have begun his own work [i.e. the criticism of Malthus] by presenting a just analysis of that which he was assailing.'[13] But none of them, unfortunately, appears to have taken up Quincey's challenge.

It is rather more surprising, however, to find a professed atheist and materialist critic of classical political economy betraying a loss of nerve and letting down his guard in the face of Malthus' Devil.

The young Engels, in his seminal 1844 essay 'Outlines of a critique of political economy', complained of the coldness, harshness and even cruelty of what he took to be the Malthusian doctrine. 'Am I to go on any longer elaborating this vile, infamous theory, this revolting blasphemy against nature and mankind?', he asked himself after depicting Malthus' theory – much in the romantic vein – as 'the crudest, most barbarous theory that ever existed, a system of despair which struck down all those beautiful phrases about love of neighbour and world citizenship'.[14]

Engels' youthful response to Rev. Malthus – 'Here at last we have the immorality of the economist brought to its highest pitch' – corresponds in a way to Marx's initial reaction to Ricardo's *Principles*. Writing in the very year in which Engels' essay was first published and in which he came to meet, in Paris, his lifelong partner, Marx observed: 'Ricardo in his book . . . Nations are merely workshops for production, and man is a machine for consuming and producing. Human life is a piece of capital. Economic laws rule the world blindly. For Ricardo men are nothing, the product everything'.[15] But, whereas in regard to Ricardo, Marx in due course changed his mind and came to see his theoretical contribution as the high point of classical economics, his position with respect to Malthus remained essentially unchanged throughout his life.

Marx, it is true, unlike the romantics, tried to work out his own, alternative theory of population. As usual, his argument hinges on a radical cleavage between the mechanisms at work in human or social processes ('History') and those applying to natural or non-human ones ('Nature'): 'An abstract law of population exists only for plants and animals, and even then only in the absence of any historical intervention by man'.[16] Hence, he maintained, different modes of production will have distinct population requirements and laws, and there will be no such thing as a truly operative law of diminishing returns on land, provided you assume first that more science and technical change will always outweigh its effects.

Yet, Marx's actual comments on Malthus' *Essay* are remarkable for their thinness and clear emotional tone. The general drift of his reaction is well-captured by remarks in a footnote to *Capital*: 'The great sensation this pamphlet caused was due solely to the fact that it corresponded to the interests of a particular party . . . [It was] declaimed in the manner of a sermon, but not containing a single original proposition of Malthus himself'.[17] Rev. Malthus, he insisted, had not been a 'man of science' like, say, Ricardo or Darwin – he had been a 'bought advocate'.

It is indeed symptomatic that in nearly all of his references to Malthus, and in his rather cursory discussions of the ideas of this 'master in plagiarism', Marx unfailingly revealed what has been already diagnosed as 'a note of hysteria',[18] by appending some form of abuse or derogatory epithet to the name of this 'shameless sycophant of the ruling classes'. And it would not perhaps be misleading to discern a belated (and costly) repercussion of the Marxist unwillingness to meet and come to terms with the Devil disclosed by the 'mountebank-parson', in that most peculiar chapter of post-war Soviet science – T.D. Lysenko's agrobiology and its rather forceful attempt to 'free' Darwin's theory of evolution from the 'ideological virus' of Malthusianism by getting rid of the 'bourgeois' notion of intra-species competition.[19]

Like the romantics before them, Marx and Engels were keen to denounce Malthus and to question his scientific integrity. It did not bother them that scientists like Darwin and Ricardo – the great luminaries of nineteenth-century science, according to Marx himself – greatly admired Malthus' achievements and had even assimilated some of his contributions into their own scientific work. In the eyes of Marx and his twentieth-century followers, Malthus remained always a 'sycophant' serving 'sinister and servile purposes'.

It is instructive to contrast the Marxist verdict on Malthus with the assessment put forward by B. Russell. Marx and his followers, as seen, depicted him as a 'plagiarist' and 'bought advocate', yet to Russell, Keynes and others it was precisely his integrity and iron (but calm) determination that stood out. According to Russell,

It is not his conclusions that are valuable, but the temper and method of his inquiry. As everyone knows, it was to him that Darwin owed an essential part of his theory of natural selection, and this was only possible because Malthus' outlook was truly scientific. His great merit lies in considering man not as the object of praise and blame, but as a part of nature, a thing with a certain characteristic behaviour from which certain consequences must follow . . . The objections which were made when his doctrine was new – that it was horrible and depressing, that people ought not to act as he said they did, and so on; as against all of them, his calm determination to treat man as a natural phenomenon marks an important advance over the reformers of the eighteenth century and the Revolution.[20]

At the same time, throughout the nineteenth century there were repeated attempts to rescue Malthus' theory from misunderstandings and misguided fire. In a letter of 1835 to Nassau Senior (who had been appointed, ten years earlier, to the first chair of political economy at Oxford) the theologian and economist Archbishop

Whately suggested: 'I want you to write a short account of Malthus' views, which, perhaps, might be subjoined to a few lines of memoir of his (I believe not eventful) life. I wish justice to be done him – 1st, against his enemies; 2nd, much more against his professed friends, who have made him a tool for noxious purposes'.[21]

It is interesting to note that, six years earlier, Senior himself had corresponded with Malthus, after sending him for comment the lectures on the theory of population he had delivered at Oxford in Easter 1828. As the correspondence with Malthus unfolded, it became increasingly clear to Senior that the object of his lectures had been in fact not Malthus' own theory, as he originally thought, but its misinterpretation and abuse by his followers. 'Undoubtedly', he replied to Malthus in a letter of 1829, 'these opinions are not fair inferences from your work; they are, indeed, directly opposed to the spirit of the greater part of it; but I think they must be considered as having been occasioned by a misconception of your reasonings. They are prevalent now: before the appearance of your writings, they were never hinted at'. And, as he was now able to discriminate between Malthus' ideas on the one hand, and what his self-proclaimed 'supporters' had made of them on the other, Senior could also see how he had laboured under misunderstanding in his lectures. '[Your] views', he wrote to Malthus in the letter which concludes the exchange, 'are as just as they are important. But they have been caricatured by most of your followers . . . These were the doctrines that I found prevalent when I began my Lectures'.[22]

Similarly Marshall, we may note, delivering a public lecture in London in 1885 on 'The pressure of population on the means of subsistence', introduced his theme stating: 'I have noticed that there is much misunderstanding as to the way in which the growth of population acts on the means of subsistence. There are indeed some who think that the economic doctrine on this subject has recently been overthrown. But I believe its assailants have not accomplished this task: they have achieved the very different and very much easier one of misunderstanding it'.[23]

So, misunderstanding Malthus was no exclusive privilege of romantic and Marxist critics of political economy. For, as we shall presently see, the supporters of Malthus' thoughts and views, as Whately and Senior had observed, were equally falling prey to misconceptions, that is, conclusions which were quite alien to the master's intentions. In an unpublished letter of 23 February 1831, addressed to the philosopher of science and lecturer on political economy at Cambridge, W. Whewell, Malthus himself expressed serious misgivings about the ways in which his ideas were being put to use by the public supporters of the Malthusian movement. He wrote: 'It is quite true as Mr [Richard] Jones observes that I have been unfortunate in my followers. I trust he is aware that the general and practical conclusions which I have myself drawn from my principles both on population and on rent, have by no means the gloomy aspect given to them by many of my readers'.[24]

The sender of this letter, it is safe to say, would have been much pleased had he been able to read, in Mill's *Autobiography*, that at least some of his utilitarian followers of the next generation were very much in tune with the practical conclusions he had derived from his theory. 'Malthus' population principle', wrote Mill recalling his youthful political agitation, 'was quite as much a banner, and point of union among us, as any opinion specially belonging to Bentham. This great doctrine, originally brought forward as argument against the indefinite improvability of human affairs, we took up with ardent zeal in the contrary sense, as indicating the sole means of realizing that improvability' (CW1,107). Mill, as already seen, was a firm believer in the power of ideas to bring about social change. Persuasion – rational and moral argument – was the road to reform and progress in human affairs. But how could he make sure that the right ideas (i.e. those of Bentham and Malthus, in his youthful view) would be rightly understood and acted upon?

In chapters 14 and 15 below, I shall conclude this illustrated taxonomy of pitfalls and unintended results in intellectual exchanges by examining some relations between this claim regarding the power of ideas on the one hand, and the problem of pure misunderstanding on the other. Before that, however, it should perhaps be made clear (to avoid any misunderstandings!) that what has happened to Malthus in the hands of a significant number of his supporters, not to speak of his romantic and Marxist critics, is by no means unique. True, he may have been, as Bonar suggested and Darwin appears to have thought as well, 'the best abused man of his age'. His *Essay* attracted more abuse and eulogy than analysis or argument; it is not hard to see, as Thomas de Quincey pointed out, that relatively little of the mass of criticism heaped upon his work actually came to grips with its content and meaning. And this, of course, is precisely what makes the reception of his *Essay* a potentially interesting case-study from the viewpoint of the logic of misunderstandings and the problem of theoretical *akrasia* in the history of ideas.

But the general argument being made here, it should be clear, is that what happened to Malthus is in effect liable to occur whenever an author's ideas manage to penetrate into the sensitive domain of beliefs which are, for whatever reasons, difficult and even painful to part with. Abundant textual evidence could be collected, for instance, and an analogous argument put together, to support the view that many of Marx's critics and followers have themselves fallen prey, in various degrees, to the effects of the Baconian Idols of the Tribe in the act of reading. A suitable opening for this exercise (and indeed for the discussion in chapters 14 and 15 below) would surely be the striking conclusion reached by Lenin in 1914, during his Swiss exile, to the effect that 'it is impossible completely to understand Marx's *Capital*, and especially its first chapter, without having thoroughly studied and understood the whole of Hegel's *Logic*'. Hence, he concluded, 'half a century later none of the Marxists understood Marx'.[25]

One cannot help wondering how Marx would have reacted to Lenin's extraordinary claim that, except of course himself after the Swiss internment, 'half a century later none of the Marxists understood Marx'. Or, yet, how he would react to Lenin's even more formidable proposal of explaining *obscurum per obscurius*, that is, the first chapter of *Capital* by 'the whole of Hegel's *Logic*'. Perhaps, it is tempting to add, Adam Smith's intriguing remark on the young prime minister's enthusiastic support for his work would not be, *mutatis mutandis*, entirely out of place in this context too. In the concluding chapters of part II, I examine how the preceding enquiry into the problem of misunderstanding in the history of ideas (chapters 8 to 12) ties up with claims about the role of political and economic philosophy in the processes of belief-formation and social change.

CHAPTER 14

Ideas into Politics, I
The transmission of abstract thought: three levels of exchange

The exchange of ideas is often a delicate business. Readers, it is true, are sometimes capable of enhancing the understanding of a given text. Lovejoy, to give a more extreme type of claim as example, has gone as far as to suggest that 'one does not, in most cases, adequately understand one author – does not see what was going on in him as he wrote – unless one understands him better than he understood himself'.[1] Authors, of course, facing claims of this nature about their work, may still think otherwise, though on occasion agreeing that a receiver has understood him (i.e. his work) better than himself.

The predominant tendency, however, seems to point in the opposite direction. The transmission of ideas, as already argued (chapter 9), normally entails a certain loss of information-content and meaning, and this 'loss or mistaking' in the process of exchange is rarely outweighed by the reader's positive contribution to a better understanding of the message at issue. On the other hand, there is the danger of over-interpreting: 'He who explains a passage in an author "more deeply" than the passage was meant has not explained the author but obscured him'.[2] This history of ideas itself, I have argued, can be seen as affording a formidable wealth of evidence regarding the scope for unintended and undesired results in the transmission of thought; for even if, as it must be the case, not all the claims made by intellectual historians stand up to scrutiny and further enquiry, the very fact that they have been made is indicative of possible trouble-spots. What misled the historian might mislead others. And as Swift pointed out long ago, echoing Locke's similar warnings (cf. p. 125 above): 'Nothing is more frequent than for Commentators to force Interpretations, which the Author never meant'.[3]

There are two basic classes of factors responsible for the loss and mistaking in the transmission of thought. First, those bearing on the *emission* of messages (chapter 10). Though I mean what I say, I may still fail to say what I mean. And if sincerity and good will do not preclude the possibility of misunderstanding, neither do clarity and precision: my attempt to ward off the limits and ambiguities of ordinary language by relying on highly formalized modes of expression is liable to backfire and cause some form of misunderstanding if it simultaneously imparts to receivers a false, that is, unintended and undesired, sense of security.

Second, and probably more relevant from the viewpoint of pure misunderstandings, there is the problem of *reception* (chapters 11 and 12). The crux of the matter here is the simple fact that decoding – e.g. hearing or reading – is no neutral absorption of thought, but a heavily selective and, as a rule, positively obtrusive activity. The receiver brings his skills and concerns to work upon previously chosen texts. He screens the whole (or part) of what is before him, and in the event sorts out what appears to 'fit well' with his concerns and current thinking. Typically, reading is carried out with an eye to those things that might merit further study and, perhaps, memorizing effort. As Kuhn has pointed out about the different modes of reading and reporting of his graduate students with different backgrounds, 'The Galileo or Descartes who appeared in the philosophers' papers was a better scientist or philosopher but a less plausible seventeenth-century figure than the figure presented by the historians'.[4]

So, for example, a grammarian and a philologist will normally look for and point to different problems and qualities while reporting on the same text, just as philosophers and poets have given surprising interpretations to each other's words and works; as it has been said, 'in the same material everyone finds what is suited to his profession – in the same field a cow looks for grass, a dog for hare, a stork for a lizard'. On first studying the Christian scriptures the young Augustine found them a rough and inferior work, only 'fit for simpletons'. 'To me', he recalled in the *Confessions* about his time as an apprentice in rhetoric, they 'seemed quite unworthy of comparison with the stately prose of Cicero, because I had too much conceit to accept their simplicity and not enough insight to penetrate their depths. It is surely true that as the child grows these books grow with him. But I was too proud to call myself a child. I was inflated with self-esteem, which made me think myself a great man'.[5]

Similarly Keynes, recalling how he and some of his Bloomsbury friends had been greatly moved in their youth by studying G.E. Moore's *Principia Ethica*, went on to acknowledge that 'what we got from Moore was by no means entirely what he offered us': 'There was one chapter in the *Principia* of which we took not the slightest notice. We accepted Moore's religion, so to speak, and discarded his morals'.[6]

The reception of Mill's *Principles* is another interesting instance of the filtering process in the transmission of ideas. The work contained a radical proposal (Book II, chapters 1 and 2) to alter the distribution of initial endowments and income in England through the curtailment of the institution of inheritance and changes in the laws of property-ownership. But as A. Bain (Mill's close friend) recalled later, Mill's expectations about the impact of his work in public debate were severely disappointed: 'What I remember most vividly of his talk pending the publication of the work, was his anticipating a tremendous outcry about his doctrines on Property. He frequently spoke of his proposals as to Inheritance and Bequest, which if carried out would pull down all large fortunes in two generations. To his surprise, however, this part of the book made no sensation'.[7] As these illustrations make clear, and they could be multiplied *ad nauseam*, reading itself is no passive or neutral activity. It settles the character of the transaction.

Of course, scientific communities have special means to ensure that losses in the transmission of ideas are kept at minimal levels and under check. The progressiveness of science as an intellectual enterprise is partly dependent on the fact that scientists engaged in a given research programme are able to communicate extremely well and quickly with one another. They have ways to prevent and monitor the occurrence of misunderstandings in the process of exchange, and hence do not normally feel the need to spend or waste much of their time interpreting each other's thoughts and meanings. A scientific community may be seen as, among other things, a community of quick and easy agreement on how to decode and put to use the results of research.

It may also be interesting to note that 'paradigm', as currently used to depict the workings of 'normal science', is a term which was originally borrowed, as Kuhn points out, from the field of linguistics, where it denotes the standard examples of word-use, verb conjugation and sentence-construction that are used to facilitate language teaching.[8] One of the vital functions of a 'scientific paradigm', it can be argued, is precisely to regulate and facilitate the *transmission* of ideas, by setting norms that ensure the easy flow of information between the practitioners of a discipline. As communication is no longer – or simply no longer felt to be – a problematic and hazardous task, so the members of a paradigm-regulated community find themselves in a position to concentrate upon, and also to co-operate more effectively, in the pursuit of a given research programme.

Yet, as some of the examples discussed above indicate, not even scientific communities are entirely proof against the occurrence of severe misunderstandings. The social sciences, like economics and political science, have no agreed paradigm (or set of assumed disciplinary norms) capable of preventing and checking the multi-plication of misapprehensions and disputes at cross-purposes between practitioners, and sometimes even the maturer scientific disciplines, like biology and medical science, have met serious problems of communication breakdowns leading to an abnormal proliferation of misunderstanding-claims within their ranks. As the examples of Darwin and others have shown, there are 'unfamiliar thoughts' in the history of science which turn out to be not so hard to get accepted as to get barely across. As Schumpeter has aptly pointed out, economics has no monopoly over this problem, even if, as he acknowledged, it surely acquires a particular virulence in it:

The first thing to be observed about all controversies between scientific parties is the large amount of mutual misunderstanding that enters into them. This element is not absent even in the most advanced sciences where homogenous training, habits of exact statement, and a high level of general competence could be expected to exclude it. But where, as in economics, conditions in all these respects are immensely less favorable than they are in mathematics or physics, men frequently have but an inadequate notion of what the other fellow really worries about. Hence a great part of the fighting is directed against positions which are indeed hostile fortresses in the imagination of the warrior but which on inspection turn out to be harmless windmills.[9]

The fact of the matter is that, as one moves away from the relatively insulated and paradigm-ruled world of 'normal science', the situation clearly tends to get worse. The natural sciences seem indeed to enjoy a great advantage in this respect: 'scientific revolutions', even if they do in fact exist,[10] are at best rare episodes, setting the stage for the next period of 'normality'. But it is already doubtful whether the disciplines dealing with social organization and behaviour would rigorously qualify as sciences according to the Kuhnian or any other currently accepted delimitation criterion. Most philosophers of science, it appears, would resist such a move. In any case, however, it seems safe to say that (a) the social sciences are already marked by a sharp decline in the ability of its practitioners to communicate and hence to co-operate satisfactorily, and (b) that the transmission of messages *across* scientific groups (as distinguished from their internal transactions) and (c) *between* intellectuals and the public at large, are on any account much more troublesome and risky affairs.

Historians of science, for example, addressing a much less defined and wider academic audience, are already more familiar with the problem of being repeatedly misunderstood. Kuhn's own assessment of the reception given to his enormously successful book, *The Structure of Scientific Revolutions*, is in a sense typical of most other 'big titles' in this field: 'Monitoring conversations, particularly among the book's enthusiasts, I have sometimes found it hard to believe that all parties to the discussion had been engaged with the same volume. Part of the reason for its success is, I regretfully conclude, that it can be too nearly all things to all people'.[11] So, like many other such exercises, this one ended up paying a very high price for its remarkable success – to have no definite meaning and yet to be 'nearly all things to all people'. As Hume once observed to Adam Smith, commenting on the great and unexpected success following the publication of the *Theory of Moral Sentiments*, 'Nothing indeed can be a stronger Presumption of Falsehood than the approbation of the multitude; and Phocion, you know, always suspected himself of some Blunder, when he was attended with the applause of the Populace'.[12]

In the history of economics, and in the social sciences in general, a *classic* has been almost by definition a work which has shown itself capable of accommodating a wide variety of different readings and hence of being reinterpreted by readers and commentators in contexts that give it a new meaning and urgency. A key ingredient in the recipe for producing a classic, in this sense, has been brilliantly set out by St Augustine:

For my part I declare resolutely and with all my heart that if I were called upon to write a book which was to be vested with the highest authority, I should prefer to write it in such a way that a reader could find re-echoed in my words whatever truths he was able to apprehend. I would rather write in this way than impose a single true meaning so explicitly that it would exclude all others, even though they contained no falsehood that could give me offence.[13]

Considering the bewildering multiplicity of interpretations that have been grafted on all the great classics in the history of economics, we may conclude that what makes an economist's work *classic* is precisely the fact that it somehow invites and allows for this astonishing multiplicity of interpretations. If this is right, then it may be said that an essential feature of these greatly successful works in the history of economic thought, that is, a necessary though of course not sufficient condition for becoming a classic in the field, has been what we may call their remarkable Augustinian plasticity.

Now, the point of the preceding analyses of the different modes and patterns of misunderstanding running through the history of ideas is not, as it is should be clear, to try and find fault with this or that interpretation of a given text, or to do justice (at last) to this or that much underrated, misread or unfairly criticized author. Rather, the aim of the discussion is to draw attention to a factor which can be of help in the attempt to take up the argument of part I and examine the foundations of a very pervasive claim in modern political and economic philosophy. In particular, the analysis undertaken can help us to bring out and state more clearly one of the basic reasons why the ideas of economists and political philosophers may not be, after all, as powerful as they have been repeatedly held to be by competing traditions in modern thought.

It may be useful to distinguish here the three basic levels in which intellectual exchanges take place. The problem at issue, it should be noted, has to do not so much with (1) the transmission of ideas *within* a community defined by access to a specialized technical language or paradigm-regulated, nor with (2) attempts to bridge and speak *across* the existing academic boundaries or to open out tunnels between them. Rather, it concerns (3) the even more formidable attempts to mould socio-economic behaviour and the institutions of practical life according to the results of abstract thought and philosophical speculation. In what follows, I shall concentrate on the transmission of ideas taking place at (3).

Power-bids of this nature, I shall argue, usually assume that existing mores, public policies and patterns of social action are at bottom the after-effects of previous systematic philosophical thought. But even if this assumption is not made, and no rival philosophy is blamed as responsible for the evils and disasters besetting human affairs, still the attempt 'to bring philosophy down from the heavens' and change society through some form of persuasion and polemical *coup* clearly presupposes the existence of a more or less straightforward and fairly unproblematic flow of ideas between deliverers and receivers.

Thus, a strong and rarely spelt out claim is being implicitly made, suggesting that there is a fluent and transparent commerce between thinking and practical minds, that is, between those 'few who take the trouble to think for themselves' on the one hand, and those few who exert leadership and hold the strings of decision-making in our public and economic affairs (the 'men of action') on the other. The last chapter of part II is devoted to a discussion of the claim that 'Ideas rule the world of human affairs and its events' and of the scope for spontaneous misunderstandings at this third and most problematic level of intellectual exchanges.

CHAPTER 15

Ideas into politics, II
Sweeping claims, the philosopher-king and pure misunderstandings

Keynes, in the much-quoted concluding paragraph of the *General Theory*, put forward his own incisive formulation of the view that 'the ideas of economists and political philosophers, both when they are right and when they are wrong, are more powerful than is commonly understood'. 'Indeed', he went on to stress, 'the world is ruled by little else': 'Practical men, who believe themselves to be quite exempt from any intellectual influences, are usually the slaves of some defunct economist. Madmen in authority, who hear voices in the air, are destilling their frenzy from some academic scribbler of a few years back. I am sure that the power of vested interests is vastly exaggerated compared with the gradual encroachment of ideas'. This process, concluded Keynes, has a built-in time-lag, 'for in the field of economic and political philosophy there are not many who are influenced by new theories after they are twenty-five or thirty years of age, so that the ideas which civil servants and politicians and even agitators apply to current events are not likely to be the newest. But, soon or late, it is ideas, not vested interests, which are dangerous for good and evil'.[1]

As seen in part I (chapter 1) above, this vivid and carefully drawn picture of 'consciously formulated ideas acting as a driving force effecting transitions from social state to social state' belongs to a distinguished and numerous family in the history of ideas. It follows a long line of roughly similar, and sometimes closely resembling, statements by leading utilitarian, Marxist and neo-liberal political and economic philosophers, all concurring to stress the overriding and unsuspected power of ideas in practical life.

In the history of economics, claims of this nature stretch back at least as far as Malthus' *Principles* (1820). 'The science of political economy', he urged introducing his book and justifying his approach to the subject, 'is essentially practical and applicable to the common business of human life . . . there are few branches of human knowledge where false views may do more harm, or just views more good'.[2] Nearly half a century later, it may be noted, Marshall would use this argument in his struggle to secure a greater support for the campaign to separate Economics from the Moral Sciences Tripos at Cambridge. The practical relevance of economic science was for Marshall – as for Malthus and Mill before him – its *raison d'être*, and he believed further that it should be its passport to academic autonomy and prestige. For economists, wrote Marshall comparing the former generation with his own, have now come to 'exert a more far-reaching and more powerful influence on ideas: and ideas fashion the course of the world ever more and more'.[3]

But Keynes' statement at the close of the *General Theory*, for all its intense and sweeping character, was not as radical as it might have been. Three points deserve to be noticed here:

(1) Unlike Marshall, Keynes never seriously entertained the notion that economics was a 'moral science' in the strong sense, that is that it could or should take both business and the trade unions in hand and teach them ethics and professional standards; he derided Marshall's 'preaching asides' and he did not share the nineteenth-century confidence in the power of the 'moral sciences' to 'civilise business' and transform individual behaviour in ordinary life.

On the other hand, it would obviously be wrong to conclude from this that Keynes held the opposite view, that is that economic and moral thinking have no real impact on the course of events and that the economist stands to his object of enquiry much in the same way as astronomers and grammarians stand to theirs, i.e. able to (partly) explain but essentially unable to bring about desired change. As he made clear, he believed that economics is a 'moral science'. For even if it does not or cannot impart virtue to agents, as the Millian-Marshallian school held, still it deals with agents who do make and act on value-judgements and who frequently fail in practice to stick to them, carried away by habit and other psychological factors. Furthermore, it deals with a set of problems like poverty, unemployment and inflation whose solution is contingent on the solution of the intellectual problems they pose for economic theorists.[4]

(2) At the same time, Keynes did not venture to go as far as to suggest that, as it has been argued, even 'common sense and the ordinary English in which it is expressed are a repository of former philosophies'. Although stressing the impact of abstract thought on human

affairs, Keynes does not appear to have held the view that this could be achieved through the conversion of large numbers of agents – 'common sense' or 'the man in the street'.

His cautiously chosen cast of actors – civil servants, politicians, journalists, business and trade union leaders, agitators and cranks (the last two replacing the 'ministers of religion' and 'heads of public or private charity' in Marshall's cast of potential customers for the 'new science of economics') – did not include the ordinary citizen, that is, the anonymous and (presumably) commonsensical 'man in the street'. Rather, he refers to the would-be leaders of opinion, those in the business of securing authority over the beliefs and opinions of their fellow-citizens and competing for power over the 'unthinking many'. The relevant contrast here, it should be noted, is with the notion voiced by socialists of various denominations before and since Marx (*pace* Lenin), and according to which social theories can and indeed ought to become 'material forces' through the *praxis* of the *masses*.

A remarkably clear and frank statement of this view can be found in the preface to the first English translation of Marx's *Capital* written by Engels in 1886. As already noticed (chapter 1), in a motion approved by the First International Marx's newly published book had been depicted as the 'Bible of the working class'. Engels, elaborating further on the analogy, wrote:

Capital is often called, on the continent, 'the Bible of the working class'. That the conclusions arrived at in this work are daily more and more becoming the fundamental principles of the great working-class movement, not only in Germany and Switzerland, but in France, in Holland and Belgium, in America, and even in Italy and Spain, that everywhere the working class more and more recognizes, in these conclusions, the most adequate expression of its condition and of its aspirations, nobody acquainted with that movement will deny. And in England, too, the theories of Marx, even at this moment, exercise a powerful influence upon the social movement which is spreading in the ranks of 'cultured' people no less than in those of the working class.

And drawing attention, later in the same preface, to the (ever) approaching crisis and the relative decline of the British industry, Engels stated:

Meanwhile, each succeeding winter brings up afresh the great question, 'what to do with the unemployed': but while the number of the unemployed keeps swelling from year to year there is nobody to answer that question; and we can almost calculate the moment when the unemployed, losing patience, will take their own fate into their own hands. Surely, at such a moment, the voice ought to be heard of a man whose whole theory is the result of a life-long study of the economic history and condition of England.[5]

As these passages clearly bring out, Marx and those who fought under his banner were attempting to articulate and give expression to what they believed were 'the dumb deep wants of the toiling class which cannot speak' (Carlyle). And although there is some evidence to show that, as it has been said, 'in his later years Marx was infuriated with supposed followers who misunderstood his intentions, or who mixed up their Marxian ideas with borrowings from Lassalle, Duhring, and others',[6] there is no evidence that he or Engels ever seriously doubted that 'the unemployed' would one day lose their patience and not only hear the voice, but understand the ideas of the Prussian exiled philosopher who felt sure he knew where their true interests really lay.

Keynes, however, did not pin his hopes on 'the toiling class which cannot speak'. His work is addressed primarily to his 'fellow economists', though he also expressed the hope that 'it will be intelligible to others'. But the real target of his message, as seen above, were the leaders of opinion in the various institutions of practical life. It is through the agency of this opinion-elite, the argument ran, that the wisdom of the few, that is the ideas of political and economic philosophers, have been (and would become) effective as catalysts and dynamos in human affairs. Thus, in his picture, the 'flock-masters', as distinct from the 'unthinking sheep', are the ones who have been (and who are) called upon to fulfil that ancient desire, viz. 'to call philosophy down from the heavens and set her in the cities of men'.[7]

(3) It should also be noted that Keynes' emphasis, in the *General Theory*, is far from being wholly negative. True, Marshall's firmly rooted belief in human perfectibility seen as a slow, yet steady and cumulative, evolution of man himself as a moral being, is gone. If it had been still possible for Marshall to look up to Germany as 'an empire in the air, that is, an empire in philosophy, literature, and music', Keynes' picture alludes already to the only too real threat posed by 'madmen in authority' and an empire in the making which had nothing airy about it.

This much darker context is well captured by the remarks made by an Oxford Greek scholar, R.W. Livingstone, in a book comparing the systems of secondary education in Britain and Germany and which had appeared when the Great War was well under way. Writing on the subject of a 'great nation on the continent besotted and maddened by false ideas', Livingstone depicted the predicament of our age as follows: 'One great danger of the modern world is our susceptibility to the general ideas that float around us, thick as bacilli, in the air, that pass our lips so often, and are so influential in our lives, that we use so readily without having analysed what we really mean by them'.[8] (As G. Ryle was to put it nearly three decades later, in the course of an extremely favourable and sympathetic review of Popper's 'powerful and important' *Open Society and Its Enemies*: 'Nazi, Fascist and Communist doctrines are descendants of the Hegelian gospel . . . [but] if philosophers are at long last immunised, historians, sociologists, political propagandists and voters are still unconscious victims of the virus'.)

Yet, in the picture put forward by Keynes in the *General Theory*, the stress is clearly laid on the potential for practical *good* stored up in the seemingly abstract and aloof ideas of economists and political philosophers. Like Malthus, Mill and Marshall before him, Keynes struggled to live up, as an economist, to the Baconian principle according to which learning should be referred to use and action, seeing that 'good thoughts, though God accept them, yet towards men are little better than good dreams, except they be put in act'. False or true, it is ideas that are 'dangerous for good and evil'. And as Whitehead had put it in *Adventures of Ideas* (published just three years before the appearance of Keynes' work), 'a general idea is always a danger to the existing order', for it issues forth and finds embodiment in a programme of reform, and from then on, as he put it, 'at any moment the smouldering unhappiness of mankind may size on some such programme and initiate a period of rapid change guided by the light of its doctrines'.[9]

This thesis, we may note, played a major role in Whitehead's philosophy. In *Science and the Modern World* he argued that in the task of critically revising the 'modes of abstraction' regulating our thinking, 'philosophy finds its niche as essential to the healthy progress of society'. Philosophy, he argued, 'is the critic of abstractions . . . a civilization which cannot burst through its current abstractions is doomed to sterility after a very limited period of progress'. Further – and like so many other critics of modern society before and after him – Whitehead singled out 'the abstractions political economy' as a chief cause of modern evils and discontent: 'It is very arguable that the science of political economy, as studied in its first period after the death of Adam Smith, did more harm than good . . . it riveted on men a certain set of abstractions which were disastrous in their influence on modern mentality. It dehumanised industry. This is only one example of a general danger inherent in modern science'.[10] Thus, Smithian economics (via its supposed 'economic man' abstraction) would have been a major determinant of the 'creed of competitive business morality' of modern society. It would have 'riveted on men' that 'practical ethics' which, by making victory in the 'undiluted fight for financial success' the accepted 'measure of brains', would have 'poisoned' not only work but leisure too.

Keynes, of course, did not share this particular diagnosis. For he surely would not blame modern economics – as the romantics before Whitehead had already done – for bringing about what it had set out to explain. Moreover, Keynes held the view that the life of money-making, though morally contemptible, was still a relatively harmless outlet for man's aggressive proclivities.[11] Rather, the important underlying agreement between Keynes and Whitehead is their firm conviction that, to quote from the latter, 'some general idea . . . inconceivable to people now living, might change our manner of life on this planet even more than the wireless has affected intercommunication'. As Keynes had already clearly stated in an 1934 article ('Poverty in plenty'), this was his own 'very confident belief'. 'We are', he wrote, 'at one of those uncommon junctures of human affairs where we can be saved by the solution of an intellectual problem, and in no other way'. In a letter of the following year to Bernard Shaw, Keynes spoke his mind and spelt out his wish:

To understand my state of mind, however, you have to know that I believe myself to be writing a book on economic theory which will largely revolutionise – not, I suppose, at once but in the course of the next ten years – the way the world thinks about economic problems. When my new theory has been duly assimilated and mixed with politics and feelings and passions, I can't predict what the final upshot will be in its effect on action and affairs.[12]

So the formula is clear. Political and economic philosophy affect the way decision-makers think about the problems of the age, and through this channel they powerfully influence the actual conduct of human affairs. There is one doctrine that may change the world. But in order to achieve this it must, first, persuade and be 'duly assimilated' by those who act and bid for power in public life.

But is this, we may ask, a tenable account of events? Is it reasonable or realistic to expect, in the light of the evidence provided by the history of ideas, that such theories and doctrines will in effect be 'duly assimilated' when they mix with 'politics and feelings and passions'? It is my contention here that this notion that 'ideas fashion the course of the world ever more and more' fails to give due weight to the problem of misunderstanding in human communication and must therefore be heavily qualified. This familiar claim, it will be argued, makes exaggerated and unwarrantable demands as regards both the transparency and the transmissibility of complex and highly abstract systems of political and economic thought.

This modern thesis that the ideas of economists and political philosophers are more powerful than we might be aware of, and that 'the world is ruled by little else', has a close kinship with a central tenet of Plato's political philosophy. In fact, it goes even further than the doctrine of the Greek Academy.

Plato, through Socrates' mouth in Books V and VI of the *Republic*, and through his own pen in the still not conclusively authenticated 'Seventh letter', set forth the famous doctrine that philosophers could and should be responsible for the government of the city-state. Using his former master as his living mouthpiece, he argued:

Unless philosophers bear kingly rule in cities, or those who are now called kings and princes become genuine and adequate philosophers, and political power and philosophy are brought together, and unless the numerous natures who at present pursue either politics or philosophy, the one to the exclusion of the other, are forcibly debarred from this behaviour, there will be no respite from evil for cities, nor, I fancy, for humanity. (*Republic*, 473)

The mission of the philosopher-king, according to this view, would be to bring together and harmonize political power and a sound knowledge of the good life, i.e. of the value of competing human goals in public and private affairs.

In order to achieve such knowledge – and before being enthroned in the seats of power – the future rulers would have to undergo a most severe elementary education, followed by two or three years of physical training; finally, from the age of twenty to thirty-five, they would be subjected to an intensive process of higher education centred on the study of pure mathematics and moral philosophy.

Moreover, the proposal was not entirely devoid of immediate implications. Plato's Academy itself, as it has been pointed out, may be seen as the philosopher's further attempt (after his failed Sicilian enterprise) to exert some influence on Greek political life, by attracting 'young men whose position and prospects were more fortunate than those of Plato's own youth', and giving them 'such training as would fit them for the art of statesmanship, as Plato conceived it'. In Plato's eyes, 'this drifting apart of the men of thought and the men of action was a disastrous calamity . . . the root of the social evils of his time'.[13]

So, like many of his modern counterparts, Plato claimed to possess knowledge that would save mankind, even if only by putting an end to major man-made disasters and catastrophic conflagrations. His argument puts forward the case for bringing power and wisdom together; the union of the two is embodied in the figure of a philosopher-king who is able and willing 'to shape the pattern of public and private life into conformity with his vision of the ideal' (*Republic*, 500). But there is, however, an important distinction to be made. For, although it is true that the Platonic argument is broadly in line with its modern counterparts, it also differs from them in one crucial respect.

Plato's political philosophy, as the passages quoted indicate, is essentially in the form of a physician's prescription or a sermon or a proposal of marriage. It is an opinion about the world as it *ought* to be if we desire to make it a good, better or less dangerous place. There is very little in it by way of positive enquiry and empirical statements about the given, i.e. the world as it already *is*.

But in the modern picture, in contrast, the marriage between philosophy and power has been persistently seen not so much as an ideal or a recipe for salvation – it has been depicted as a *fait accompli*. The medicine has been duly swallowed and the sermon has been not only listened to and taken in but even acted upon. Although philosophers obviously did not become kings themselves, yet their ideas have contaminated (or inoculated) the 'spirit of the age', captured the minds of rulers, ministers and voters and brought about momentous results. Whereas Plato had argued that philosophers ought to become rulers, others have come to argue that they (including Plato himself) are already ruling. It is this conviction that has led even an otherwise more cautious philosopher like Ryle to assert (following here Popper and the Austrian neo-liberal school), that 'The apriorist dream of a method which shall be proof against mistakes is a delusion from the start. It is also a nightmare in the result. Berchtesgaden and the Kremlin fulfil the promise of the *Republic* and the *Laws*'.[14]

Thus, the modern claim turns out to be even bolder than the Platonic one. Plato offers the philosopher-king as a remedy for the man-made ills of this world. He did not make philosophy the cause of our troubles, nor did he blame his rivals (e.g. Isocrates or the sophists) for what went wrong. As W. Guthrie observed: 'In Plato's opinion it was not they [the sophists] who should be blamed for infecting the young with pernicious thoughts, for they were doing no more than mirror the lusts and passions of the existing democracy'.[15] In the *Phaedrus*, it is true, he speaks of Pericles' debt to Anaxagoras for his excellence in speech (270a), and it may even be true, though the evidence for this is extremely frail, that Plato, out of envy, would have 'wished to burn all the writings of Democritus that he could collect'. But what he never did was to explain existing evils as the result of 'philosophical errors' or indoctrination.

In the 'Seventh letter', for example, he relates how he had found it difficult, in his youth, to take active part in public life and still retain his sense of integrity: 'The corruption of written law and established custom was proceeding at an astonishing rate, so that I, who began by being full of enthusiasm for a political career, ended by growing dizzy at the spectacle of universal confusion'.[16] The diagnosis here is clearly one of anomy and apostasy. He speaks of confusion and a severe lack of concern with principles, but not of a bad philosophical regimen or the adoption of wrong-headed dogmas and tenets. This view seems to be consistent with the one vented in the *Republic*. Life in the cave-world, as Plato saw it, was no grand clash of philosophical theories. The returning philosopher finds life in the cave, 'as it is in most existing states', a bizarre chase of shadows hunting shades – a dream, as he finely put it, 'where men live fighting one another about shadows and quarreling for power, as if that were a great prize' (*Republic*, 520).

But in the modern picture, on the contrary, philosophy has been persistently represented, first of all, as the cause of our troubles. And of course each such diagnosis is accompanied by its own – and equally philosophical – corrective therapy. Thus Popper's historicist philosophers have promulgated a set of beliefs in the 'Inexorable Laws of Historical Destiny', which have claimed 'countless victims' in the recent past, while Lukács, in his turn, accuses the 'destroyers of Reason' and makes them largely responsible and to blame for the tragic lapse of Germany into 'irrationalism' in the inter-war period – 'a philosophical stance', he asserts, 'cannot be innocent'.[17]

Similarly, Hayek's Cartesian constructivists are found at work, insidiously sapping the very foundations of a 'free and open society', while Whitehead and many others have not hesitated to make 'our old friend Adam Smith' and his followers ultimately responsible for the 'rat race' presiding over modern commercial society and even for the environmental decay that it has brought in its trail. The common denominator in all these pictures (and many others have been cited) is the assumption that philosophy has married power, even if so far the union has proved, for the most part, an unhappy one. The ideas of political and economic philosophers, it is claimed, have 'dominated the world', that is, 'the world outside, not perhaps of the street, but of history – a world in which simple unifying ideas and ideals in religion, politics and science have wrought tremendous, profound social transformations'.[18]

In the remainder of this chapter and in the conclusion to part II the chief aim will be the attempt to clarify and drastically qualify claims of this nature by drawing attention to the communication demands underlying them – the problem of pure misunderstanding.

It may be well to begin by recalling the Lockean principle cited in the introduction to part II: 'Though every thing said in the Text be infallibly true, yet the Reader may be, nay cannot chuse but be very fallible in the understanding of it.'[19] Locke's reference to the problem of human fallibility in the act of decoding and understanding thoughts and conclusions reached by other minds brings us to an ancient problem in the history of philosophy.

Socrates (see the epigraph to part II) would never commit to writing the living search-procedure of a dialogue. To do so, he appears to have held, would imply (at best) giving hostages to fortune and (at worst) courting misunderstandings. Plato, his most famous disciple, abandoned this 'hands off' approach to communication and made full use of his literary gifts and skills to convey his doctrines. But he would still refrain from openly introducing himself or his views into his dialogues, many of which are, in any case, in the form of reported conversations (X telling Y that W and Z said so and so).

Yet, as Popper, Ryle and other philosophical opponents of Plato and Platonism have not hesitated to claim in their attempts to explain the rise of totalitarianism (and 'to make sense of it'): 'The very things for which Socrates lived and died are the things which Plato tries to demolish with words put into Socrates' mouth.'

Although arguing against justice he [Plato] convinced all righteous men that he was its advocate. Not even to himself did he fully admit that he was combating the freedom of thought for which Socrates had died; and by making Socrates his champion he persuaded all others that he was fighting for it . . . And he achieved the somewhat surprising effect of convincing even great humanitarians of the immorality and selfishness of their creed.[20]

These are, obviously, wild guesses. It is hard to conceive what could be the basis for making them. For, to begin with, nearly all that we can know about Socrates' political philosophy is what Plato himself chose to write down in his dialogues. Moreover, how can one possibly know that 'not even to himself' did Plato 'fully admit' what he was doing? There simply is no evidence – or 'hot line' to Plato's and Socrates' minds – to support these claims; indeed, the very cocksure certainty with which they are made betrays their fundamental unreliability.

But even if the statements by Popper and Ryle were true, and Plato did really misapprehend or cynically misrepresent, in his last writings, the teachings of his master, how can one be so sure as to accuse Plato's doctrines of far-off political mischiefs, without even pausing to consider whether what Plato did to Socrates was not also done to him, in turn, by his readers? Should not then Socrates himself be summoned back to the accused's dock and charged with the consequences of the misuse of his teachings, this time by Plato and the Academy? The logic of the argument that turns 'the spell of Plato' (via Hegel!) into 'the fountain head of most modern irrationalism and totalitarianism', is essentially the same as would lead us to the conclusion that, to give even more extreme examples, the Spanish Inquisition 'fulfils the promise' (Ryle's expression) of Jesus Christ, and cruelty to animals is the 'crowning' (Lukács) of the Augustinian doctrine according to which 'Christ himself shows that to refrain from the killing of animals is the height of superstition'.

It is interesting to note that in their last meeting, in 1946, Hayek and Keynes exchanged views on the question of the possible misuse of ideas even by one's own alleged followers. 'I asked him', reported Hayek about the conversation, 'whether he was not alarmed about the use to which some of his disciples were putting his theories. His reply was that these theories had been greatly needed in the 1930s, but if these theories should ever become harmful, I could be assured that he would quickly bring about a change in public opinion'.[21] Obviously, the problem with Keynes' jocular and dismissive reply is that soon after that he was dead, and hence absolutely unable to exert any control on the uses, misuses and interpretations of his legacy. What is missing from Hayek's report, however, is how *he* would respond if a similar question were put to him. Considering that it is the destiny – or doom – of all great economic philosophers to be endlessly reinterpreted, no matter how seemingly simple their doctrines, would it be reasonable to make them in any meaningful sense responsible for the uses to which their followers may come to put their theories?

The history of ideas, as I have tried to argue in part II, teaches one sure and important lesson, viz. there is no such a thing as the one and only true interpretation of a philosophical or economic work. The reasons for this may be seen as threefold:

1 The time-factor affecting the intergenerational transmission of abstract thought. As suggested in chapter 8, the readings and interpretation of philosophical and economic works are bound to vary through time, as the linguistic, intellectual and practical contexts change and thus induce readers to assign new – and often unexpected – meanings to a given message. Plato, again, is a case in point:

Arm yourself with a stout pair of blinkers and a sufficient but not excessive amount of scholarship, and by making a suitable selection of texts you can prove Plato to be almost anything that you want him to be. By the skillful use of this method Plato has been revealed at various times as a complete sceptic and as a complete mystic, as a pupil of Hegel and as a pupil of Aquinas, as a Cambridge Platonist and as one of Nature's Balliol men, as an early Christian and as a very early Nazi. Each of these partisan Platos has his title-deeds, he can produce for you a nice little anthology of texts to prove his claim: for all these artificial *homunculi* have been constructed out of fragments of Plato himself.[22]

Of course, the story could have been told with a different cast of characters and the nominal values in the formula filled in with a distinct batch of protagonists and schools. The relevant point to stress is that there is no shortage of qualified names and labels in the history of ideas to construct essentially analogous plots. This is the reason why the art of preserving some knowledge of what past texts and masters might have meant, not of course for us, but in their own age, has become a specialist's job.

2 The fact that authors can only be partially aware of what they are doing. As discussed in chapter 10, it is impossible to say one thing only. In a few cases, authors have come to agree that they had said things they did not mean or even think of. On the other hand, attempts to evade this problem by setting up highly formalized and unambiguous communication techniques have often run into fresh and unforeseen problems like for instance self-complacent irrelevancy and the false-security type of misunderstanding.

The exact sciences, it is true, are able to circumvent most potential trouble-spots in the transmission of ideas by establishing a set of rules to prevent misunderstandings and to check the multiplication of interpretation-claims in the exchanges taking place within the specific community. However, as suggested in chapter 14, there are no paradigms smoothing over the transmission of ideas between academic communities; further, the problem of communication can only grow as the *salto mortale* takes place and the attempt is made to transform social behaviour or persuade decision-makers to reform the institutions of practical life.

3 As seen in chapters 11 and 12 and illustrated in chapter 13, the fixation of belief in ordinary life is powerfully affected by sub-rational dispositions and motivations. As Bacon observed, the human understanding is no 'dry light': our feelings, wishes and desires 'imbue and corrupt our understanding in innumerable and sometimes imperceptible ways'. This is the reason why, as Hume and Adam Smith pointed out, our beliefs and opinions 'are apt to be most partial when it is of most importance that they should be otherwise' (TMS,157), and particularly when some form of self-appreciation is involved.

Hence, ambitious 'young men in a hurry', who are eager and about to launch their careers as civil servants, politicians, journalists, agitators, business and trade union leaders, are not at all likely to approach (or even strive to approach) the writings of political and economic philosophers as Platonic readers, that is, capable of detaching themselves from all other desires and emotions and animated solely by the desire for truth. The very capacity for self-assertion which is required to rise in the competitive arena of politics and the market-place is bound to interfere in the process of belief-formation, by checking the ability to lose or transcend oneself in order to learn something from minds different from one's own. The political process itself works as a powerful filter of economic ideas. As Marshall perceptively pointed out about the way governments traditionally tended to use and misapply economic theories: 'Political bias then, as always, had a great power of enabling people to see just those parts of economic truth which fitted in with their policy, and to remain honestly blind to those which did not'.[23] Bacon's Idols of Tribe beset the human understanding at all ages; they affect not only, as he emphasised, 'the commerce of the mind with things', but also (as I have tried to show) the commerce between minds.

The scope for serious misapprehensions and misconceptions, it is also argued, tends to increase when what is being conveyed is not a piece of factual information, nor a technical contribution within a shared and specialized research programme, but a line of thought or conjecture bordering on one's 'fortress of certainties' or illusions, i.e. those beliefs which have some command upon our emotions and overlap with our sense of identity. 'It is sweet to keep our thoughts out of the range of hurt', it has been said. Pure misunderstanding, I have tried to suggest, is one of the mechanisms through which we achieve the protection of our relevant thoughts.

Obviously, the discussion in part II is by no means meant to deny the fact that the quality of transmission and reception can improve, or that some readings are more careful, closer and truer to the original message than others. Indeed, the very notion of misunderstanding would be deprived of its meaning were it not for the assumption of a common background of understanding against which it stands.

The contention here is rather that the intellectualist bias of the argument which represents philosophy as 'the most powerful material force, although it works very slowly' stands out clearly once the formidable problems bearing on the transmission of abstract thought and their proper use and understanding by users are brought to the fore. For the specific interpretation a given text receives will depend, as a rule, not only on the author's intentions and clarity but also, and to a large degree, on (i) the exigencies of practical life ('problems of the age') and (ii) the peculiar interests, goals and concerns of its individual users. Receivers, not authors, set and vary the meaning of what is being said.

Conclusion to part II

Urged in 1934 by Bernard Shaw to re-read Marx's *Capital* and unearth for himself its scientific treasures, Keynes responded as follows:

My feelings about *Das Kapital* are the same as my feelings about the *Koran*. I know that it is historically important and I know that many people, not all of whom are idiots, find it a sort of Rock of Ages and containing inspiration. Yet when I look into it, it is to me inexplicable that it can have this effect. Its dreary, out-of-date, academic controversialising seems so extraordinarily unsuitable as material for the purpose. But then, as I have said, I feel just the same about the *Koran*. How could either of these books carry fire and sword round half the world? It beats me. Clearly there is some defect in my understanding.[1]

Indeed, according to Keynes' own observation, in the fields of political and economic philosophy there are not many who are still open to genuine dialogue and persuasion 'after they are twenty-five or thirty years of age'. That, we may note, was the age at which Plato's philosopher-kings would undergo the last stage of their strenuous training for power. But the comparison between religious and economic texts which 'carry fire and sword round half the world' merits further examination.

Hegel, in his lectures on the philosophy of history, gives part of the answer to Keynes' question. Referring to the use of abstract principles like 'Reason', 'Justice' and 'Liberty' in early nineteenth-century political and public debate, he held:

At no time so much as in our own, have such general principles and notions been advanced, or with greater assurance. If in days gone by, history seems to present itself as a struggle of passions; in our time – though displays of passion are not wanting – it exhibits partly a predominance of the struggle of notions assuming the authority of principles; partly that of passions and interests essentially subjective, but under the mask of such higher sanctions.[2]

Similarly Pareto, writing almost a century later, would attempt to draw attention to the role of rationalization in belief-formation and social action. His position, it appears, was even more radical than the one adopted by Hegel in the passage just quoted:

Men follow their sentiment and their self-interest, but it pleases them to imagine that they follow reason. And so they look for, and always find, some theory which, *a posteriori*, makes their actions appear to be logical. If that theory could be demolished scientifically, the only result would be that another theory would be substituted for the first one, and for the same purpose; a new form would be used, but the actions would remain the same . . . Theories have only a limited effect in the determination of man's actions; self-interest and passions play a much greater role, and some obliging theory is always found in the nick of time to justify them.[3]

But rationalizing – i.e. the use of philosophical and economic doctrines to support and justify beliefs and opinions which are emotionally welcome to oneself – is not all. Pure misunderstanding, as I have tried to show, must also be taken into account: (a) one manages somehow to 'defuse' all adverse-looking facts and thoughts, in particular those which for some reason feel like shaking the very soil of one's convictions, and (b), one is able to 'enlist' to one's cause, as 'higher sanctions', authorities and ideas which can only fit in by being severely misinterpreted.

The belief that the truth has been found is a matchless powerhouse of self-confidence and motivation. Thus, much like the 'sacred books' of old, economic and philosophical texts find themselves handled as if they were pieces of wax in men's hands. Defunct economists are raised from the dead, and the visions of idiosyncratic academics find their way to most improbable banners, manifestos and platforms. It takes several phases of filtering, reinterpreting and misunderstanding for their abstract ideas to gather practical force.

More than any other class of authors, poets are familiar with the phenomenon of misunderstanding. For if it is true, as the young Hume had it, that poets are 'liars by profession' who 'always endeavour to give an air of truth to their fictions' (THN,121), and that 'all poetry is misrepresentation' (Bentham), it may still be the case that readers – and not only of poetry – are a suitable match. Baudelaire, in his journals, observed: 'The world only goes round by misunderstanding. It is by universal misunderstanding that all agree. For if, by ill luck, people understood each other, they would never agree'.[4]

Like Pareto's point about the role of rationalization in the process of belief-formation, this is an extreme view and it would certainly be wrong to construe it as the final word on the matter. But it offers, I think, an important corrective to the (understandable) tendency of economic philosophers of left and right to overestimate the role of political and economic ideas in social change. In this discussion about the scope for misunderstandings in the transmission of abstract thought, I have tried to suggest that the poet's remark may contain an important lesson for those who sincerely believe in the power of economic philosophy to change the course of human affairs. Much has been said about the assault of thoughts upon the unthinking. But this must be qualified in the light of the problem of misunderstanding: the no less important, though much overlooked, assault upon thoughts by those who feel they must act.

Notes

1 FROM HUME TO HAYEK

1 See THN,487 and 2ndE,300. On the family and the notion of self-interest see also Marshall's discussion in PEc,5: 'In a modern society the obligations of family kindness become more intense, though they are concentrated on a narrower area'; A.K. Sen, 'Economics and the family'; B. Williams, *Ethics and the Limits of Philosophy*: '*we* can represent a self-interest as much as *I*; and who *we* are depends on the extent of identification in a particular case, and on the boundaries of contrast' (p.15).

2 See *The Letters of David Hume*, vol. 1, p. 32; J.H. Burton, *Life and Correspondence of David Hume*, vol. 1, pp. 112–15. On the orthodox Christian (esp. Wishart's) criticism of Hume's philosophy see P. Russell, 'Skepticism and natural religion in Hume's *Treatise*'. On the relations between Hutcheson, Hume and Adam Smith see R.F. Teichgraeber III's detailed and careful discussion in *'Free Trade' and Moral Philosophy*. See also J. Bonar, *Philosophy and Political Economy*, Bk II, chs. 6 and 8; W.L. Taylor, *Francis Hutcheson and David Hume as Predecessors of Adam Smith*; A.S. Skinner, *A System of Social Science*, esp. pp. 14–15 and pp. 46–8; D. Forbes, 'Hume and the Scottish Enlightenment'; E Rotwein's introduction to *Hume's Writings on Economics*, pp. xcix-ciii.

3 Keynes, 'Malthus' in *Collected Writings*, vol. 10, p. 79n: 'If anyone will take up again Paley's *Principles* he will find, contrary perhaps to his expectations, an immortal book'. There is evidence that Paley's *Principles* and *Wealth of Nations* were the two main works discussed by G. Pryme in his course in Cambridge from 1828 (see J.P. Henderson, 'George Pryme, the first professor of political economy at Cambridge', esp. p. 13). On Paley's influence in the United States up to the mid-nineteenth century see J. Viner, *The Role of Providence in the Social Order*, p. 74.

4 Paley, *Principles* (20th ed., 1814), vol. 1, p. 1 and p. 66. In the appendix referred to by Paley, Hume expressed his doubts 'whether virtue could be taught or not'. On the sophist and the Socratic approach to this issue see W.K. Guthrie, *Sophists*, ch. 10. D. LeMahieu's *The Mind of William Paley* gives a commentary on his thought as a whole; for a brief account of

Paley's ethics and its place in English utilitarianism see H. Sidgwick, *History of Ethics*, pp. 236f. On the relations Paley-Malthus-Darwin-Marshall see B. Thomas, 'A plea for an ecological approach to economic growth', pp. 293–4. On Paley-Malthus-Darwin see R. Young, 'Malthus and the evolutionists', esp. pp. 114–18.

5 Paley, *Principles*, pp. xxiii-xxiv and p. xxiii.

6 L. Stephen, *English Utilitarians*, vol. 3, p. 31.

7 Bentham, *Chrestomathia* (1817), p. 230; 'Anarchical fallacies; being an examination of the declarations of rights issued during the French Revolution' in *Works*, vol. 2, p. 497. See also his *The Book of Fallacies* (edited by J.S. Mill and F. Place and first published in English in 1824): 'By a single word or two . . . what hostility has been produced! how intense the feeling of it! how full of mischief, in all imaginable shapes, the effects!' (in *Works*, vol. 2, p. 438). For a perceptive interpretation of Bentham's project of linguistic reform see J. Rée's *Philosophical Tales*, pp. 97–106.

8 Mill, 'Essay on liberty' (1859) in *Three Essays*, p. 86. A sympathetic discussion of this essay is I. Berlin's engaging 'Mill and the ends of life' in *Four Essays*. For a systematic commentary on Mill's contributions as a whole see A. Ryan, *John Stuart Mill*.

9 Mill, *Considerations on Representative Government*, quoted by S. Collini in 'The tendency of things: Mill and the philosophic method', p. 150; Collini's article gives a careful analysis of Mill's views on social change and on the relations between his theories in logic and economics. See also Mill's early essay (not included in the Toronto edition) *The Spirit of the Age* (1831): 'All persons, from the most ignorant to the most instructed . . . have their minds more or less under the dominion of one or other, or all, of the influences which have just been mentioned. All bow down . . . to the authority of superior minds, or the interpreters of the divine will, or of their superiors in rank and station'. (pp. 61–2) On Mill's debt to and criticism of Bentham see also, besides his two essays on Bentham and the *Autobiography*: E. Neff, *Carlyle and Mill*, ch. 9; Viner, 'Bentham and Mill: the utilitarian background'; J. Riley, *Liberal Utilitarianism*, Part II.

10 Marx, 'Theses on Feuerbach' (1845) in *Early Writings*, p. 423 and *Writings of the Young Marx*, p. 257. On the relations between Marx and the 'left Hegelians' see D. McLellan, *The Young Hegelians and Marx*. On Marx's way to the 'critique of earth' via the 'critique of heaven' see A.Th. Van Leeuwen, *Critique of Heaven*.

11 See *Karl Marx: Interviews and Recollections*, ed. McLellan, p. 13. The discussion took place in a meeting of the Communist League held in Brussels on the evening of 30 March 1846; the report is given by P. Annenkov, a Russian militant who attended the meeting. For the background of this event see R. Payne, *Marx*, esp. pp. 133f. See also M. Bakunin's account of Marx's political activities and of their competition for the leadership in the meetings of the First International: '[Marx] has

the fault of all professional scholars: he is *doctrinaire*. He has an absolute faith in his theories . . . This self-adoration in his absolute and absolutist theories has a natural corollary in the hate that Marx nurtures not only against the bourgeoisie but against all – even revolutionary socialists – who contradict him and dare to follow a line of ideas different from his theories' (*Interviews and Recollections*, p. 116–17).

12 Marx, *Grundrisse*, p. 463. Cf. J. Elster's comment on this passage in *Making Sense of Marx*, p. 106. The Hegelian content of this work is discussed by McLellan in the introduction to his abridged edition of the notebooks (pp. 2–15). On Hegel's reading and knowledge of British political economy and on his conception of labour and freedom in general see G. Lukács, *The Young Hegel*, esp. Part II, ch. 5 and Part III, chs. 5 to 7 and J. Hyppolite, 'Alienation and objectification: commentary on Lukács's *The Young Hegel*' in *Studies on Marx and Hegel*, pp. 70–90.

13 Marx, *Capital*, vol. 1, pp. 167–8 and p. 280. On the composition of the *Grundrisse* (the 800-page notebooks which contain Marx's breakthrough in the study of capitalist economies) see his letter of 8 December 1857 to Engels (*Collected Works*, vol. 40, p. 217). There was a 'commercial crisis' in England and Marx made up his mind to believe that it might bring about a working-class insurgency and a revolutionary situation. In a further letter to Lassale (still then a friend) he wrote: 'The present commercial crisis has impelled me to set to work seriously on my outlines of political economy, and also to prepare something on the present crisis' (*Works*, vol. 40, p. 226).

14 The motion was raised by J.P. Becker, a Swiss delegate to the Brussels Congress of the First International. See P. Lafargue, 'Reminiscences of Marx' (1890), p. 85. See also G.M. Stekloff, *History of the First International*, ch. 9: 'At the Brussels Congress, the communists secured a notable victory [over Proudhon's followers] . . . The Brussels Congress passed a vote of thanks to Marx for his *Capital* and recommended the workers to master its teachings' (p. 130 and p. 400n).

15 The interview is reproduced *in toto* in McLellan, *Karl Marx: Interviews and Recollections*; the quotation is on p. 112.

16 It is interesting to compare Marx's reaction to D. Ricardo and J.S. Mill. In his *Principles* (1817), Ricardo had left a tight, anatomic body of economic theory which was remarkably unobtrusive in so far as social and economic philosophy was concerned: the ideal skeleton, so to speak, to be fleshed out and put to work by a radical philosopher willing to bring down the system. But Mill's *Principles*, on the contrary, could not have been more obtrusive precisely in the domain of social and economic philosophy where Marx wanted to have a free, active hand. A footnote in *Capital* barely disguises Marx's own ambition, and his jealousy of the impact of Mill's work: 'When we compare the text of [Mill's] *Principles* with the Preface to the first edition, where he announces himself as the Adam Smith of his day, we do not know what we should be most

astonished at, the naivety of the man or that of the public which accepted him in good faith as the new Adam Smith, for he bears about as much resemblance to Adam Smith as General Williams [a British commandant who had recently been humiliatingly defeated by the Russians in Turkey] does to the Duke of Wellington'. (p. 221n) In the light of this, it does not seem hard to see who else, besides Mill, was by then fancying himself as 'the Adam Smith of his day'.

17 Marx, *Early Writings*, p. 257. Commenting on this passage in his *Philosophy and Myth in Karl Marx* R.C. Tucker remarks: 'For him [Marx] the proletariat remained always what he had once called it, the material weapon of philosophy or reality striving toward thought. But this was *his* thought' (p.231).

18 See his letter of 28 October 1808 to F.I. Niethammer (Hegel's close friend since the theology seminary at Tubingen University and who had an important role in the publication saga of the 1807 *Phenomenology*); the letter appears in W. Kaufmann's *Hegel*, p. 323. On the notion, alluded to by Marx in *Capital*, that 'reflection begins *post festum*' and that 'when philosophy paints grey in grey, a form of life has aged' see Hegel's preface to the *Philosophy of Right*.

19 Robinson, *Economic Philosophy*, p. 10. On the 'inefficiency of complete egoism' see R. Matthews, 'Morality, competition and efficiency' pp. 292f. D. Braybrooke, *Ethics in the World of Business*; Sen, 'The profit motive'; M. Morishima, *Why Has Japan 'Succeeded'?*

20 Robinson, *Freedom and Necessity*, p. 122.

21 Robinson, *Freedom and Necessity*, p. 122; *Economic Philosophy*, p. 25. On the distinction between genuine disagreement and being at cross-purposes see R. Bambrough, *Conflict and the Scope of Reason*, p. 6; G. Ryle, *Dilemmas*, p. 11.

22 Robbins, *The Great Depression*, pp. 199–200. (I would like to thank Richard Wright for drawing my attention to this passage.) For a detailed account and discussion of the public debate on economic policy in England in the 1920s and early 1930s, and in particular on the disagreements between Keynes and Robbins in this context see P.F. Clarke, *The Keynesian Revolution in the Making*. On Robbins' intellectual development and relations with the Austrian economists see D.P. O'Brien's *Lionel Robbins*.

23 Mises, *Liberalism*, p. 50. This work, it should perhaps be noted, contains some disturbing statements about what Mises perceived as the role of Fascism in barring the spread of communist regimes and thus 'saving European civilization': 'The merit that Fascism has thereby won for itself will live on eternally in history. But though its policy has brought salvation for the moment, it is not of the kind which could promise continued success. Fascism was an emergency makeshift. To view it as something more would be a fatal error'. (p. 51) It is even more surprising that this 'vindication' of the historical role of 'Fascism and similar

movements aiming at the establishment of dictatorships', though presumably written for the 1927 Austrian edition of the book, was not revised by the author for the many subsequent editions and translations.

24 Hayek, *Law, Legislation and Liberty*, vol. 3, p. 173. The remark on Hume is from his *Studies*, p. 264. Introducing his *magnum opus*, the three-volume *Law, Legislation and Liberty*, he wrote: 'On these issues which will be my main concern, thought seems to have made little advance since David Hume and Immanuel Kant' (vol. 1, p. 6).

25 Hayek, *Counter Revolution of Science*, p. 87. For a succinct account of Hayek's thought as a whole see N.P. Barry, 'Restating the liberal order: Hayek's philosophical economics'. The origins of his disillusionment with pure economic theory and interest in philosophical issues are discussed by B.J. Caldwell in 'Hayek's transformation'.

26 Hayek, *Law, Legislation and Liberty*, vol. 1, pp. 69–70. Cf. his remarks in *Counter Revolution of Science*: 'We are still, largely without knowing it, under the influence of ideas which have almost imperceptibly crept into modern thought because they were shared by the founders of what seemed to be radically opposed traditions... But while the ideas of Hume and Voltaire, of Adam Smith and Kant, produced the liberalism of the nineteenth century, those of Hegel and Comte, of Feuerbach and Marx, have produced the totalitarianism of the twentieth' (p. 206).

27 Hayek, *Counter Revolution of Science*, p. 206.

28 Popper, *Open Society and its Enemies*, vol. 2, Addendum (1961), p. 383; 'The history of our time: an optimist's view' in *Conjectures and Refutations*, p. 373. See also his remarks in an 1970 interview with B. Magee: 'Magee: So your thesis is this: we are all practising philosophers in the sense that we all hold philosophical theories and act on them. But usually we are not aware that what we are doing is uncritically accepting the truth of a theory./Popper: Yes./ M: And some of these theories are true, you say, while others are not only false but harmful. And you say the real task for philosophy is to examine critically our often unconscious philosophical prejudices and to correct them where correction is needed./ P: Exactly. Incidentally, I do not think that the need to correct what professional philosophers say would be a sufficient excuse for philosophy to exist' (*Modern British Philosophy*, p. 91).

2 THE SCIENTIFIC CHALLENGE: 'MAN-MACHINE'

1 Plato's *Phaedo*, 98e. This and the following point on Epicurus are made by J. Passmore in *Science and its Critics*, pp. 10–13. On Socrates and the birth of moral philosophy see Sidgwick, *History of Ethics*, p. xviii: 'It is in and through the teaching of Socrates that moral philosophy came to occupy in Greek thought the central position which it never afterwards lost: Socrates is the main starting-point from which all subsequent lines of Greek ethical thought diverge'; Hegel, *History of Philosophy*, vol. 1, p. 388:

'Reflective morality adds to natural morality the reflection that this is the good and not that . . . Socrates in this way gave rise to moral philosophy'. On the contrast between the Socratic and scientific perspectives see also F. Nietzsche's remark that 'Fundamentally, morality is hostile to science: Socrates was so already – and for this reason, that science takes things seriously that have nothing to do with "good" and "evil", consequently makes the feeling for "good" and "evil" seem less important' (*Will to Power*, § 443, p. 245).

2 *Epicurus*, ed. C. Bailey, p. 91. The passage quoted is from a letter to his disciple Menoeceus. On Epicurean ethical and political thought, and its relation to early Greek atomism see J. Nichols Jr, *Epicurean Political Philosophy*; F. Lange, *History of Materialism*.

3 Marx, *The Difference Between the Democritean and the Epicurean Philosophy of Nature* (1841) in *Works*, vol. 1, p. 30: 'The confession of Prometeus: "In simple words, I hate the pack of gods" is [philosophy's] own confession, its own aphorism against all heavenly and earthly gods who do not acknowledge human self-consciousness as the highest divinity. It will have none other beside'. On Marx's defence of the Epicurean 'swerving' of the atoms see Leeuwen's detailed study of Marx's doctoral thesis and related notebooks in *Critique of Heaven*, esp. ch. 5; B. Farrington, *The Faith of Epicurus*, ch. 7.

4 Descartes, *Philosophical Letters*, pp. 244–5. On the background of the correspondence between More and Descartes see E. Cassirer, *The Platonic Renaissance in England*, pp, 132–3 and pp. 142–8; A. Koyré, *From the Closed World to the Infinite Universe*, pp. 110–24. On Descartes' views on determinism see Lange's *History of Materialism*, pp. 215–49; E.A. Burtt, *Metaphysical Foundations of Modern Science*, pp. 105f.

5 Descartes' *Lettres*, p. 245. Cf. on this issue Paley's discussion of the 'right to the flesh of animals' (*Principles*, pp. 96–100). See also the section 'meat or mercy?' in K. Thomas, *Man and the Natural World*, pp. 287–300; S. Clark, *The Moral Status of Animals*, esp. pp. 37–51.

6 Bacon, *Advancement of Learning*, p. 55 and p. 114. On Bacon and the notion of technical progress as salvation see B. Farrington, *Bacon: Philosopher of Industrial Science*; R. Attfield, *Ethics of Environmental Concern*, ch. 5.

7 Boyle, quoted by Burtt in *Metaphysical Foundations*, p. 183 and p. 194. On the relations between Boyle and the Baconian movement see also G.N. Clark, *Science and Social Welfare in the Age of Newton*, esp. p. 13 and pp. 80–2.

8 On the relations between Hobbes and Descartes see Burtt, *Metaphysical Foundations*, pp. 126–30; Lange, *History of Materialism*, pp. 270–90.

9 La Mettrie, *L'Homme Machine*, p. 162 and p. 197. For an account and discussion of the evolution of La Mettrie's thought see A. Vartanian's excellent introductory essay to his critical edition of this work. See also Passmore, *Science and its Critics*, esp. pp. 13–14; K. Thomas, *Man and the Natural World*, p. 123 and p. 33 on his debt to Descartes.

10 D'Holbach, *The System of Nature*, p. 38 and p. 40. On the relation between La Mettrie and d'Holbach, their place in eighteenth-century thought and some of the responses provoked by their work see Cassirer, *Philosophy of the Enlightenment*, pp. 65–73; Lange, *History of Materialism*, Bk I, Part IV, chs. 1–4.

11 La Mettrie, 'Discourse sur le bonheur', quoted by Cassirer in *Philosophy of the Enlightenment*, pp. 69–70n. This essay, first published in 1748 as *Anti-Seneque*, is discussed at length in A. Thomson, *Materialism and Society in the Mid-Eighteenth Century*, pp. 45f. On *L'Homme Plante* and its place in the development of La Mettrie's thought see A. Vartanian's introductory essay, section 3. On the 'chain of being' construct from Plato to Leibniz and its use in eighteenth-century biology see A.O. Lovejoy, *The Great Chain of Being*, chs. 6–8. And on St Francis and the complex issue of Christian attitudes to the non-man in the world see C. Glacken, *Traces on the Rhodian Shore*, esp. pp. 214–16; R. Attfield, 'Christian attitudes to nature', pp. 369–86.

12 D'Holbach, *The System of Nature*, pp. 40–1.

13 Goethe, *Poetry and Truth*, pp. 363–4. It is interesting to compare the young Marx's reaction to La Mettrie: 'In La Mettrie's works we find a synthesis of Cartesian and English materialism. He makes use of Descartes's physics in detail. His *L'Homme Machine* is a treatise after the model of Descartes's animal-machine'. But then Marx goes on, not to argue, but simply to dismiss offhandedly La Mettrie's work as mere 'mechanical materialism', and to contend (referring now to Locke, Condillac and Helvetius) that 'If man is shaped by environment, his environment must be made human' (see *The Holy Family* (1845) in *Works*, vol. 4, pp. 130–1).

14 This and the following paragraphs ae based on information obtained from the following sources: Lange, *History of Materialism*; Vartanian's introduction to his edition of *L'Homme Machine*; Thomson, *Materialism and Society*. The account of La Mettrie's death in the next paragraph is from Vartanian's introduction, p. 12; cf. Thomson, *Materialism and Society*, p. 48.

15 Vartanian's introduction to *L'Homme Machine*, p. 97.

16 La Mettrie, 'Discours preliminaire' (reproduced in French in Thomson's *Materialism and Society*), p. 219 and 222. (I would like to thank Hugo Tucker for his help in translating these passages). Cf. Nietzsche's remark in *Human All Too Human*, §50: 'The strongest knowledge (that of the total unfreedom of the human will) is nonetheless the poorest in successes: for it always has the strongest opponent, human vanity' (p. 226).

17 Voltaire, 'On Mr Locke' in *Philosophical Letters*, p. 58. On the relations between La Mettrie and Voltaire (the epigraph of the first edition of *L'Homme Machine* is from Voltaire's 'Epitre a Monsieur de Genonville') see Thomson, *Materialism and Society*, pp. 161–5.

3 THE SCIENTIFIC CHALLENGE: 'ECONOMIC MAN'

1 Although it is highly probable (as the editors of Smith's EPS suggest) that in this passage he is referring to La Mettrie, there are other possibilities. Cf. e.g. Le Camus's *Médecine de L'Esprit* (1753), which proposes to cure, by physical means, 'les défauts des opérations de l'entendement et de la volonté qui dépendent des vices de l'organisation' (see Thomson, *Materialism and Society*, p. 29). The definition of morality in medical terms, and of virtue as 'the health of the soul', dates back to the Stoic philosopher Ariston of Chios in the third century BC. He held that 'it is idle to hand on moral precepts' (see J. Rist, *Stoic Philosophy*, pp. 31–2 and pp. 74–8).

2 Smith's intention, at one stage, to dedicate WN to Quesnay is reported by D. Stewart in his 'Account of the life and writings of Adam Smith' (in EPS): 'If he had not been prevented by Quesnay's death, Mr Smith had once an intention (as he told me himself) to have inscribed to him his *Wealth of Nations*' (EPS,304). Hume, however, did not share Smith's admiration. In a 1769 letter to the Abbé Morellet he depicted Quesnay and his school in harsh terms: 'They are the set of men the most chimerical and most arrogant that now exist, since the annihilation of the Sorbonne' (*Letters*, vol. 2, p. 205). On Hume–Smith and the physiocrats see also D. Deleule, *Hume et la Naissance du Liberalisme Economique*, pp. 287f.

3 Quesnay's 1765 essay 'Natural right' is reproduced and translated by R.L. Meek in *The Economics of Physiocracy*. The passages quoted on this and the preceding paragraph are from pp. 49–54.

4 Quesnay, 'Natural right', p. 54. On the philosophical foundations of physiocracy and its relations to the seventeenth-century 'natural law' tradition see Bonar, *Philosophy and Political Economy*, Bk II, chs. 7–9; M. Beer, *An Inquiry Into Physiocracy*; R. Kuntz, *Capitalismo e Natureza*.

5 In the 1790 edition of TMS, Smith dropped the references he had made to La Rochefoucauld's moral philosophy as a 'licentious system'. On Smith's views about the 'ideas of the profligate Mandeville' see also his letter to the short-lived *Edinburgh Review* (1755–6), where he compares the *Fable* with Rousseau's essay on inequality (EPS,250–1). In his discussion of those systems of moral philosophy which tended to equate virtue with benevolence (i.e. actions aimed at the good of all intelligent beings), Smith criticized Hutcheson, on similar grounds, for holding the view that 'Self-love was a principle which could never be virtuous in any degree or in any direction': 'Regard to our own private happiness and interest, too, appear upon many occasions very laudable principles of action . . . Carelessness and a want of oeconomy are universally disapproved of, not, however, as proceeding from a want of benevolence, but from a want of the proper attention to the objects of self-interest' (TMS,304). On this point see also Skinner, 'Moral philosophy and civil

society', pp. 42–7 and the introduction to TMS by D.D. Raphael and A.L. Macfie, esp. pp. 10–15.

6 Aristotle, *Nicomachean Ethics*, 1169a13–17 (p.237). My account of Aristotle's ethical thinking is largely based on J.L. Ackrill's lucid and useful introduction to *Aristotle's Ethics*. See note 16 of ch. 5 below.

7 Smith's quote, as the editors of WN point out, is from Cicero's *De Divinatione*, ii. 58. But there has been no lack of ancient and modern variations on this theme, beginning with Aristotle's *Metaphysics*, 1074b10: 'In all likelihood every skill and every philosophy has been discovered many times over and again perished' (quoted by E.R. Dodds in *The Ancient Concept of Progress*, p. 14). See also Descartes, *Discourse on Method* (1637): 'But I had been taught, even in my College days, that there is nothing imaginable so strange or so little credible that it has not been maintained by one philosopher or other' (*Works*, vol. 1, p. 90); B. de Fontenelle's remark in his *Digression sur les Anciens et let Modernes* (1688) to the effect that 'We are under obligation to the ancients for having exhausted almost all the false theories that could be formed' (quoted by C.L. Becker, *The Heavenly City*, p. 135); Goethe's lines in *Faust*, Part II: 'Depart, "original" enthusiast!/ How would this insight peeve you: whatsoever/ A human being thinks, if dumb or clever,/ Was thought before him in the past' (quoted by W. Kaufmann, *Hegel*, p. 191); F. Schelling's 'there is no absurdity which does not find some spokesmen' (quoted by Lovejoy, *The Great Chain of Being*, p. 319); E. Gellner's 'There is no rubbish great enough not to have been asserted by someone' (*Legitimation of Belief*, p. 15).

8 Malthus, *Principles*, p. 1. On the relations between Malthus' economics and his moral philosophy see Bonar, *Malthus and His Work*, Bks II and III. The differences between Malthus and Ricardo are best seen in their correspondence, esp. letters 199 and 200 of January 1817 in *Works of David Ricardo*, vol. 7, pp. 119–24. See also D. Winch, 'Higher maxims: happiness versus wealth in Malthus and Ricardo', pp. 63–89.

9 See Mill's 'On the definition of political economy; and on the method of investigation proper to it' in CW4,322–3. See also J.K. Whitaker, 'J.S. Mill's methodology', esp. p. 1044.

10 In later editions of the *Principles*, Mill would soften his views on the United States and drop this passage on 'dollar-hunting'. But he held up, however, his case against the 'struggle for riches' as an end – or the end – of life: 'the best state for human nature is that in which, while no one is poor, no one desires to be richer, nor has any reason to fear being thrust back, by the efforts of others to push themselves forward'. This point is taken up in chapter 4 below.

11 Tocqueville, *Democracy in America*, vol. 2, pp. 161–2. Reviewing Tocqueville's work in 1840, Mill described it as 'the beginning of a new era in the scientific study of politics' (CW18,156). For rather similar views on the American 'material restlessness' and 'strenuous indolence'

see F. Nietzsche, *The Gay Science* (1882), § 329, pp. 258–60; B. Russell, *The Conquest of Happiness*, esp. p. 51.

12 Schumpeter, *History of Economic Analysis*, p. 531. On the reception of Mill's work see N.B. de Marchi, 'The success of Mill's *Principles*', pp. 119–57. In a letter of 20 March 1852 to K.H. Rau, Mill declared: 'I confess that I regard the purely abstract speculations of political economy . . . as of very minor importance compared with the great practical questions which the progress of democracy and the spread of Socialist opinions are pressing on, and for which both the governing and the governed classes are very far from being in a fit state of mental preparation . . . There is therefore abundance of occupation for moral and political teachers such as we aspire to be' (CW14,87).

13 On the propensity to barter and exchange and its roots in human psychology see the important passages in his *Lectures on Jurisprudence*, p. 352 and TMS,336. The much-quoted expression 'result of human action, but not of human design' is from Adam Ferguson's *An Essay on the History of Civil Society* (1767): 'Every step and every movement of the multitude, even in what are termed enlightened ages, are made with equal blindness to the future; and nations stumble upon establishments, which are indeed the result of human action, but not the execution of any human design'. (p. 187) See, however, on Ferguson's *History*, Hume's unfavourable opinion in letters to his friend Hugh Blair (*Letters*, vol. 2, pp. 11–12 and p. 133).

14 Marshall, *Memorials*, pp. 154–5.

15 Jevons, 'Brief account of a general mathematical theory of political economy', p. 282. See also, on this early paper, Jevons' own remarks in the introduction to his *Theory of Political Economy* (1871), esp. p. 2. On Jevons' thought see: E.F. Paul, 'Jevons: economic revolutionary and political utilitarian'; R. Collison Black, 'Jevons and the foundation of modern economics' in *The Marginal Revolution in Economics*, pp. 98–113.

16 This concept of 'the economic type of action' is based on R.G. Collingwood's discussion in 'Economics as a philosophical science'.

17 Edgeworth, *Mathematical Psychics*, p. 16.

18 See the introductory discussion by F. Hahn and M. Hollis to *Philosophy and Economic Theory*, p. 4.

19 F. Bacon, *Cogitata et Vita* (c. 1607), a posthumously published Latin manuscript, translated and reproduced *in toto* by B. Farrington in *The Philosophy of Francis Bacon*; the quotation is on p. 93. On the Baconian philosophy of science see also T.S. Kuhn's illuminating discussion in 'Mathematical versus experimental traditions in the development of physical science', esp. pp. 48f.

20 Edgeworth, *Mathematical Psychics*, p. 104 and p. 15. See also his article 'Mathematical method in political economy': 'The idea of applying mathematics to human affairs may appear at first sight an absurdity worthy of Swift's Laputa' (p. 711).

21 Edgeworth, *Mathematical Psychics*, p. 12.
22 Cf. Keynes, 'Edgeworth' in *Collected Writings*, vol. 10, p. 256: 'Edgeworth wished to establish theorems of intellectual and aesthetic interest, Marshall to establish maxims of practical and moral importance'.
23 Schumpeter, 'Marshall' in *Ten Great Economists*, p. 97. Commenting on Schumpeter's assertion, N. Georgescu-Roegen remarked: 'No doubt it was a strange ambition after all for Marshall to insist upon respect for relevance instead of succumbing to the temper of his age' (*The Entropy Law*, p. 321).
24 The sources of these three statements are as follows: R. Matthews, 'Morality, competition and efficiency', p. 292; Robinson, *Economic Philosophy*, p. 53; Williams, *Ethics and the Limits of Philosophy*, p. 184. All three are of course critical of the claim according to which 'what ought to happen is that everyone pursue his or her own interest'.

4 ECONOMIC MAN AND MAN-MACHINE

1 On the origins and rise of neo-classical economics see *The Marginal Revolution in Economics*, eds. R.C. Black, A.W. Coats and C.D. Goodwin; P. Deane, 'The scope and method of economic science'; M. Dobb, 'The trend of modern economics'; S.G. Checkland, 'Economic opinion in England as Jevons found it'; G. Stigler, 'The development of utility theory'. See also on (iii) M. Milgate, 'On the notion of "intertemporal equilibrium"'; Hahn, 'Reflections on the invisible hand'.
2 See also *Memorials*, pp. 154–5; *Industry and Trade*, p. 658. For a succinct account of Marshall's economics see O'Brien, 'Marshall'. The most comprehensive reconstruction of and commentary on his economic and social thought is given by D. Reisman in *Economics of Alfred Marshall* and *Progress and Politics*. On Marshall's intellectual enterprise as a whole see also T. Parsons, 'Economics and sociology: Marshall in relation to the thought of his time'; Winch, 'A separate science: polity and society in Marshall's economics'.
3 On ethics as the 'mistress' of economics see Marshall's 'Speech at the meeting of the British Economic Association'; see also his 'Distribution and exchange' (the quote is on p. 54). On the relation between consumption and production see Parsons, 'Wants and activities in Marshall', and Marx's similar remark that 'It is not what is made but how and by what instruments of labour that distinguishes different economic epochs' (*Capital*, p. 286).
4 Marshall, *Industry and Trade*, pp. 664–5; cf. p. 704. See also T. Parsons, 'The motivation of economic activities', esp. pp. 50–68.
5 Jevons, 'The future of political economy' (1876) in *Principles*, pp. 196–9; *Theory of Political Economy* (1879), p. xvii and p. 21. For discussions of the Jevonian 'mechanics of utility and self-interest' see also Black, 'Jevons and the development of marginal utility analysis'; P. Mirowski, 'Physics and the marginalist revolution'.

6 Robbins, *Nature and Significance of Economic Science*, pp. 83–6. For a criticism of this position see K. Boulding's 'Economics as a moral science'. On the relation between ethics and neo-classical economics see also P. Wicksteed, 'The scope and method of political economy'.

7 Pareto, *Manual*, p. 113 and p. 120.

8 On Marshall's impact on British economics see N. Jha, *The Age of Marshall*. For studies on his thought see Keynes, 'Marshall' in *Collected Writings*, vol. 10, pp. 161–231; J. Whitaker, 'Some neglected aspects of Marshall's economic and social thought'; P. Dooley, 'Marshall: fitting the theory to the facts'; G. Harcourt, 'Marshall, Sraffa and Keynes: incompatible bedfellows?'; J. Hirshleifer, 'Economics from a biological viewpoint'.

9 Marshall, 'Distribution and exchange', p. 44; PEc, 622. On the place and significance of Bk V see his letter of April 1891 to the Dutch economist N. Pierson in *Early Writings*, ed. J. Whitaker, vol. 1, p. 98; 'Distribution and exchange', p. 52; the preface to the 1891 edition of PEc, where he stated that 'to myself personally the chief interest of the volume centres in Book V'.

10 R. Sperry, *Science and Moral Priority*, p. 100.

11 Robbins, 'Economics and political economy' (1981) reprinted in *Nature and Significance*, p. xvi.

12 Pareto, *Manual*, pp. 29–31 and p. 180. Pareto's full discussion of 'non-logical conduct' is in his *The Mind and Society*, vol. 1, chs. 2–3. Non-logical actions and the tendency to disguise them through some form of rationalization are also briefly discussed in his *Manual*, ch. 2. For interpretations of his thought see *The Other Pareto*, ed. P. Bucolo; W.J. Samuels, *Pareto on Policy*.

13 Huxley in *Method and Results*, p. 244; see also his essay 'On Descartes' in ibid., esp. pp. 192–3. For a survey of the mind-brain issue in nineteenth-century science see R. Young, *Mind, Brain and Adaptation*.

14 Locke, *Essay Concerning Human Understanding*, Bk II, ch. 21, p. 244 and p. 266. Cf. Hume's lstE,90. For a comment on ch. 21 of Locke's *Essay* see J. Colman, *Locke's Moral Philosophy*, ch. 8.

15 Sperry, *Science and Moral Priority*, p. 30–1 and p. 39. Cf. on this issue K. Boulding's comment: 'On the question of the relation between the physical and chemical structure of an organism and its knowledge structure, I am prepared to be agnostic. It is, of course, an article of faith among physical scientists that there must be somewhere a one-to-one correspondence between the structures of the physical body and the structures of knowledge. Up to now [1956], there is nothing like empirical proof or even very good evidence for this hypothesis'. (*The Image*, p. 17) See also P. Strawson's conclusion in *Skepticism and Naturalism*: 'We shall certainly learn more and more about the general causal dependence of the conscious enjoyment or exercise of our various experiential capacities (e.g. for vision, memory, recognition) on physical mechanisms, even though we are not likely to establish, and there would

be little interest in establishing, extended point-to-point correspon-
dences between particular (token) experiences, as fully described in the
idiom of personal histories, and physiological (token) events, as fully
described in the idiom of physical histories' (p. 64). See also A. Hardy,
The Spiritual Nature of Man, esp. p. 8f. For a survey of current research on
the physical basis of the mind see J.Z. Young, *Philosophy and the Brain*.

16 Hollis, editor's introduction to *Philosophy and Economic Theory*, eds. F.
Hahn and M. Hollis, p. 13.

17 Marx, *Early Writings*, p. 314.

18 Whitehead, *Science and the Modern World*, p. 15.

19 Cleanthes, disciple of Zeno and his successor as head of the Stoic School
in the third century BC, quoted by Rist, *Stoic Philosophy*, p. 127; according
to Zeno, 'man is like a dog tied to a cart; if he does not walk along he will
be pulled along' (p. 127).

20 Whitehead, *Adventures of Ideas*, p. 27.

21 Gellner, *Legitimation of Belief*, p. 187.

22 The sources for the quotations in this paragraph are: Berlin, 'Two
concepts of liberty' in *Four Essays*, p. 119 (see also pp. ix-xxxvii); T.M.
Knox, *Action*, p. 175 (see also p. 237); Burtt, *Metaphysical Foundations*, p.
17.

23 James, *Pragmatism* (1907), p. 9. In this passage James is quoting G.K.
Chesterton.

5 THE LOGIC OF THE ECONOMIC SITUATION

1 Linnaeus, from *Nemesis Divina* (c. 1750), a collection of notes found in a
private library in Kalmar by the mid-nineteenth century and now in the
Upsala University Library. This passage is quoted by his biographer K.
Hagberg in *Carl Linnaeus*, pp. 231–2. There appear to be remarkable
similarities between some passages in *Nemesis Divina* and Adam Smith's
account of scientific change in his history of astronomy (EPS,33–53).

2 Porphyry, 'On the life of Plotinus and the arrangement of his work', p. 1.
Cf. Plato's *Phaedrus*, 249d, which refers to man's soul in the body as 'the
oyster in his shell'. Cf. however, on the interpretation of Plotinus'
philosophy, Cleanthes' remark in Hume's *Dialogues Concerning Natural
Religion*, p. 179.

3 Locke, *Essay Concerning Human Understanding*, p. 239.

4 Epictetus, *The Encheiridion* [Manual], vol. 2, p. 495.

5 J. Steuart, *An Inquiry into the Principles of Political Oeconomy* (1767), vol. 1, p.
51.

6 Smith, 'Of the external senses' in EPS,165: 'But all the appetites which
take their origin from a certain state of the body, seem to suggest the
means of their own gratification; and, even long before experience, some
anticipation or preconception of the pleasure which attends that
gratification'. See also TMS,27–31 and Hume's 2ndE,301. On the

Aristotelian taxonomy see Aristotle, *Historia Animalium*, p. 589a: 'The life of animals, then, may be divided into two acts – procreation and feeding; for on these two acts all their interests of life concentrate'. On the use of this notion in eighteenth-century biology see J. Larson, *Reason and Experience*, p. 27.

7 On Seneca's failings and the disconcerting rift between his preaching and his behaviour see V. Sorensen, *Seneca*, esp. pp. 166–70. In his dialogue 'Of peace of mind', Seneca held that 'wealth is the most fertile source of human sorrows' and that 'the best amount of property to have is that which is enough to keep us from poverty, and which yet is not far removed from it' (*Minor Dialogues*, p. 267). Yet during his time as Nero's preceptor and regent of the Empire, he became one of the richest men in Rome. Challenged to account for this fact he replied: (a) that 'there is no need to sing the praises of what is wrong just because you cannot live up to what is right', (b) that 'the wise man does not show his independence by owning nothing, but by not being owned by anything' and (c) that he had never said he was a wise man. For an engaging collection of case-studies on the rift between sublime thought and ordinary life see P. Johnson, *Intellectuals*.

8 Paley, *Principles*, pp. 104–5. 'It is the utility of any moral rule alone', he held, 'which constitutes the obligation of it' (p. 72).

9 T. Carlyle, *Chartism* (1839) in *Selected Writings*, p. 168. The 'blank in the lottery of life' passage is from Malthus, *First Essay on Population* (1798), p. 204. On the notion of economic life as a game resembling 'a perfectly fair lottery', and involving a great deal of 'unmerited disappointment' by the participants see Smith's WN, 122; Marx, *Early Writings*, p. 309; Hayek, *Law, Legislation and Liberty*, vol. 2, p. 71; F.K. Knight, 'The ethics of competition', pp. 623–4.

10 Malthus, *Principles*, p. 403.

11 Hegel, *Philosophy of History* (1830–1), p. 82. As a possible source for both Malthus and Hegel see the remarks by A. von Humboldt in *Political Essay on the Kingdom of New Spain* (1808), vol. 1, esp. pp. 122s: '. . . the inhabitants of the warm region (tierra caliente) will never awake from the state of apathy in which for centuries they have plunged, till a royal cedula shall order the destruction of the banana plantation'. See also Marx, *Capital*, p. 649: 'Where nature is too prodigal with her gifts, she "keeps [man] in hand, like a child in leading-strings". Man's own development is not in that case a nature-imposed necessity'; Hume's 'Of commerce' (1752): 'What is the reason, why no people, living between the tropics, could ever yet attain to any art or civility, or reach even any police in their government, and any militarity discipline; while few na-tions in the temperate climates have been altogether deprived of these advantages? It is probable that one cause of this phaenomenon is the warmth and equality of weather in the torrid zone, which render clothes and houses less requisite for the inhabitants, and thereby remove, in part,

that necessity, which is the great spur to industry and invention'
(*Hume's Writings on Economics*, ed. Rotwein, pp. 17–18).

12 F. Nietsche, *The Gay Science* (1882), § 205, p. 207; cf. § 329, pp. 358–60.
See also R. McGinn, 'Nietzsche on technology'. The young Marx wrote:
'. . . each person speculates on creating a new need in the other, with the
aim of forcing him to make a new sacrifice and seducing him into a new
kind of enjoyment and hence into economic ruin' (*Early Writings*, p. 358).

13 Ruskin, *Unto This Last* (1860), § 243, p. 73. Cf. the Epicurean view that
'The wealth demanded by nature is both limited and easily procured;
that demanded by idle imaginings stretches on to infinity' (*Epicurus*, ed.
Bailey, p. 99).

14 Engels, 'On authority' (1874) in *Writings on Politics and Philosophy*, p. 483.

15 A good illustration of Marx's belief that, by changing the social relations
of production and having more technical progress, the labour-process
could be radically transformed, is in *Capital* p. 607: 'Mirabeau's
"Impossible! Never use that ridiculous word to me!" is particularly
applicable to modern technology'.

16 Aristotle, *Nicomachean Ethics*, 1096a5 (p. 7); 1099a32 (p. 17); 1110a2–3
(p. 48). See also 1178a29–30: 'The liberal man will need money for the
doing of his liberal deeds, and the just man too will need it for the
returning of services (for wishes are hard to discern, and even people who
are not just pretend to wish to act justly)' (p. 266–7). In his chapter on
Aristotle in *Philosophy and Political Economy*, Bonar renders (quite freely)
the line at 1099a32 as: 'It is hard to be good without an income' (p. 32).
See also Ackrill's introduction to *Aristotle's Ethics*, pp. 13–36; H. Arendt,
The Human Condition, pp. 12–15.

17 N. Machiavelli, *The Prince* (1532), ch. 15, p. 110. See also Keynes, *General
Theory*, pp. 156–7; Elster, *Sour Grapes*, esp. p. 24f: 'Practical morality is
largely about "second best" choices'. For a superbly illustrated survey of
ethical problems and dilemmas in corporate business see Braybrooke,
Ethics in the World of Business.

18 Marx, *Capital*, p. 736. The structuralist vein in Marx's analysis of the
capitalist mode of production is examined at length in J. Zeleny, *La
Estrutura Logical de 'El Capital' de Marx*.

19 Apart from its well-known occurrence in WN,456, Smith also deployed
the 'invisible hand' metaphor, for different purposes, in TMS, 184 and
EPS,49. For a discussion of its uses and meanings in Smith's work see
A.L.Macfie, 'The invisible hand of Jupiter'. Cf. Hume, 1stE,69
('invisible intelligent principle') and 1stE,108 ('original hand of nature'). See also N. Malebranche, *The Search After Truth* (1674): 'Thus, our
reason should constantly recognize this invisible hand that fills us with
goods, and is hidden from our minds under sensible appearances' (p.
311); S. Jenyns, *Origin of Evil* (1757):'yet has the Almighty so contrived
the nature of things, that happiness is distributed with a more equal hand
. . . It is a cordial administered by the gracious hand of Providence' (pp.

64–5); especially J. Butler, 'Sermon upon human nature' (1729):'so by acting merely from regard to reputation, without any consideration of the good of others, men often contribute to public good . . . they are plainly instruments in the hands of another, in the hands of Providence, to carry on ends, the preservation of the individual and good of society, which they themselves have not in their view or intention' (p. 391).

20 Cf. J. Passmore, *Man's Responsibility for Nature*, p. 187: 'Our society has officially denounced greed while in practice subscribing to Horace's maxim: "By right means if you can, but by any means make money".' The source is *Epistles* (I, i, ll.65–6).

21 This discussion is based on Hayek's path-breaking contributions to modern economic theory in 'Economics and knowledge' (1937) and 'The use of knowledge in society' (1945). For the context and a commentary on these seminal articles see B. Caldwell, 'Hayek's transformation'.

22 Knight, 'The ethics of competition', p. 602.

23 Nietzsche, *The Gay Science*, § 42, p. 108. See also *Daybreak*, § 204: 'What one formerly did "for the sake of God" one does now for the sake of money, that is to say, for the sake of that which now gives the highest feeling of power and good conscience' (p. 123).

6 THE PASSIONS OF THE IMAGINATION: THE DETERMINANTS OF BELIEF

1 B. Willey, *The Eighteenth Century Background*, p. 126. See also S.C. Brown, 'The "principle" of natural order', esp. pp. 56–76.

2 Voltaire, *Philosophical Letters*, p. 5. Cf. Hume's remarks on the Quakers as 'the most egregious, though, at the same time, the most innocent enthusiasts that have yet been known' (E,75–6). Locke's attack on 'enthusiasm', in particular against the Protestant extremists, is in the chapter he added to the fourth edition of his *Essay* (ch. 19); on the background to this attack see M. Cranston, *John Locke*, esp. pp. 277–8. A very detailed study of the semantic changes of 'enthusiasm' in the history of ideas is given by S.I. Tucker, *Enthusiasm*.

3 Hegel, *History of Philosophy*, vol. 1, p. xiii; *Theologische Jugendschriften*, quoted in R. Plant, *Hegel*, p. 47. The first point is fully stated in his *Philosophy of Nature* (1830), pp. 191–220. On Hegel's early writings on religion and their place in his thought see Hyppolite, *Introduction à la Philosophie de L'Histoire de Hegel*, chs. 2 and 3.

4 Marx, *Difference Between the Democritean and the Epicurean Philosophy of Nature* in *Works*, vol. 1, p. 104. Cf. Plato's *Apology*, 24.

5 Smith, WN,796. For a comment on this sentence see Raphael, 'Adam Smith: philosophy, science and social science', p. 81. See also Hume's remark in E,579.

6 Aristotle, *Physics*, 185a11.

7 Swift, *A Tale of a Tub* (1710), p. 105. In his early *Lectures on Rhetoric* Smith refers to Swift as 'the plainest as well as the most proper and precise of all the English writers . . . All his works shew a complete knowledge of his Subject' (p. 42).

8 L. Wittgenstein, *On Certainty*, § 253, p. 33e. See also J. Annas and J. Barnes, *The Modes of Scepticism*, esp. p. 92; G.H. von Wright, 'Wittgenstein on certainty'. On the source and background for Hume's motto see E.C. Mossner, *Life of David Hume*, p. 78 and p. 296.

9 The verses quoted are from A. Pope's 'Epitaph intended for Newton's tomb' (*Poetical Works*, vol. 2, p. 342). Hume's remark on Newton's achievement is in his *History of England* (1776), vol. 6, p. 542. This passage has been quoted by the following authors: Mossner, *Life of David Hume*, p. 75; N. Kemp Smith, *The Philosophy of David Hume*, p. 52; Brown, 'The "principle" of natural order', pp. 59–60; Passmore, *Science and Its Critics*, p. 5 and *Hume's Intentions*, p. 43.

10 The letter to Lord Kames (Henry Home) is dated 2 December 1737 and appears in *Letters*, vol. 1, p. 25 and Burton, *Life and Correspondence*, vol. 1, p. 62. The expression 'illusions of philosophical enthusiasm' is from 2ndE,343. On the importance of the science of man see also Malebranche, *The Search After Truth*, p. 291 and esp. p. xxv: 'Of all the human sciences, the science of man is the most worthy. Yet this science is neither the most cultivated nor the most complete that we possess; ordinary men neglect it altogether. Even among those who take pride in science, there are very few who apply themselves to this science, and there are still fewer who apply themselves to it with any success'. On the origins of Hume's project in THN and its relations to Hobbes' science of man see P. Russell, 'Hume's *Treatise* and Hobbes's *Elements of Law*'.

11 Hume, *Dialogues*, p. 149. For similar passages see THN,267–74 and 1stE,9, 106 and 158–9: 'The great subverter of Pyrrhonism or the excessive principles of scepticism is action, and employment, and the occupations of common life'. On the origins of this argument and the history of scepticism see Annas and Barnes, *The Modes of Scepticism*; they hold that 'Hume's attitude to scepticism is complex . . . but there is no doubt that his philosophy is informed by and founded upon the sceptical arguments which derive from Sextus [Empiricus]' (p. 6).

12 Marx, *Early Writings*, p. 326. Cf. Hume, E,179n and *Dialogues*, p. 150.

13 In his 'Abstract' of THN Hume wrote: 'Tis not, therefore, reason, which is the guide of life, but custom' (THN,652); see also his *History of England*, vol. 3, p. 192: 'But in opposition to these reasons and many more which might be collected Henry [VIII] had custom and precedent on his side, the principle by which men are almost wholly governed in their actions and opinions'. Cf. Malebranche, *The Search After Truth*, pp. xx–xxi; *Early Writings of Charles Darwin*, p. 84: 'Men are called creatures of reason, [but] more appropriately they would be creatures of habit'. See also on Hume's THN and his account of human conduct Teichgraeber III, '*Free Trade*' and Moral Philosophy', esp. p. 85 and p. 97.

14 A.-N. de Condorcet, *Sketch for a Historical Picture of The Progress of the Human Mind*, p. 163 and pp. 168–9.

15 Hayek, *Law, Legislation and Liberty*, vol. 3, pp. 175–6.

16 Smith, EPS,48 and TMS,157. Cf. Montaigne's 'I plainly perceive we lend nothing unto devotion but the offices that flatter our passions' (*Essays* (1580), p. 222). Smith is quoting from Malebranche's *The Search After Truth*: 'That all the passions seek their own justification; the judgements they cause us to make to justify them'. (pp. 399–403) See also C. McCracken, *Malebranche and British Philosophy*, esp. pp. 254–90.

17 B. de Spinoza, *Tractatus Politicus* (1677) in *Political Works*, p. 263. On his use of *affectus* see S. Hampshire, 'Spinoza and the idea of freedom'.

18 Spinoza's *Ethics* was originally called *Ethica Ordine Geometrico Demonstrata*. On Hume's and Smith's approach to the study of history and on its relevance for their science of man and society see Skinner, 'Natural history in the age of Smith'; Rotwein's introduction to *Hume: Writings on Economics*, pp. xxi-xxxi; Cassirer, *Philosophy of the Enlightenment*, pp. 226–8; Becker, *The Heavenly City*, p. 3.

19 La Rochefoucauld, *Maxims* (1665), § 460, p. 95; § 43, p. 42; § 8, p. 38.

20 Spinoza, *Ethics*, p. 130. Cf. J. Ray, *Three Physico-Theological Treatises* (1713): 'A Passion, I call it [Shame], because the Body, as in other Passions, suffers from it, and that in a peculiar manner; it causing a sudden motion of the Blood to the outward Parts, especially the Face, which is called Blushing, and a Dejection of the Eyes'. (quoted in Lovejoy, *Reflections on Human Nature*, p. 165) On the notion of passion (*pathe*) in the history of Greek philosophy see E.R. Dodds, *The Greeks and the Irrational*, pp. 181–95 and pp. 211–16.

21 Bacon, *Advancement of Learning*, p. 71 and 'Of adversity' in *Essays*, p. 11. See also Smith, TMS,252–3; Lucretius' *De Rerum Natura*, Bk III, ll. 55–8; 'It is more fitting to watch a man in doubt and danger, and to learn of what manner he is in adversity; for then at last a real cry is wrung from the bottom of his heart: the mask is torn off and the truth remains behind'.

22 Teichgraeber III, *'Free Trade' and Moral Philosophy*, p. 172. On this particular type of misunderstanding of WN see also G. Himmelfarb, *The Idea of Poverty*, ch. 2.

23 See in particular his *Lectures on Rhetoric*, p. 173; also pp. 145–6 on the different methods of scientific exposition and their merits. In WN,768–9, Smith refers to 'The beauty of a systematical arrangement of different observations connected by a few common principles'. For an interesting parallel between the pleasure derived from 'a well composed concerto' and from 'a great system in any other science' see his 'Of the imitative arts' (EPS,204–5).

24 See Hume's 'Of curiosity, or the love of truth' (THN,451). See also THN,422–3: 'When the soul applies itself to the performance of any action, or the conception of any object, to which it is not accustom'd, there is a certain unpliableness in the faculties, and a difficulty of the

spirit's moving in their new direction. As this difficulty excites the spirits, 'tis the source of wonder, surprize, and of all the emotions, which arise from novelty'. This passage, we may note, contradicts W. Wightman's account of the origins of Smith's philosophy of science in 'Adam Smith and the history of ideas', esp. p. 56. For Smith's philosophy of science see EPS,33–53 and WN,767–8. On the importance of his history of astronomy for an understanding of his works see, apart from the two editorial introductions to EPS, the following works: Skinner, 'Science and the role of the imagination'; Raphael, '"The true old Humean philosophy" and its influence on Adam Smith'; I. Lakatos, 'Newton's effect on scientific standards', esp. p. 222.

25 Keynes, *Collected Writings*, vol. 9, p. 329.

7 THE PASSIONS OF THE IMAGINATION: THE ECONOMIC AGENT

1 On Smith's theory of structural economic change and his views on how it affects economic and socio-political institutions see Skinner, 'Historical theory'; R.L. Meek, 'Smith, Turgot, and the "four stages theory"'.

2 On the role of sub-rational motives in Smith see Winch, *Adam Smith's Politics*, esp. pp. 165–9: 'Smith does not make use of the construct known as "economic man"' (p. 167); Coats, 'Adam Smith's conception of self-interest in economic and political affairs'; Viner, *The Role of Providence*, pp. 77–85; Bonar, *Philosophy and Political Economy*, pp. 171–5; Lovejoy, *Reflections on Human Nature*, pp. 213–15 and pp. 258f. On the Humean origins of Smith's economic psychology see Teichgraeber III, '*Free Trade' and Moral Philosophy*, esp. p. 85 and pp. 97f; Skinner, *A System of Social Science*, pp. 14–15; Rotwein's introduction to *Hume: Writings on Economics*, pp. xxxii–liii: 'the passion for gain . . . is essentially in the nature of a desire to accumulate symbols of successful endeavour' (p. xlv); Forbes, 'Hume and the Scottish Enlightenment', esp. pp. 99–101.

3 Malebranche, *The Search After Truth* (first edn 1674; first English trans. 1694), p. 290. In his early *Lectures on Rhetoric*, Smith observed: 'Such is the temper of men, that we are rather disposed to laugh at the misfortunes of our inferiors than take part in them' (p. 24). Cf. Lucretius, *De Rerum Natura*, Bk V, ll. 1114–16: 'for, for the most part, however, strong men are born, however beautiful their body, they follow the lead of the richer man'. Three copies of Lucretius' work were found in Smith's library: see J. Bonar, *A Catalogue of the Library of Adam Smith* and H. Mizuta, *Adam Smith's Library*.

4 Cf. Aristotle, *Nicomachean Ethics*, 1155a4–8: 'For without friends no one would choose to live, though he had all other goods; even rich men and those in possession of office and of dominating power are thought to need friends most of all' (p. 192).

5 Bentham, *Introduction to the Principles of Morals and Legislation* (1789), p. 11.

6 On the notions of 'positional goods' and 'positional jobs' see F. Hirsch, *Social Limits to Growth*.

7 On this important point see Bonar, *Philosophy and Political Economy*, p. 172: 'Men struggle for wealth in a great mesure because they take an illusory view of the pleasures obtainable by it, and they are thus decoyed into a course of action which has beneficent consequences due to no human designing'; Winch, *Adam Smith's Politics*, p. 91: 'Smith's scepticism towards material enjoyments is a major feature of this work [TMS], and is by no means absent in the *Wealth of Nations*. Beyond certain "necessities and conveniences of the body" Smith maintained that the pursuit of material benefits was in large measure delusory to the individuals involved . . . But Smith acknowledged that the illusion, though derived from a corruption of our moral sentiments, was an important one to society because it "rouses and keeps in continual motion the industry of mankind."'

8 Cf. Montaigne's 'An apologie of Raymond Sebond': 'Oh men, most braine-sicke and miserable, that endeavour to be worse than they can!' (*Essays*, p. 223).

9 Malthus, *First Essay*, p. 228–9: 'The first object of the mind is to act as purveyor to the wants of the body'.

10 Malthus, *First Essay*, p. 261–2. Cf. Paley, *Principles*, p. 23: 'happiness does not consist in the pleasures of sense', i.e. 'animal gratifications of eating, drinking, and that by which the species is continued'. See also Epictetus, *The Encheiridion*, vol. 2, p. 535.

11 The expression 'obscurantism of pleasure' is from R. Barthes, *The Pleasure of the Text*, p. 46: 'One out of every two Frenchmen, it appears, does not read; half of France is deprived – deprives itself of the pleasure of the text . . . It would be better to write the grim, stupid, tragic history of all the pleasures which societies object to or renounce: there is an obscurantism of pleasure'. Cf. Nietzsche, *The Gay Science*, § 328–9, pp. 258–60; Russell, *The Conquest of Happiness*, p. 53: 'Men and women appear to have become incapable of enjoying the more intellectual pleasures . . . It is not only work that is poisoned by the philosophy of competition; leisure is poisoned just as much'.

12 S. Freud, 'Creative writers and day-dreaming' (1907), p. 145. Cf. on this point: Thucydides, 'Pericles' funeral speech': '. . . sorrow is not felt at the loss of what has never been enjoyed, but at the deprivation of joys which long experience has made familiar' (44–5); Seneca, 'Peace of mind': '. . . you will find that those upon whom Fortune has never smiled are more cheerful than those whom she has deserted' (*Minor Dialogues*, p. 267); Spinoza, *Ethics*, p. 134: '. . . it is not within the free power of the mind to remember or forget a thing at will'. On Freud's so-called 'discovery of the unconscious' see I. Dilman, *Freud and the Mind*.

13 See Aristotle's *Metaphysics*, 982b. Hegel had already been very fond of this view and referred to this Aristotelian passage at least three times, viz:

Philosophy of Nature, vol. 1, p. 194; *Philosophy of History*, p. 80; *History of Philosophy*, p. 135. See also G. Duncan, *Marx and Mill*, pp. 185–6; Arendt, *The Human Condition*, p. 132–5.

14 W. Godwin, *Thoughts Occasioned by the Perusal of Dr Parr's Spital Sermon*, p. 73.

15 Hume, 'A dissertation on the passions', pp. 188–9. This passage, as indeed the 'Dissertation' as a whole, is, for the most part, a verbatim copy of parts of Bk II of THN; in the quote given here, for example, apart from changes in punctuation, he substituted 'a well-proportioned animal in a forest' for 'an animal in a desert' (cf. THN,303–4). But in the 'Dissertation' (first published in 1757 as one of the *Four Dissertations* complementing the two *Enquiries*), Hume appended an important note (p. 486) on the relation of property as 'the relation which has the greatest influence on these passions [i.e. of pride and vanity]', and which did not appear in THN.

16 Hume, 'A dissertation on the passions', p. 486.

17 Marx, *Grundrisse*, p. 173: 'The less time society requires to produce wheat, cattle, etc., the more time it wins for other production, material or mental. Just as in the case of an individual the multiplicity of its development, its enjoyment and its activity depends on economization of time. Economy of time, to this all economy ultimately reduces itself'.

18 Keynes, *Collected Writings*, vol. 9, p. 327.

19 See Marshall, *Memorials*, p. 339.

20 See Carlyle, *Selected Writings*, pp. 222–6.

21 Nietzsche, *Daybreak*, § 179, p. 108. Cf. Bentham, *Rationale of Reward* in *Works*, vol 2, p. 253: 'Prejudice apart, the game of push-pin is of equal value with the arts and sciences of music and poetry. If the game of push-pin furnish more pleasure, it is more valuable than either'; also Mill, CW10,113–14. On the notion of capabilities see Sen, 'Rights and capabilities' and 'Goods and people'. And on the impotence of governments to bring about certain social states see Elster, *Sour Grapes*, pp. 86f.

CONCLUSION TO PART I

1 E. Young, *Night-Thoughts* (1744), Night IV, p. 298.
2 Malthus, *First Essay*, p. 252 and p. 254.

8 UNDERSTANDING MISUNDERSTANDINGS

1 See Alexander Pope, *Correspondence*, vol. 4, pp. 171–2.
2 J. Rae, *Life of Adam Smith*, p. 403. The point is a commonplace in most biographies of Smith and Pitt. But for a more careful and detailed discussion see J. Ehrman, *The Younger Pitt*, esp. p. 249: 'It would be rash to claim too precise an effect for Adam Smith's great work. Its influence

was seminal rather than specific. One can seldom be confident that a given act of policy stemmed directly from his advice'.

3 The story is Addington's at first hand and the *locus in quo* is H. Dundas' house in London. Its first appearance in print is in G. Pellew's *Life and Correspondence of Henry Addington*, vol. 1, p. 151. Although no date is given, Ehrman holds 'the occasion must have been in 1787' (p. 512n). The story has been retold by the following authors: Rae, *Life of Adam Smith*, p. 405; F. Hirst, *Adam Smith*, p. 228; Himmelfarb, *The Idea of Poverty*, pp. 73–4; and Raphael, *Adam Smith*, p. 27. On Pitt-Smith see also C.R. Fay, *Adam Smith and the Scotland of his Day*, pp. 35–8; Winch, *Adam Smith's Politics*, pp. 7–8.

4 Bagehot, 'William Pitt' (1861) in *Works*, vol. 3, p. 130. See also J. Burrow, 'Sense and circumstances: Bagehot and the nature of political understanding', esp. p. 178: 'This is Bagehot's portrait of the younger Pitt. He is the ideal type of the relation between ideas and action, combining, in Bagehot's account, qualities normally divided among opposed types of men'.

5 Lovejoy, *Great Chain of Being*, pp. 22–3; Koyré, *Closed World*, p. 246; Locke, *Essay Concerning Human Understanding*, p. 480 and p. 496.

6 Lovejoy, *Great Chain of Being*, p. 14.

7 Nietzsche, *Daybreak*, § 47, p. 32. The comparison between words and coins is borrowed from F.M. Cornford, *The Unwritten Philosophy*, p. 40.

8 See Willey, *The Eighteenth Century Background*, p. 2. See also R.W. Harris, *Reason and Nature in the Eighteenth Century*; R. Feingold, *Nature and Society*, esp. ch. 2; R. Williams, *Keywords*, pp. 184–9. The most comprehensive work on the meanings of 'Nature' is still probably Lovejoy and G. Boas, *Primitivism and Related Ideas in Antiquity*, pp. 103–16 and the appendix ('Some meanings of "Nature"') where some sixty-six senses are given. On the Marxian-dialectical use of 'nature' see A. Schmidt, *The Concept of Nature in Marx*.

9 Lewis, *Studies in Words*, p. 5.

10 Kuhn, *The Essential Tension*, p. xii.

11 Wittgenstein, *Culture and Value*, p. 79e and p. 43e. Cf. G.E. Moore's curious remark in 'Wittgenstein's lectures in 1930–33', pp. 2–3: 'Of these discussions in Austria I only know that Ramsey told me that, in reply to his questions as to the meaning of certain statements [in the *Tractatus*], Wittgenstein answered more than once that he had forgotten what he had meant by the statement in question'.

12 Hayek, *Law, Legislation and Liberty*, vol. 1, p. 32 (cf. above note 26 of ch. 1, part I); Lukács, 'On the responsibility of intellectuals', p. 268; for a full statement of Lukács' thesis – i.e. 'Germany's path to Hitler in the sphere of philosophy', and Hitlerism as 'the ideological and political "crowning" of the development of irrationalism' – see his *The Destruction of Reason*, esp. pp. 11f.

13 Cassirer, *The Myth of the State*, p. 248. Pondering on the success and revival

of Hegel's philosophy in Germany and elsewhere, Schumpeter concluded that it was 'beyond anything I might be able to account for. I
could explain temporary success in Germany of the philosopher who is
credited with the saying: "Of all my pupils only one has understood me;
and this one has misunderstood me"' (*History of Economic Analysis*, p.
413).

14 Robbins, *Theory of Economic Policy*, pp. 4–5. For a comment on this passage
see A. Gerschenkron, 'History of economic doctrines and economic
history', p. 6.

15 Stigler, *Memoirs of an Unregulated Economist*, p. 216 and p. 214.

16 On the misconstruction of the past as a 'spurious present' see L. Kruger,
'Why do we study the history of philosophy', esp. pp. 79–85. See also
Kuhn, 'The relations between the history and the philosophy of science'.
For applications of the more sophisticated Kuhnian approach to the
history of economics see P. Deane, *The Evolution of Economic Ideas*; A.K.
Dasgupta, *Epochs of Economic Theory*.

17 Pareto, *Manual*, p. 94. Cf. J.A. Hobson's similar treatment of belief-
formation in Clarke, *Liberals and Social Democrats*, esp. p. 223. The
comparison between 'classics' and 'aristocrats' is borrowed from A.
Flew's introduction to Malthus' *Essay*, p. 8. As Malthus' publishers wrote
in the advertisement to *A Summary View* (1830), 'It has been frequently
remarked, that no work has been so much talked of by persons who do
not seem to have read it, as Malthus' *Essay on Population*' (*Introduction to
Malthus*, ed. D. Glass, p. vii and p. 117).

9 CONTRACTS AND TRAPS

1 Bacon, *Valerius Terminus*, a posthumously published Latin manuscript
quoted and translated by Farrington in *Francis Bacon*, p. 60. The term
'conceit' here is used in its older sense, meaning conception or
judgement.

2 Nietzsche, *Human All Too Human*, § 153, p. 248.

3 Bartlett, *Remembering*, p. 175.

4 Locke, *Essay*, p. 489 and p. 504. The manuscript memorandum (to John
Freke) is quoted by Cranston in *Locke*, p. 415; see also pp. 273–4 on the
notion of equivocal agreement.

5 Carlyle, *Selected Writings*, p. 155.

6 Bacon, *Advancement of Learning*, p. 134.

7 Bacon, *Cogitata et Visa*, p. 79 (on this work see above note 19 of ch. 3, part
I).

8 On the Socratic lesson see Plato's *Phaedo* 91b–c: 'if you take my advice,
you'll care little for Socrates but much more for the truth: if I seem to you
to say anything true, agree with it; but if not, resist it with every
argument you can, taking care that in my zeal I don't deceive you and

myself alike, and go off like a bee leaving its sting behind'. Cf. *Epicurus*, ed. C. Bailey, p. 117 and Popper's remark that 'our falsifications indicate the points where we have touched reality, as it were' (*Conjectures and Refutations*, p. 116). The paradox in 'trying to impress' is from Elster, *Sour Grapes*, p. 66.

9 T.S. Eliot, *The Use of Poetry and the Use of Criticism*, p. 109. La Rochefoucauld's remark is from *Maxims*, § 487, p. 98.

10 Both letters (dated 2 and 5 July 1866) are in *More Letters of Charles Darwin*, vol. 1, pp. 267–71.

11 Both letters are in *Life and Letters of Charles Darwin*, vol. 2, pp. 316–18.

12 Bonar, *Malthus and his Work*, p. 1. See also the 'Memoir' by Bishop Otter, appended to the second edition of Malthus' *Principles*, esp. p. xvi: 'For some time, indeed, he may be said to have stood alone upon the ground he had taken. The tide of public opinion ran obstinately against him'.

10 ON THE MISUSE OF LANGUAGE

1 Bacon, *Advancement of Learning*, p. 128. The name Tartar referred originally to the followers of Genghis Khan who invaded China in the thirteenth century, but was later applied to other foreign invaders; I have not been able to trace any explanation of the 'Tartar's bow'. The notion of thinking with one's pen is from Wittgenstein, *Culture and Value*, p. 17e. See also P. Ziff's lucid discussions of meaning and understanding in *Understanding Understanding*.

2 Smith, *Lectures on Rhetoric*, p. 203, pp. 206–7 and p. 214. Smith's essay was first published in 1761 in *Philological Miscellany* and then appended to the third edition of TMS (1767).

3 Hegel, *Philosophy of Right*, p. 270. Holderlin's remark is quoted by M. Hamburger in 'Holderlin', p. 60. According to Hamburger, 'Those who saw Holderlin only as an inspired visionary failed to notice his extraordinary capacity for self-criticism and for critical reflection on his own work. As his essays and letters show, Holderlin repeatedly questioned, modified or even rejected the premises of his art' (*Art as Second Nature*, p. 57).

4 Letter of 21 November 1807 to K.L. von Knebel in W. Kaufmann, *Hegel*, p. 322. In his letter, Knebel (the translator of Lucretius into German) had said: 'Truly, we consider you one of the first thinkers of our age; but we wish that you might have supported the spiritual force with more physical form' (p. 320).

5 Nietzsche, *The Gay Science*, § 173, p. 201; *Beyond Good and Evil*, § 290, p. 229. Cf. his remarks in *Daybreak*, § 193, where he discusses Hegel's way of writing and 'the bad style peculiar to him'. See also his letter of 22

January 1875 to his sister: 'Am I so difficult to understand and so easy to misunderstand in all my intentions, plans and friendships? Ah, we lonely ones and free spirits – it is borne home to us that in some way or other we constantly appear different from what we think. Whereas we wish for nothing more than truth and straightforwardness, we are surrounded by a net of misunderstanding' (*Selected Letters*, p. 101).

6 See *The Letters of David Hume*, vol. 1, p. 187. J. Stewart, the recipient, was then Professor of Natural Philosophy at Edinburgh University. See Mossner, 'The continental reception of Hume's *Treatise*'; also Hume's remark, in a letter of 6 July 1759 to Adam Smith, that 'If my past Writings do not sufficiently prove me to be no Jacobite, ten Volumes in folio never would'.

7 Cf. Kaufmann's sympathetic reading of this aphorism: 'Hegel was almost certainly not thinking of himself . . . we are all condemned, as Hegel sees it, to try to comprehend what man has thought up to our time and to relive, in condensed form, the experiences of the world spirit' (*Hegel*, p. 365).

8 See Keynes, *General Theory*, p. 33 and p. 378. On this point see also, among others: Robinson, 'History versus equilibrium'; T. Balogh, *The Irrelevance of Conventional Economics*; Georgescu-Roegen, *The Entropy Law*, esp. pp. 330ff; Mises, 'Comments about the mathematical treatment of economic problems': 'The equations of mathematical economics are . . . useless for all practical purposes. But they are also valueless as knowledge' (pp. 97–8).

9 Locke, *Essay Concerning Human Understanding*, p. 494. On Bacon's philosophy of science see Farrington, *Francis Bacon*; Kuhn, 'Mathematical versus experimental traditions in the development of physical science'; Broad, *The Philosophy of Francis Bacon*.

10 Both letters are in *Memorials*, p. 422 and p. 427. Their recipient was A.L. Bowley, a former student of Marshall and then Professor of Economics at the LSE.

11 Keynes, *General Theory*, p. 371.

12 P. Dasgupta and F. Hahn, 'To the defence of economics', p. 590. The article is a reply to A.S. Eichner's criticism in a piece called 'The lack of progress in economics'.

13 Hahn, 'Living with uncertainty in economics', p. 833.

14 Keynes, 'The general theory of employment' in *Collected Writings*, vol. 14, p. 111.

15 *The Early Writings of Charles Darwin*, pp. 195–6. See also H.E. Gruber's comments on this passage in his *Darwin on Man*, p. 251. For Huxley's reaction see E. Mayr's introduction to his edition of the *Origin*, p. xv. His review of the *Origin*, first published in 1860, is in *Darwiniana*, vol. 2, pp. 22–79. For Darwin's own short-list of those who had grasped his theory rather than misunderstood it see the letters referred to in note 11 of ch. 9 above.

16 Marshall, *Economics of Industry*, p. 30. Bagehot's remark is from his

'Malthus' (1880) in *Collected Works*, vol. 11, p. 341.
17 Nietzsche, *Human All Too Human*, § 532, p. 183.

11 ERRORS AND ILLUSIONS

1 Arrow, 'Classificatory notes on the production and transmission of technical knowledge', p. 174.
2 The proposed distinction between errors and illusions is based on Freud, *The Future of an Illusion*, p. 27.
3 Malthus, *First Essay*, p. 210; Marx, *Capital*, vol. 1, p. 766–7n (emphasis added in both). On the history of ideas about the age of the Earth see G. Davies, *The Earth in Decay*, pp. 12–18. On Malthus' marriage and children see the memoir by Bishop Otter, published in the second edition (1836) of Malthus' *Principles*.
4 Smith's assertion is from TMS,140. Hegel's is from *Philosophy of History*, p. 26 and p. 36. On Smith's position see also his statement in TMS,235 ('the very suspicion of a fatherless world, must be the most melancholy of all reflections') and the position taken by the Deist Cleanthes in Hume's *Dialogues Concerning Natural Religion*, p. 228: 'Health is more common than Sickness: Pleasure than Pain: Happiness than Misery. And for one Vexation, which we meet with, we attain, upon Computation, a hundred Enjoyments'. On Hegel's criticism of hedonism and defence of the view that in history 'periods of happiness are empty pages' see H. Marcuse, 'On hedonism'; on the development of his philosophy of history see J. Hyppolite, *Introduction à la Philosophie de L'Histoire de Hegel*.
5 Bacon, *Novum Organum*, § 44, p. 18 and § 49, p. 23; *Advancement of Learning*, pp. 126–7; *Novum Organum*, § 49, p. 23 and § 46, p. 20. Cf. the Cartesian views that 'there is nothing entirely within our power but our own thoughts' and that 'there is nothing which is easier for me to know than my mind' (*Works*, vol. 1, p. 97 and p. 157).
6 La Rochefoucauld, *Maxims*, § 513, p. 105.
7 B. Russell, 'The place of science in a liberal education', p. 57.
8 Bacon, *Advancement of Learning*, pp. 128–9.
9 Viner, *The Role of Providence in the Social Order*, pp. 18–19; see also p. 85.
10 Peirce, 'The fixation of belief', p. 11. For a detailed analysis of this article see W.B. Gallie, *Peirce and Pragmatism*; according to Gallie: 'The philosophical movement known as pragmatism is largely the result of James's misunderstanding of Peirce' (p. 30).
11 Hayek, *Law, Legislation and Liberty*, vol. 1, p. 61; Myrdal, 'The trend towards economic planning', p. 40. Incidentally, Hayek and Myrdal were jointly awarded the Nobel Prize in Economics in 1974.
12 Darwin, *Autobiography*, p. 123.
13 Bacon, 'Of truth' in *Essays*, pp. 1–2. For the philosopher's word of caution see Wittgenstein's letter of 16 November 1944 in N. Malcolm, *Wittgenstein*, p. 94.

12 THE PROTECTION OF BELIEF

1 R. Bambrough, *Moral Scepticism and Moral Knowledge*, pp. 113–14. The examples quoted in the next paragraph are from p. 113 and p. 115. On the notion of *akrasia* see also Ackrill's introduction to *Aristotle's Ethics*; Dodds, *The Greeks and the Irrational*, pp. 183f; and D. Evans, 'Moral weakness'.

2 Dostoyevsky, *The Gambler*, p. 31 and p. 128; *Diary of a Writer*, p. 270.

3 Bacon, quoted by Broad in *The Philosophy of Francis Bacon*, p. 49. Cf. Nietzsche, *Human All Too Human*, § 15:' . . . strong belief demonstrates only its strength, not the truth of that which is believed' (p. 19). In a letter of 1876, Nietzsche described himself as 'a man who longs for nothing more than daily to be rid of some comforting belief' (*Selected Letters*, p. 111). See also Pareto's remark in a private letter that: 'I learnt above all to be distrustful of emotions so that now, if something agrees with my feelings, I only become suspicious and seek arguments against it with greater care than if it were contrary to my feelings' (*The Other Pareto*, p. 178).

4 See the fragments of Heraclitus. According to J. Burnet, 'The dry light is the wisest soul' is a corruption of Heraclitus' *ipsissima verba*; the correct form would be 'The dry soul is the wisest and best' (*Early Greek Philosophy*, p. 138 and 138n2). See also T. Fowler's note in his edition of *Novum Organum*, p. 225n77. In *The Advancement of Learning*, Bacon refers to 'Heraclitus the profound' as his source for the 'dry light' metaphor (p. 8); in 'Of truth', he wrote, 'A mixture of a lie doth ever add pleasure' (*Essays*, p. 2).

5 Darwin, *Autobiography*, p. 125.

6 Popper, *Open Society*, vol. 2, addendum, p. 394. Explaining his position he added: 'As it was, I wrote about Hegel in a manner which assumed that few would take him seriously' (p. 394). Locke's observation is quoted by Cranston in *Locke*: 'He emphasised the danger of the habit of conversing "but with one sort of men" and of reading "but one sort of books". Men who did so, Locke said, "canton out to themselves a little Goshen in the intellectual world, where light shines, and, as they conclude, day blesses them; but the rest of that vast *expansum* they give up to night and darkness; and so avoid coming near it"' (p. 419).

7 Montaigne, 'An apologie of Raymond Sebond' in *Essays*, p. 224.

8 J.N. Findlay, *Hegel*, p. 272. Hegel's statements are from *Philosophy of Nature*, vol. 3, pp. 22–3; in a note, M. Petry comments: 'In denying that "man has formed himself out of the animal", Hegel is evidently rejecting the theory of evolution put forward by Lamarck'. (p. 230) See also on this point Findlay's introduction to Miller's translation of Hegel's work, p. xv; C. Taylor, *Hegel and Modern Society*, p. 28n.

9 For Darwin's letter (13 July 1856) see *More Letters*, vol. 1, p. 94. In a letter of 11 January 1844 to Hooker, Darwin had first vented his belief that species were not immutable – 'it is like confessing a murder', he added in

parentheses. In a further letter to Hooker (13 September 1864) he said: 'You have represented for many years the whole great public to me'. See also R. Colp, Jr., *To Be An Invalid*, p. 55. The link between Rev. Taylor and Darwin follows up a hint by J.R. Moore in his contribution to *Charles Darwin*, p. 176 and p. 188. Rev Taylor had been a Queen Margaret's Foundation Scholar at St John's College, Cambridge and in 1813 took his BA. His main work was *The Devil's Pulpit* (1831); the line quoted in the last paragraph is from his sermon 'The cup of salvation': 'Well have they [his prosecutors] sought to hold me up to public execration, by fastening on me the opprobrius title of The Devil's Chaplain: since, like the Devil, I am playing the Devil with their craft, and do tempt ye to take, pluck, and eat of that forbidden fruit of the Tree of Knowledge (p. 227).

10 Darwin, *Autobiography*, p. 57. See also his *Early Writings*, p. 125.
11 Montaigne, 'An apologie of Raymond Sebond' in *Essays*, p. 222.
12 Keynes, *Collected Writings*, vol. 2, p. 6. Cf. C. Glacken, *Traces on the Rhodian Shore*, p. 647: 'Western thought has never been the same since Malthus'.

13 ON MISUNDERSTANDING MALTHUS

1 Ruskin, *Unto This Last*, § 279, p. 84 and § 183, p. 57. The letter quoted is to C.E. Norton (3 April 1871) in *Ruskin Today*, p. 118. I have also used in this paragraph expressions from P. Shelley's preface to 'Laon and Cythna' and W. Hazlitt's 'Mr Malthus', p. 270.
2 Malthus, *First Essay*, p. 350.
3 Coleridge, *Table Talk*, vol. 2, p. 88. This same passage is also quoted by Keynes in his biographical sketch of Malthus (*Collected Writings*, vol. 10, p. 85) and by H.A. Boner in *Hungry Generations*, p. 123.
4 See Emerson, 'Poetry and imagination' in *Complete Works*, p. 603, emphasis added and slightly adapted. Cf. however his attack on Malthus in 'Works and days' (esp. p. 409). Coleridge's marginal notes have been fully printed (with the corresponding passages from the 1803 *Essay*) in G. Potter's 'Unpublished marginalia in Coleridge's copy of Malthus' *Essay on Population*'; the expressions cited are on p. 1063 and p. 1065: 'I am weary of confuting such childish Blunders'.
5 Hazlitt, *A Reply to the 'Essay on Population'*, p. 5. See also his letter of November 1823 to the editors of the *London Magazine*; this letter is reprinted *in toto* in Quincey, *Collected Writings*, vol. 9, pp. 20–2. The same point would be made again by Hazlitt in his portrait of 'Mr Malthus': 'Nothing could in fact be more illogical (not to say absurd) than the whole of Malthus' reasoning applied as an answer . . . to Godwin's book, or to the theories of other Utopian philosophers' (p. 272).
6 Southey, 'Malthus' *Essay on Population*', p. 298; 'On the state of the poor',

p. 93 and p. 150n. On the context of the review and his use of Coleridge's marginalia see Boner, *Hungry Generations*, pp. 45–50: 'Yesterday', wrote Southey to a friend in January 1804, 'Malthus received, I trust, a mortal wound from my hand'.

7 Shelley, preface to 'Laon and Cythna', quoted by Boner in *Hungry Generations*, p. 87.

8 Coleridge, *The Friend*, p. 240. See also Carlyle's *Chartism*, where he describes the 'Benthamee-Malthusian' teaching as leading to the 'practical inference' that 'nothing whatever can be done in it [the present sea of troubles] by man, who has simply to sit still, and look wistfully to "time and general laws" and thereupon, without so much as recommending suicide, coldly takes its leave of us' (*Selected Writings*, p. 221).

9 Malthus, *Principles*, p. 16. See also his letter of 26 January 1817 to Ricardo: 'I certainly am disposed to refer frequently to things as they are, as the only way of making one's writings practically useful to society, and I think also the only way of being secure from falling into the errors of the taylors of Laputa, and by a slight mistake at the outset arrive at conclusions the most distant from truth' (Ricardo, *Works*, vol. 7, pp. 121–2); Bonar, *Malthus and His Works*, p. 213: 'To Malthus the discovery of truth was less important than the improvement of society. When an economical truth could not be made the means of improvement, he seems to have lost interest in it'; Winch, 'Higher maxims: happiness versus wealth in Malthus and Ricardo'.

10 R.M. Young, 'Malthus and the evolutionists', p. 132. See also Bonar, *Philosophy and Political Economy*, p. 211; *Malthus and His Work*, p. 5.

11 Malthus, *First Essay*, p. 260 and his letter to Ricardo in note 9 above. On his views on progress see S. Levin, 'Malthus and the idea of progress'; D. LeMahieu, 'Malthus and the theology of scarcity'; E. Santurri, 'Theodicy and social policy in Malthus'; S. Rashid, 'Malthus's *Principles* and British economic thought'. Lenin's remark is from *Collected Works*, vol. 33, p. 229.

12 Coleridge, *A Lay Sermon*, p. 140.

13 Quincey, 'Malthus on population' in *Collected Writings*, vol. 9, p. 17. On his economic writings and friendship with Coleridge see A. Japp, *Thomas de Quincey*.

14 Engels, *Collected Works*, vol. 3, p. 437 and p. 420. According to Engels, 'this theory ill conforms with the Bible's doctrine of the perfection of God and of His creation' (p. 437). On Malthus's theology see however J. Pullen, 'Malthus' theological ideas and their influence on his principle of population'.

15 Marx, *Early Writings*, p. 306.

16 Marx, *Capital*, vol. 1, p. 784.

17 Marx, *Capital*, vol. 1, p. 766n. Marx's writings dealing with Malthus have been edited and translated by R. Meek in *Marx and Engels on*

Malthus. See also the long and rather dogmatic introduction by H. Parsons to *Marx and Engels on Ecology.* It is suggestive that Schmidt's *The Concept of Nature in Marx* does not contain a single reference to Malthus.

18 The diagnosis is by T.W. Hutchison in *The Politics and Philosophy of Economics*, p. 2.

19 See Z. Medvedev, *The Rise and Fall of Lysenko*, esp. pp. 166–7: 'According to Lysenko, Darwin invented this [intra-species] competition when the book of the reactionary, Malthus, happened to fall into his hands'. For a recent misinterpretation of Malthus see e.g. Himmelfarb, *The Idea of Poverty*: 'When Malthus enunciated the principle of population, he took it to apply to men but not to plants and animals: it was mankind that increased geometrically while food supply (plants and animals) increased only arithmetically' (p. 128). Yet, Malthus himself had written: 'Among plants and animals the view of the subject is simple. They are all impelled by a powerful instinct to the increase of their species; and this instinct is interrupted by no reasoning, or doubts about providing for offspring. Wherever therefore there is liberty, the power of increase is exerted; and the superabundant effects are repressed afterwards by want of room and nourishment, which is common to animals and plants; and among animals, by becoming prey to others' (*First Essay*, p. 27). So, Himmelfarb misunderstood Malthus and, yet, she went on to claim that 'Darwin himself did not realize' what he was doing when he applied Malthus' theory 'with manifold force to the whole animal and vegetable kingdoms'.

20 Russell, 'The place of science in a liberal education', pp. 37–8.

21 See E.J. Whately, *Life and Correspondence of R. Whately*, vol. 1, p. 301. (I would like to thank Richard Brent for drawing my attention to this letter.)

22 Senior, *Two Lectures on Population*, pp. 81–9.

23 Marshall, *Early Economic Writings*, vol. 2, p. 388.

24 This unpublished letter to Whewell is now in Trinity College Library, Cambridge, Whewell Papers, Add. Mss. c. 53/2.

25 Lenin, 'Conspectus of Hegel's *Science of Logic*' in *Collected Works*, vol. 38, p. 180.

14 IDEAS INTO POLITICS: THREE LEVELS OF EXCHANGE

1 Lovejoy, *Reflections on Human Nature*, p. 68.

2 Nietzsche, *Human All Too Human*, § 17, p. 309.

3 Swift, *A Tale of a Tub*, X, p. 118n. Swift classified readers into three classes, viz. 'the Superficial, the Ignorant, and the Learned', but 'wise Philosophers', he wrote, 'hold all Writings to be fruitful in the proportion they are dark . . . The Words of such Writers being like Seed, which, however scattered at random, when they light upon a fruitful Ground,

will multiply far beyond either the Hopes or Imagination of the Sower'
(p. 118).

4 Kuhn, 'The relations between the history and the philosophy of science',
p. 7.

5 Augustine, *Confessions*, p. 60 and p. 304. See also Seneca's *Epistulae*, 108,
quoted by V. Sorensen in *Seneca*, p. 77.

6 Keynes, 'My early beliefs' in *Collected Writings*, vol. 10, pp. 436–7. On
Bloomsbury-Keynes-Moore see also R. Harrod, *The Life of J.M. Keynes*,
p. 80; D. Moggridge, *Keynes*, pp. 13–26; P. Levy, *Moore and the Cambridge
Apostles*, esp. pp. 6–7.

7 A. Bain, *J.S. Mill*, quoted by Robbins in *Theory of Economic Policy*, p. 151n.

8 On this point see Kuhn's important preface to *The Essential Tension*, esp.
p. xix, and his essay 'Second thoughts on paradigms'. On the concept of
paradigms see also M. Masterman, 'The nature of a paradigm'.

9 Schumpeter, *History of Economic Analysis*, p. 815. On the existence of deep
methodological differences in the history of economics see Bonar,
Philosophy and Political Economy; Caldwell, *Beyond Positivism*.

10 On the origins and some of the problems of this concept see I. Cohen,
'The eighteenth-century origins of the concept of scientific revolution':
'For some three centuries there has been a more or less unbroken
tradition of viewing scientific change as a sequence of revolutions' (p.
257). Cf., however, among others, Blaug's statement that 'the distinctive
feature of Kuhn's methodology is not the concept of paradigms that
everyone has siezed on, but rather that of "scientific revolutions" as
sharp breaks in the development of science, and particularly the notion
of a pervasive failure of communications during periods of "revolutionary crises"' ('Kuhn versus Lakatos', p. 403).

11 Kuhn, 'Second thoughts on paradigms', p. 293: 'I conclude that a gestalt
switch divides readers of my book into two or more groups . . . For that
excessive plasticity, no aspect of the book is so much responsible as its
introduction of the term "paradigm".'

12 See *The Letters of David Hume*, vol. 1, p. 305.

13 Augustine, *Confessions*, p. 308.

15 IDEAS INTO POLITICS: CLAIMS AND MISUNDERSTANDINGS

1 Keynes, *General Theory*, pp. 383–4.

2 Malthus, *Principles*, p. 9.

3 Marshall, *Memorials*, p. 297. On his campaign for the separation of
Economics from the Moral Sciences see his 'A plea for the creation of a
curriculum in economics'. See also J. Maloney, 'Marshall, Cunningham,
and the emerging economics profession'; P. Groenewegen, 'Marshall and
the establishment of the Cambridge Economic Tripos'; Winch, 'A
separate science: polity and society in Marshall's economics'.

4 In his pamphlet 'A plea', for example, Marshall suggested that: 'Economic training may give a high intellectual tone to business life' (p. 169). See also 'Social possibilities of economic chivalry' in *Memorials*. On Keynes' view that economics is a moral science see his letters of 4 and 16 July 1938 to R. Harrod (*Collected Writings*, vol. 14, pp. 295–7 and pp. 299–301) and his remark that 'If economists could manage to get themselves thought of as humble, competent people, on a level with dentists, that would be splendid' (ibid., vol. 11, p. 332). The outstanding work on Keynes' intellectual evolution and the interplay between theory and policy in his thinking is Clarke's *The Keynesian Revolution in the Making*.

5 Engels, preface to the first English translation of Marx's *Capital*, pp. 112–13.

6 D. Morgan, 'The "orthodox" Marxists', p. 6. Cf. F. Mehring, *Karl Marx*, p. 530: '[Marx] was dissatisfied with the way in which his sons-in-law represented his ideas . . . as far as he was concerned he was certainly not a Marxist'. See also Tucker, *Philosophy and Myth in Marx*, esp. p. 231.

7 This is how Cicero described Socrates' achievement in philosophy (*Tusculan Disputations*, p. 435).

8 Livingstone, *A Defence of Classical Education*, p. 108.

9 Whitehead, *Adventures of Ideas*, p. 24. Bacon's remark above is from *Essays*, p. 24.

10 Whitehead, *Science and the Modern World*, pp. 85–6 and p. 288. Cf. B. Russell, *The Conquest of Happiness*, pp. 49–51 and pp. 54–5; unlike Whitehead, Russell did not blame modern science or modern economics for the 'rat race'.

11 See his *General Theory*, p. 374 and his remarks on the money-motive in 'Economic possibilities for our grandchildren' (*Collected Writings*, vol. 9, p. 329). On the history of this view and its eighteenth-century background see A.O. Hirschman, *The Passions and the Interests*.

12 Keynes, *Collected Writings*, vol. 13, p. 492. The letter to B. Shaw (1 January 1935) is in *Collected Writings*, vol. 28, p. 42. See also *Dialogues of Whitehead*, p. 281.

13 Cornford, 'Plato's commonwealth', p. 57. Cf. his introduction to his translation of the *Republic*, p. xxii. See also Burnet's discussion of Plato's attitude to the practical life in his contribution to *The Legacy of Greece*, ed. Livingstone, pp. 83–5.

14 Ryle, review of Popper's *Open Society* in *Mind*, 56 (1947), p. 172.

15 Guthrie, *The Sophists*, p. 21. See also *Republic*, 493a.

16 Plato's 'Seventh letter', 325 (p. 114). On the issue of the authenticity of the letters see A.E. Taylor, *Plato*, pp. 15–16. See also Dodds, 'The sophistic movement and the failure of Greek liberalism'. On the 'Socratic problem' see Taylor, *Plato*, esp. pp. 24–5; Koyré, *Discovering Plato*; Cornford, *Before and After Socrates*.

17 See Popper's dedicatory in *The Poverty of Historicism*; Lukács, *The Destruction of Reason*, p. 32. 'Every thinker', argued Lukács, 'is responsible

to history for the objective substance of his philosophizing. Thus the subject-matter which now presents itself to us is Germany's path to Hitler in the sphere of philosophy . . . Only now can we understand how Hitler contrived a demagogic popularization of all the intellectual motives of entrenched philosophical reaction, the ideological and political "crowning" of the development of irrationalism' (p. 4 and p. 11).

18 E. Gellner, *Legitimation of Belief*, p. 21.

19 Locke, *Essay Concerning Human Understanding*, pp. 489–90.

20 Ryle, review of Popper's *Open Society*, p. 169; Popper, *Open Society*, vol. 1, p. 199.

21 Hayek, *A Tiger by the Tail*, p. 103. See also J. Buchanan *et al.*, *The Consequences of Mr Keynes*, esp. pp. 48–51.

22 Dodds, 'Plato and the irrational', p. 107.

23 Marshall, *Industry and Trade*, p. 724. See also A. Downs, *The Economic Theory of Democracy*, esp. p. 112; A. Cairncross, 'Economics in theory and practice'. It may be useful to remark that in a recent editorial article ('The dangerous science', 17 June 1989, pp. 19–20) *The Economist* updates Marshall's point about the natural blindness of decision-makers and discusses four concrete cases of what it calls 'knowledge abuse' involving the political hijacking of economic theories: the Laffer curve, exchange rates policy, incomes policy and strategic trade policy. It describes economic theorists as 'a misunderstood profession' and asks: 'Shocking, isn't it, that economists can be more ignorant about politics than politicians are about economics?'

CONCLUSION TO PART II

1 Keynes, *Collected Writings*, vol. 28, p. 38. The letter is dated 2 December 1934.

2 Hegel, *Philosophy of History*, p. 35.

3 Pareto, *Manual*, p. 95 and p. 342.

4 Baudelaire, 'My heart laid bare' in *Intimate Journals*, p. 89. Cf. Goethe, *Poetry and Truth*, p. 436 and p. 524. On the view that poets are poor interpreters of their own work see Socrates' remarks in *Apology*, 22 and *Protagoras*, 374e. For Bentham's assertion that 'all poetry is misrepresentation' see *Works*, vol. 2, pp. 253–4: 'Truth, exactitude of every kind, is fatal to poetry'.

Bibliography

Ackrill, J.L. (ed.) *Aristotle's Ethics*, London, 1973.

Annas, J. and J. Barnes *The Modes of Scepticism*, Cambridge, 1985.

Arendt, H. *The Human Condition*, Chicago, 1958.

Aristotle, *The Nicomachean Ethics*, trans. D. Ross, Oxford, 1980.

Historia Animalium, trans. D. Ross, Oxford, 1910.

Metaphysics, trans. C. Kirwan, Oxford, 1971.

Physics, trans. W. Charlton, Oxford, 1971.

Arrow, K.J. 'Classificatory notes on the production and transmission of technical knowledge' in *Essays in the Theory of Risk-Bearing*, London, 1971.

'Rationality of self and others in an economic system', mimeo, 1986.

Attfield, R. 'Christian attitudes to nature' in JHI 44(1983), 369–86.

The Ethics of Environmental Concern, Oxford, 1983.

Augustine, St *Confessions*, trans. R.S. Pine-Coffin, Harmondsworth, 1961.

Bacon, F. *The Advancement of Learning*, ed. A. Johnston, Oxford, 1974.

Novum Organum, ed. T. Fowler, Oxford, 1899 and English version, London, 1844.

Essays or Counsels Civil and Moral, London, 1906.

Cogitata et Visa in *The Philosophy of F. Bacon*, trans. B. Farrington, Liverpool, 1964.

Bagehot, W. *Collected Works*, ed. Normam St John Stevas, vols. 3 and 11, London, 1965–78.

Bailey, C. (ed.) *Epicurus: The extant remains*, Oxford, 1926.

Balogh, T. *The Irrelevance of Conventional Economics*, London, 1982.

Bambrough, J.R. *Conflict and the Scope of Reason*, Hull, 1974.

Moral Scepticism and Moral Knowledge, London, 1979.

Barry, N.P. 'Restating the liberal order: Hayek's philosophical economics' in *Twelve Contemporary Economists*, eds. J.R. Shackleton and G. Locksley, London, 1981.

Barthes, R. *The Pleasure of the Text*, trans. R. Miller, New York, 1975.

Bartlett, F.C. *Remembering*, Cambridge, 1961.

Baudelaire, C. *Intimate Journals*, trans. C. Isherwood, San Francisco, 1983.

Becker, C.L. *The Heavenly City of the Eighteenth Century Philosophers*, New Haven, 1932.

234   *Bibliography*

Beer, M. *An Inquiry into Physiocracy*, London, 1939.
Bentham, J. *Chrestomathia*, London, 1817.
    Works, ed. J. Bowring, vol. 2, Edinburgh, 1843.
    An Introduction to the Principles of Morals and Legislation, eds. J.H. Burns and
        H.L.A. Hart, London, 1982.
Berg, M. *The Machinery Question and the Making of Political Economy*,
    Cambridge, 1980.
Berlin, I. *Four Essays on Liberty*, Oxford, 1969.
    'Marx's *Kapital* and Darwin' in JHI 39(1978),519.
Black, R.D.C. 'Jevons and the foundation of modern economics' in *The
    Marginal Revolution in Economics*, eds. R.D.C. Black, A.W. Coats and C.
    Goodwin, Durham, 1973.
    'Jevons and the development of the marginal utility analysis in British
        economics', mimeo, 1985.
Black, R.D.C., A.W. Coats and C. Goodwin (eds.) *The Marginal Revolution
    in Economics*, Durham, 1973.
Blaug, M. *Economic Theory in Retrospect*, Cambridge, 1968.
    'Kuhn versus Lakatos, or paradigms versus research programmes in the
        history of economics' in HOPE7(1975), 399–432.
Bonar, J. *Philosophy and Political Economy*, London, 1922.
    Malthus and His Work, London, 1924.
    A Catalogue of the Library of Adam Smith, London, 1932.
Boner, H. *Hungry Generations*, New York, 1955.
Boulding, K. *The Image: Knowledge in life and society*, Michigan, 1956.
    'Economics as a moral science' in *American Economic Review* 59(1969), 1–12.
Bowler, P.J. 'The changing meaning of "evolution"' in JHI 36(1975),
    95–114.
    'Malthus, Darwin, and the concept of struggle' in JHI 37(1976), 631–50.
Braybrooke, D. *Ethics in the World of Business*, Totowa, 1983.
Broad, C.D. *The Philosophy of Francis Bacon*, Cambridge, 1926.
Brown, S.C. 'The "principle" of natural order: or what the enlightened
    sceptics did not doubt' in *Philosophers of the Enlightenment*, ed. S.C.
    Brown, Sussex, 1979.
Buchanan, J., J. Burton and R. Wagner, *The Consequences of Mr Keynes*,
    I.E.A., London, 1978.
Bucolo, P. (ed. and trans.) *The Other Pareto*, London, 1980.
Burnet, J. *Early Greek Philosophy*, London, 1930.
Burrow, J. 'Sense and circumstances: Bagehot and the nature of political
    understanding' in *That Noble Science of Politics*, eds. S. Collini, D. Winch
    and J. Burrow, Cambridge, 1983.
Burton, J.H. *The Life and Correspondence of David Hume*, Edinburgh, 1846.
Burtt, E.A. *The Metaphysical Foundations of Modern Science*, London, 1932.
Butler, J. 'Sermon upon human nature' in *The Analogy of Religion*, London,
    1889.
Caldwell, B. *Beyond Positivism*, London, 1982.
    'Hayek's transformation' in HOPE 20 (1988), 513–44.

Cairncross, A. 'Economics in theory and practice' in *American Economic Review* 75(1985), 1–14.

Carlyle, T. *Selected Writings*, ed. A. Shelston, Harmondsworth, 1971.

Carnap, R. 'The elimination of metaphysics through logical analysis of language' in *Logical Positivism*, ed. A.J. Ayer, London, 1959.

Cassirer, E. *The Philosophy of the Enlightenment*, trans. F. Koelln and J.P. Pettegrove, London, 1951.

The Platonic Renaissance in England, trans. J.P. Pettegrove, London, 1953.

The Problem of Knowledge, trans. W. Woglom and C. Hendel, New Haven, 1950.

The Myth of the State, trans. C. Hendel, New Haven, 1946.

Cavanaugh, M.A. 'Scientific creationism and rationality' in *Nature* 315(1985), 185–9.

Checkland, S.G. 'Economic opinion in England as Jevons found it' in *Manchester School* 19(1951), 143–69.

Cicero, M.T. *Tusculan Disputations*, trans. J. King, Loeb, 1927.

Clark, G.N. *Science and Social Welfare in the Age of Newton*, Oxford, 1949.

Clark, S.R.L. *The Moral Status of Animals*, Oxford, 1984.

Clarke, P.F. *Liberals and Social Democrats*, Cambridge, 1978.

The Keynesian Revolution in the Making: 1924–1936, Oxford, 1988.

Coats, A.W. 'Adam Smith's conception of self-interest in economic affairs' in HOPE 7(1975), 132–6.

Cohen, I.B. 'The eighteenth century origins of the concept of scientific revolution' in JHI 37(1976), 257–88.

Coleman, W. 'Providence, capitalism, and environmental degradation: English apologetics in an era of economic revolution' in JHI 37(1976), 27–44.

Coleridge, S.T. *Specimens of the Table Talk of the Late S.T. Coleridge*, ed. H.N. Coleridge, London, 1935.

The Friend in *Collected Works*, ed. B.E. Rooke, vol. 4, London, 1969.

A Lay Sermon in *Collected Works*, ed. R. White, vol. 6, London, 1972.

Collingwood, R.G. 'Economics as a philosophical science' in *International Journal of Ethics* 36(1925),162–85.

The Idea of Nature, Oxford, 1960.

Collini, S. 'The tendency of things: John Stuart Mill and the philosophic method' in *That Noble Science of Politics*, eds. S. Collini, D. Winch and J. Burrow, Cambridge, 1983.

Colman, J. *John Locke's Moral Philosophy*, Edinburgh, 1983.

Colp Jr, R. 'Multiple independent discovery: the Darwin-Marx letter' in JHI 40(1979), 479.

To Be An Invalid: The illness of Charles Darwin, Chicago, 1977.

Condorcet, A.-N. de *Sketch for a Historical Picture of the Progress of the Human Mind*, trans. J. Barraclough, Westport, 1979.

Cornford, F.M. 'Plato's commonwealth' in *The Unwritten Philosophy*, Cambridge, 1967.

Before and After Socrates, Cambridge, 1932.

Cranston, M. *John Locke*, Oxford, 1985.

Cropsey, J. 'Adam Smith and political philosophy' in *Essays on Adam Smith*, eds. A.S. Skinner and T. Wilson, Oxford, 1976.

Darwin, C. *Autobiography*, ed. N. Barlow, London, 1958.

Early Writings of Charles Darwin, transcribed and annotated by P.H. Barret with a commentary by H.E. Gruber, Chicago, 1974.

The Life and Letters of Charles Darwin, ed. F. Darwin, London, 1887.

More Letters of Charles Darwin, ed. F. Darwin, London, 1903.

Dasgupta, A.K. *Epochs of Economic Theory*, Oxford, 1983.

Dasgupta P. and F. Hahn 'To the defence of economics' in *nature* 317 (1985), 589–90.

Davies, G. *The Earth in Decay: British Geomorphology, 1578–1878*, London 1969.

Deane, P. *The Evolution of Economic Ideas*, Cambridge, 1978.

'The scope and method of economic science' in *Economic Journal* 93(1983),1–12.

Deleule, D. *Hume et la Naissance du Liberalisme Économique*, Paris, 1979.

Descartes, R. *Philosophical Letters*, trans. A. Kenny, Oxford, 1970.

Philosophical Works, trans. E.S. Haldane and G. Ross, vol. 1, Cambridge, 1931.

Dilman, I. *Freud and the Mind*, Oxford, 1984.

Dobb, M. *Theories of Value and Distribution Since Adam Smith*, Cambridge, 1973.

'The trend of modern economics' in *A Critique of Economic Theory*, eds. E. Hunt and J. Schwartz, Harmondsworth, 1972.

Dodds, E.R. *The Greeks and the Irrational*, Berkeley, 1951.

'The sophistic movement and the failure of Greek liberalism' and 'Plato and the irrational' in *The Ancient Concept of Progress*, Oxford, 1985.

Dooley, P.C. 'Alfred Marshall: fitting the theory to the facts' in *Cambridge Journal of Economics* 9(1985), 245–55.

Dostoyevsky, F. *The Gambler*, trans. J. Coulson, Harmondsworth, 1966.

The Diary of a Writer, trans. B. Brasol, Haslemere, Surrey, 1984.

Downs, A. *An Economic Theory of Democracy*, New York, 1957.

Duncan, G. *Marx and Mill*, Cambridge, 1973.

Edgeworth, F.Y. *Mathematical Psychics*, London, 1881.

'John Stuart Mill' and 'Mathematical method in political economy' in *Palgrave's Dictionary of Political Economy*, London, 1894–9.

Ehrman, J. *The Younger Pitt: The years of acclaim*, London, 1969.

Eliot, T.S. *The Use of Poetry and the Use of Criticism*, London, 1964.

Elster, J. *Ulysses and the Sirens*, Cambridge, 1979.

Sour Grapes, Cambridge, 1983.

Making Sense of Marx, Cambridge, 1985.

Emerson, R.W. *Complete Works*, ed. A.C. Hearn, Edinburgh, 1907.

Engels, F. 'On authority' in *Marx and Engels: Basic writings on politics and philosophy*, ed. L.S. Feuer, London, 1959.

'Outlines of a critique of political economy' in *Collected Works*, vol. 3, London, 1975.

Evans, D. 'Moral weakness' in *Philosophy* 50(1975), 295–310.

Epictetus *The Encheiridion*, trans. W.A. Oldfather, vol. 2, Loeb, 1928.

Farrington, B. *The Faith of Epicurus*, London, 1967.

Francis Bacon: Philosopher of industrial science, London, 1951.

Fay, C.R. *Adam Smith and the Scotland of His Day*, Cambridge, 1956.

Feingold, R. *Nature and Society: Later Eighteenth Century Uses of the Pastoral and Georgic*, Sussex, 1978.

Ferguson, A. *An Essay on the History of Civil Society*, ed. D. Forbes, Edinburgh, 1966.

Fetter, F.W. 'The influence of economists in parliament on British legislation from Ricardo to John Stuart Mill' in *Journal of Political Economy* 83(1975), 1051–64.

Findlay, J.N. *Hegel: A re-examination*, London, 1958.

Fingarette, H. *Self-Deception*, London, 1969.

Flew, A.G.N. (ed.) *Malthus's Essay on Population*, Harmondsworth, 1970.

David Hume: Philosopher of moral science, Oxford, 1986.

Foley, V. *The Social Physics of Adam Smith*, West Lafayette, 1976.

Forbes, D. 'Hume and the Scottish enlightenment' in *Philosophers of the Enlightenment* ed. S.C. Brown, Sussex, 1979.

'Sceptical Whiggism, commerce and liberty' in *Essays on Adam Smith*, eds. A.S. Skinner and T. Wilson, Oxford, 1976.

Fraser, L.M. *Economic Thought and Language*, London, 1937.

Freud, S. 'Creative writers and day-dreaming' in *Complete Works*, ed. J. Strachey, vol. 9, London, 1959.

The Future of an Illusion, ed. J. Strachey, London, 1962.

Gallie, W.B. *Peirce and Pragmatism*, Harmondsworth, 1952.

Gide, C. and C. Rist *A History of Economic Doctrines*, trans. R. Richards, London, 1948.

Gellner, E. *Legitimation of Belief*, Cambridge, 1974.

Georgescu-Roegen, N. *The Entropy Law and the Economic Process*, Cambridge, Mass., 1971.

Gerschenkron, A. 'History of economic doctrines and economic history' in *American Economic Review* 59(1969), 1–17.

Gillespie, N.C. *Darwin and the Problem of Creation*, Chicago, 1979.

Glacken, C.J. *Traces on the Rhodian Shore*, Berkeley, 1967.

Glass, D.V. (ed.) *Introduction to Malthus*, London, 1953.

Godwin, W. *Thoughts Occasioned by the Perusal of Dr Parr's Spital Sermon*, Christ Church, April 15, 1800, London, 1801.

Goethe, J.W. von *Poetry and Truth*, trans. R. Heitner, New York, 1987.

Goodhue, E.W. 'Economics as a social philosophy' in *International Journal of Ethics* 36(1925), 54–70.

Gordon, B. *Political Economy in Parliament, 1819–1823*, London, 1976.

Goudge, T.A. 'The concept of "evolution"' in *Mind* 63(1954), 16–25.

Grampp, W.D. 'Adam Smith and the economic man' in *Journal of Political Economy* 56(1948), 315–36.

Groenewegen, P. 'Alfred Marshall and the establishment of the Cambridge Economic Tripos' in HOPE 20(1988), 627–67.

Gruber, H.E. *Darwin on Man*, Chicago, 1981.

Guthrie, W.K. *The Sophists*, Cambridge, 1971.

Hagberg, K. *Carl Linnaeus*, trans. A. Blair, London, 1952.

Hahn, F. and M. Hollis (eds.) *Philosophy and Economic Theory*, Oxford, 1979.
On the Notion of Equilibrium in Economics, Cambridge, 1973.
'Reflections on the invisible hand' in *Lloyds Bank Review* 144(1982), 1–21.
'Living with uncertainty in economics' in *Times Literary Supplement*, 1 August 1986, 833–4.
'On some economic limits in politics', mimeo, 1986.

Hamburger, M. *Art as Second Nature*, Manchester, 1975.

Hampshire, S. 'Spinoza and the idea of freedom' in *Studies in Spinoza*, ed. S.P. Kashap, Berkeley, 1972.

Harcourt, G. 'Marshall, Sraffa and Keynes: incompatible bedfellows?' in *The Social Science Imperialists*, ed. P. Kerr, London, 1982.

Hardy, A. *The Spiritual Nature of Man*, Oxford, 1979.

Harris, R.W. *Reason and Nature in the Eighteenth Century*, London, 1968.

Harrod, R. *The Life of John Maynard Keynes*, London, 1951.

Hayek, F.A. *The Counter Revolution of Science*, Glencoe, Ill., 1952.
The Sensory Order, London, 1952.
Studies in Philosophy, Politics and Economics, London, 1967.
A Tiger by the Tail: The Keynesian legacy of inflation, I.E.A., London, 1972.
New Studies in Philosophy, Politics, Economics and the History of Ideas, London, 1978.
Law, Legislation and Liberty, vols. 1, 2 and 3, London, 1982.
'Economics and knowledge' in *Economica* 4(1937), 33–54.
'The use of knowledge in society' in *American Economic Review* 35(1945), 519–30.

Hazlitt, W. 'Mr Malthus' in *The Spirit of the Age*, London, 1910.
A Reply to the 'Essay on Population' by the Revd T.R. Malthus. In a Series of Letters; to which are added extracts from the Essay, London, 1807.

Hegel, G.W.F. *Philosophy of Right*, trans. T.M. Knox, Oxford, 1952.
Lectures on the History of Philosophy, trans. E.S. Haldane, London, 1892.
The Philosophy of History, trans. J. Sibree, New York, 1956.
The Philosophy of Nature, trans. M.J. Petry, London, 1969.

Henderson, J.P. '"Just notions of political economy": George Pryme, the first professor of political economy at Cambridge' in *Research in the History of Economic Thought and Methodology*, ed. W.J. Samuels, vol. 2, Greenwich, Conn., 1984.

Hetherington, N.S. 'Isaac Newton's influence on Adam Smith's natural laws in economics' in JHI 44(1983), 487–505.

Himmelfarb, G. *The Idea of Poverty*, New York, 1984.

Hirsch, F. *Social Limits to Growth*, London, 1977.

Hirschman, A.O. *The Passions and the Interests*, Princeton, 1977.

Hirshleifer, J. 'Economics from a biological viewpoint' in *Journal of Law and Economics* 20(1977), 1–52.

Hirst, F.W. *Adam Smith*, London, 1904.

Holbach, P.T. d' *The System of Nature*, trans. H.D. Robinson, New York, 1970.

Hont, I. and M. Ignatieff, 'Needs and justice in the *Wealth of Nations*' in *Wealth and Virtue*, Cambridge, 1983.

Holmes, R. *Coleridge*, Oxford Past Masters, 1982.

Humboldt, A. von *Political Essay on the Kingdom of New Spain*, trans. J. Black, New York, 1966.

Hume, D. *A Treatise of Human Nature*, ed. L.A. Selby-Bigge, Oxford, 1978.
An Enquiry Concerning Human Understanding, ed. L.A. Selby-Bigge, Oxford, 1975.
An Enquiry Concerning the Principles of Morals, ed. L.A. Selby-Bigge, Oxford, 1975.
Essays Moral, Political and Literary, ed. E.F. Miller, Indianapolis, 1985.
Dialogues Concerning Natural Religion, ed. J.V. Price, Oxford, 1976.
The History of England, ed. W. F. Todd, Indianapolis, 1983–5.
'A dissertation on the passions' in *Essays and Treatises on Several Subjects*, Edinburgh, 1800.
The Letters of David Hume, ed. J.Y.T. Greig, Oxford, 1932.
New Letters of David Hume, eds. R. Klibansky and E.C. Mossner, Oxford, 1954.

Hutchinson, T.W. *Economics and Economic Policy in Britain, 1946–1966*, London, 1968.
The Politics and Philosophy of Economics, Oxford, 1981.

Huxley, T.H. 'On the hypothesis that animals are automata and its history' and 'On Descartes's "Discourse touching the method of using one's reason rightly and seeking scientific truth"' in *Methods and Results*, London, 1894.
'The *Origin of Species*' in *Darwiniana*, vol. 2, London, 1899.

Hyppolite, J. *Studies on Marx and Hegel*, New York, 1973.
Introduction à la Philosophie de L'Histoire de Hegel, Paris, 1947.

Japp, A. *Thomas de Quincey: His life and writings*, London, 1890.

James, W. *Pragmatism and The Meaning of Truth*, Cambridge, Mass., 1975.

Jenyns, S. *A Free Enquiry into the Nature and Origin of Evil*, London, 1757.

Jevons, W.S. 'Brief account of a general mathematical theory of political economy' in *Journal of the Statistical Society of London* 29(1866), 282–7.
Papers and Correspondence, ed. R.D.C. Black, vols. 4, 6 and 7, London, 1977–81.
The Theory of Political Economy, ed. H.S. Jevons, New York, 1965.
The Principles of Economics, ed. H. Higgs, London, 1905.
'Evolution and the doctrine of design' in *Popular Science Monthly*, May 1874, 98–100.

Jha, N. *The Age of Marshall*, London, 1973.

Johnson, P. *Intellectuals*, London, 1988.

Kamenka, E. (ed.) *Intellectuals and Revolution*, London, 1979.

Kaufmann, W. *Hegel*, London, 1966.

Kelsen, H. *Society and Nature*, London, 1943.

Kemp Smith, N. *The Philosophy of David Hume*, London, 1941.

Keynes, J.M. *Collected Writings*, general ed. D.E. Moggridge, London, 1971–82.
The General Theory of Employment, Interest and Money, London, 1973.

Kittrel, E.R. '"Laissez-faire" in English classical economics' in JHI 17(1966), 610–20.

Knight, F.K. 'The ethics of competition' in *Quarterly Journal of Economics* 37(1923), 579–624.

Knox, T.M. *Action*, London, 1968.

Koyré, A. *From the Closed World to the Infinite Universe*, Baltimore, 1968.
Discovering Plato, trans. L. Rosenfield, New York, 1945.

Kruger, L. 'Why do we study the history of philosophy' in *Philosophy in History*, eds. R. Rorty, J. Schneewind and Q. Skinner, Cambridge, 1984.

Kuhn, T.S. *The Structure of Scientific Revolutions*, Chicago, 1970.
'The relations between the history and the philosophy of science'; 'Mathematical versus experimental traditions in the development of physical science'; and 'Second thoughts on paradigms' in *The Essential Tension*, Chicago, 1977.

Kuntz, R.N. *Capitalismo e Natureza*, São Paulo, 1982.

Lafargue, P. 'Reminiscences of Marx' in *Reminiscences of Marx and Engels*, Moscow, 1959.

Lakatos, I. 'Newton's effect on scientific standards' in *The Methodology of Scientific Research Programmes*, eds. J. Worrall and G. Currie, Cambridge, 1978.

La Mettrie, J.O. de *L'Homme Machine*, ed. A. Vartanian, Princeton, 1960.
'Discours Preliminaire' in A. Thomson, *Materialism and Society in the Mid-Eighteenth Century*, Paris, 1981.

Lange, F.A. *The History of Materialism*, trans. E.C. Thomas, London, 1925.

La Rouchefoucauld, Duc de *Maxims*, trans. L. Tancock, Harmondsworth, 1967.

Larson, J.L. *Reason and Experience: The representation of natural order in the work of Carl von Linneaus*, Berkeley, 1971.

Leeuwen, A. Th. van *Critique of Heaven*, London, 1972.

LeMahieu, D.L. *The Mind of William Paley*, Nebraska, 1976.
'Malthus and the theology of scarcity' in JHI 40(1979), 467–74.

Lenin, V.I. *Collected Works*, vols. 33 and 38, London, 1957–61.

Levin, S. 'Malthus and the idea of progress' in JHI 17(1966), 92–108.

Levy, P. *Moore and the Cambridge Apostles*, Oxford, 1981.

Lewis, C.S. *Studies in Words*, Cambridge, 1967.

Livingstone, R.W. (ed.) *The Legacy of Greece*, Oxford, 1922.
A Defence of Classical Education, London, 1916.

Locke, J. *An Essay Concerning Human Understanding*, ed. P. Nidditch, Oxford, 1975.

Louis, F.D. *Swift's Anatomy of Misunderstanding*, London, 1981.

Lovejoy, A.O. *The Great Chain of Being*, Cambridge, Mass., 1964.
Reflections on Human Nature, Baltimore, 1961.
Essays in the History of Ideas, Baltimore, 1955.

Lovejoy, A.O. and G. Boas *Primitivism and Related Ideas in Antiquity*, Baltimore, 1935.

Low, J.M. 'An eighteenth-century controversy in the theory of economic progress' in *Manchester School* 20(1952), 311–30.

Lucretius *De Rerum Natura*, trans. C. Bailey, Oxford, 1910.

Lukács, G. 'On the responsibility of intellectuals' in *Marxism and Human Liberation*, ed. E. San Juan Jr, New York, 1973.
The Destruction of Reason, trans. P. Palmer, London, 1980.
The Young Hegel, trans. R. Livingstone, London, 1975.

Mabbott, J.D. 'Interpretations of Mill's utilitarianism' in *Theories of Ethics*, ed. P. Foot, Oxford, 1967.

McCraken, C.J. *Malebranche and British Philosophy*, Oxford, 1983.

Machiavelli, N. *The Prince*, trans. N.H. Thomson, Oxford, 1913.

Macfie, A.L. 'The invisible hand of jupiter' in JHI 32(1971), 595–9.

McGinn, R. 'Nietzsche on technology' in JHI 41(1980), 679–91.

McLellan, D. (ed.) *Karl Marx: Interviews and Recollections*, London, 1981.
The Young Hegelians and Karl Marx, London, 1969.

McWilliams-Tullberg, R. 'Marshall's "tendency to socialism"' in HOPE 7(1975), 75–111.

Magee, B. *Modern British Philosophy*, London, 1971.

Malcolm, N. *Ludwig Wittgenstein*, Oxford, 1984.

Malebranche, N. *The Search After Truth*, trans. T. Lennon and P. Olscamp, Ohio, 1980.

Maloney, J. 'Marshall, Cunningham, and the emerging economics profession' in *Economic History Review* 29(1976), 440–51.

Malthus, T.R. *Principles of Political Economy*, London, 1836.
First Essay on Population, ed. J. Bonar, London, 1926.
A Summary View of the Principle of Population in *Introduction to Malthus*, ed. D.V. Glass, London, 1953.
An Essay on the Principle of Population, London, 1958.
Unpublished letter to W. Whewell, Trinity College Library, Cambridge, Whewell Papers, Add. Mss. c. 53/2.

Marchi, N.B. de 'The success of Mill's *Principles*' in HOPE 6(1974), 119–57.

Marcuse, H. 'On hedonism' in *Negations*, Boston, 1968.

Marshall, A. *Principles of Economics*, London, 1949.
Industry and Trade, London, 1919.
The Economics of Industry, London, 1896.
Early Economic Writings, 1867–1890, ed. J.K. Whitaker, London, 1975.
Memorials of Alfred Marshall, ed. A.C. Pigou, London, 1925.
'A plea for the creation of a curriculum in economics and associated branches of political science' in *Principles of Economics*, ed. C.W. Guillebaud, variorum edition, London, 1961.

'Speech at the meeting of the British Economic Association' in *Economic Journal* 3(1893), 387–90.

'Distribution and exchange' in *Economic Journal* 8(1898), 37–59.

Unpublished MS on a projected book on Economic Progress, transcribed by H.-M. Neimeyer, Marshall Library, Cambridge.

Marx, K. *Collected Works*, vols. 1, 4 and 40, London, 1975–83.

   Early Writings, trans. R. Livingstone and G. Benton, London, 1975.

   Writings of the Young Marx on Philosophy and Society, 1835–1847, eds. L. Easton and K. Guddat, New York, 1967.

   Grundrisse, trans. M. Nicolaus, London, 1973.

   Capital: A critique of political economy, vol. 1, trans. B. Fowkes, London, 1976.

   Theories of Surplus Value, Moscow, 1969.

   Karl Marx: Interviews and Recollections, ed. D. McLellan, London, 1981.

   Marx and Engels on Malthus, trans. R.L. and D. Meek, London, 1953.

   Marx and Engels on Ecology, ed. H.L. Parsons, Westport, 1977.

Masterman, M. 'The nature of a paradigm' in *Criticism and the Growth of Knowledge*, eds. I. Lakatos and A. Musgrave, Cambridge, 1970.

Matthews, R.C.O. 'Morality, competition and efficiency' in *Manchester School* 49(1981), 289–309.

Medvedev, Z.A. *The Rise and Fall of T.D. Lysenko*, trans. I. Lerner, New York, 1969.

Meek, R.L. 'Smith, Turgot, and the "four stages theory"' in HOPE 3(1971), 9–27.

   The Economics of Physiocracy, London, 1962.

Mehring, F. *Karl Marx*, trans. E. Fitzgerald, London, 1936.

Menger, C. *Principles of Economics*, trans. J. Dingwall and B. Hoselitz, New York, 1976.

Milgate, M. 'On the notion of "intertemporal equilibrium"' in *Economica* 46(1979), 1–10.

Mill, J.S. *Collected Works*, general ed. J.M. Robson, Toronto, 1963–78.

   The Spirit of the Age, ed. F.A. Hayek, Chicago, 1942.

   Mill on Bentham and Coleridge, ed. F.R. Leavis, London, 1950.

   Autobiography, ed. H. Taylor, London, 1873.

   Three Essays, ed. R. Wollheim, Oxford, 1975.

Mini, P.V. *Philosophy and Economics*, London, 1974.

Mirowski, P. 'Physics and the marginalist revolution' in *Cambridge Journal of Economics* 8(1984), 361–79.

Mises, L. von *Liberalism in the Classical Tradition*, trans. R. Raico, San Francisco, 1985.

   'Comments about the mathematical treatment of economic problems' in *Journal of Libertarian Studies* 1(1977), 97–100.

Mizuta, H. *Adam Smith's Library*, Cambridge, 1967.

Moggridge, D.E. *Keynes*, London, 1980.

Montaigne, M. *Essays of Montaigne*, trans. J. Florio [1603], London, 1885.

Moore, G.E. 'Wittgenstein's lectures in 1930–33' in *Mind* 63(1954), 1–15.

Moore, J.R. '1859 and all that' in *Charles Darwin 1809–1882*, eds. R.C. Chapman and C.T. Duval, Wellington, 1982.

Morgan, D.W. 'The "orthodox" Marxists: first generation of a tradition' in *Ideas Into Politics*, eds. R. Bullen, H. von Strandmann and A. Polonsky, London, 1984.

Morishima, M. *Why Has Japan 'Succeeded'?*, Cambridge, 1982.

Mossner, E.C. *The Life of David Hume*, Oxford, 1954.

'The continental reception of Hume's *Treatise*' in *Mind* 56 (1947). 31–43.

Murdoch, I. *The Sovereignty of Good*, London, 1970.

Myrdal, G. 'The trend towards economic planning' in *Manchester School* 19(1951), 1–42.

Neff, E. *Carlyle and Mill: An introduction to Victorian thought*, London, 1964.

Nichols Jr, J. *Epicurean Political Philosophy*, Ithaca, 1976.

Nietzsche, F. *Human All Too Human*, trans. R.J. Hollingdale, Cambridge, 1986.

Daybreak, trans. R.J. Hollingdale, Cambridge, 1982.

The Gay Science, trans. W. Kaufmann, New York, 1974.

Beyond Good and Evil, trans. W. Kaufmann, New York, 1966.

The Will to Power, trans. W. Kaufmann and R.J. Hollingdale, New York, 1968.

Selected Letters, trans. A. Ludovici, London, 1985.

O'Brien, D.P. 'Marshall, 1842–1924' in *Pioneers of Modern Economics in Britain*, eds. D.P. O'Brien and J.R. Presley, London, 1981.

Lionel Robbins, London, 1988.

Paley, W. *The Principles of Moral and Political Philosophy*, London, 1814.

Pareto, V. *Manual of Political Economy*, trans. A.S. Schwier, New York, 1971.

The Mind and Society, trans. A. Bongiorno and A. Livingstone, vol. 1, London, 1935.

The Other Pareto, trans. P. Bucolo, London, 1980.

Parsons, H.L. (ed.) *Marx and Engels on Ecology*, Westport, 1977.

Parsons, T. 'Wants and activities in Marshall' and 'Economics and sociology: Marshall in relation to the thought of his time' in *Quarterly Journal of Economics* 46(1931–2), 101–40 and 316–47.

'The motivation of economic activities' in *Essays in Sociological Theory*, New York, 1964.

Passmore, J. *Hume's Intentions*, London, 1952.

Man's Responsibility for Nature, London, 1980.

Science and Its Critics, London, 1978.

Paul, E. Frankel 'Jevons: economic revolutionary and political utilitarian' in JHI 40(1979), 267–83.

'Adam Smith: a reappraisal' in *Journal of Libertarian Studies* 1(1977), 289–306.

Payne, R. *Marx*, London, 1968.

Peirce, C.S. 'The fixation of belief' in *Philosophical Writings*, ed. J. Buchler, New York, 1955.

Pellew, G. *Life and Correspondence of the Right Honourable Henry Addington, First Viscount Sidmouth*, vol. 1., London, 1847.

Plant, R. *Hegel*, London, 1973.

Plato, *Apology*, trans. R.W. Livingstone, Oxford, 1938.

  Phaedo, trans. R.S. Bluck, London, 1955.

  Protagoras, trans. C.C.W. Taylor, Oxford, 1976.

  Phaedrus, trans. R. Hackforth, Cambridge, 1952.

  Republic, trans. A. Lindsay, London, 1976 and F. Cornford, Oxford, 1941.

  'Seventh Letter' in *Phaedrus*, trans. W. Hamilton, Harmondsworth, 1973.

Pope, A. *Poetical Works*, vol. 2, Glasgow, 1785.

  Correspondence, ed. G. Sherburn, vol. 4, Oxford, 1956.

Popper, K.R. *The Open Society and Its Enemies*, New York, 1963.

  Conjectures and Refutations, London, 1963.

  The Poverty of Historicism, London, 1961.

Porphyry, 'On the life of Plotinus and the arrangement of his work' in *The Enneads*, trans. S. Mackenna, London, 1930.

Potter, G. 'Unpublished marginalia in Coleridge's copy of Malthus' *Essay on Population*' in *Publications of the Modern Language Association* 51(1936), 1061–8.

Prenant, M. *Biology and Marxism*, trans. C. Greaves, London, 1938.

Pullen, J. 'Malthus's theological ideas and their influence on his principle of population' in HOPE 13(1981), 39–54.

Quesnay, F. 'Natural right' in *The Economics of Physiocracy*, ed. R.L. Meek, London, 1962.

Quincey, T. de *Collected Writings*, ed. D. Masson, vol. 9, London, 1897.

Rae, J. *Life of Adam Smith*, New York, 1965.

Raphael, D.D. *Adam Smith*, Oxford Past Masters, 1985.

  'Adam Smith and "the infection of David Hume's society"' in JHI 20(1969), 225–48.

  'Adam Smith: philosophy, science, and social science' in *Philosophers of the Enlightenment*, ed. S.C. Brown, Sussex, 1979.

  '"The true old Humean philosophy" and its influence on Adam Smith' in *David Hume*, ed. G.P. Morice, Edinburgh, 1977.

  'The just and the charitable' in *Times Literary Supplement*, 15 June 1984, 672.

Rashid, S. 'Malthus's *Principles* and British economic thought' in HOPE 13(1981), 55–79.

Rée, J. *Philosophical Tales*, London, 1987.

Reisman, D.A. *The Economics of Alfred Marshall*, London, 1986.

  Alfred Marshall: Progress and Politics, London, 1987.

Ricardo, D. *Works and Correspondence*, ed. P. Sraffa, Cambridge, 1952–73.

Riley, J. *Liberal Utilitarianism*, Cambridge, 1988.

Rist, J.M. *Stoic Philosophy*, Cambridge, 1969.

Robbins, L. *The Great Depression*, London, 1935.

  An Essay on the Nature and Significance of Economic Science, London, 1984.

  The Evolution of Modern Economic Theory, London, 1970.

The Theory of Economic Policy in English classical political economy, London, 1965.

Robinson, J. *Economic Philosophy*, Harmondsworth, 1964.

Freedom and Necessity, London, 1970.

'History versus equilibrium' in *Thames Polytechnic Papers* 1(1974).

Robson, J.M. *The Improvement of Mankind*, Toronto, 1968.

Rose, S., L. Kamin and R. Lewontin *Not In Our Genes*, Harmondsworth, 1984.

Rotwein, E. (ed.) *Hume: Writings on economics*, Edinburgh, 1955.

Ruskin, J. *Unto This Last*, London, 1862.

Munera Pulveris, London, 1907.

Ruskin Today, ed. K. Clark, Harmondsworth, 1982.

Russell, P. 'Hume's *Treatise* and Hobbes's *Elements of Law*' in JHI 46(1985), 51–63.

'Skepticism and natural religion in Hume's *Treatise*' in JHI 49(1988), 247–65.

Russell, B. *The Conquest of Happiness*, London, 1930.

'John Stuart Mill' in *Mill*, ed. J. Schneewind, London, 1969.

'The place of science in a liberal education' in *Mysticism and Logic*, London, 1963.

'Philosophy and politics' in *Unpopular Essays*, London, 1950.

Ryan, A. *John Stuart Mill*, London, 1974.

The Philosophy of the Social Sciences, London, 1970.

Ryle, G. *Dilemmas*, Cambridge, 1954.

Review of Popper's *Open Society* in *Mind* 56(1947), 167–72.

Samuel, V. *Belief and Action: An everyday philosophy*, Harmondsworth, 1939.

Samuels, W.J. *Pareto on Policy*, Amsterdam, 1974.

'The history of economic thought as intellectual history' in HOPE 6(1974), 303–23.

Santurri, E. 'Theology and social policy in Malthus' in JHI 43(1982), 315–30.

Schmidt, A. *The Concept of Nature in Marx*, trans. B. Fowkes, London, 1971.

Schumpeter, J. *History of Economic Analysis*, ed. E. Schumpeter, London, 1954.

'Science and ideology' in *American Economic Review* 30(1949), 345–59.

Ten Great Economists: From Marx to Keynes, London, 1952.

Sen, A.K. 'Description as choice' in *Oxford Economic Papers* 32(1980), 353–69.

'Rational fools: a critique of the behavioural foundations of economic theory' in *Philosophy and Economic Theory*, eds. F. Hahn and M. Hollis, Oxford, 1979.

'Economics and the family'; 'The profit motive'; 'Rights and capabilities'; and 'Goods and people' in *Resources, Values and Development*, Oxford, 1984.

On Ethics & Economics, Oxford, 1987.

Seneca, *Minor Dialogues*, trans. A. Stewart, London, 1889.

Senior, N. *Two Lectures on Population* delivered before the University of Oxford in Easter Term, 1828. To which is added a correspondence between the author and T.R. Malthus, London, 1829.

Sidgwick, H. *Outlines of the History of Ethics*, London, 1931.

Simon, H.A. 'From substantive to procedural rationality' in *Philosophy and Economic Theory*, eds. F. Hahn and M. Hollis, Oxford, 1979.

Skinner, Q. *Machiavelli*, Oxford Past Masters, 1981.

Skinner, A.S. 'Science and the role of the imagination'; 'Moral philosophy and civil society'; and 'Historical theory' in *A System of Social Science: Papers Relating to Adam Smith*, Oxford, 1979.

'Natural history in the age of Smith' in *Political Studies* 15(1967), 32–48.

'Adam Smith and the American economic community' in JHI 37(1976), 59–78.

Smith, A. *Theory of Moral Sentiments*, eds. D.D. Raphael and A.L. Macfie, Oxford, 1976.

An Inquiry into the Nature and Causes of the Wealth of Nations, eds. R.H. Campbell and A.S. Skinner; textual ed. W.B. Todd, Oxford, 1976.

Essays on Philosophical Subjects, eds. W.P.D. Wightman, J.C. Bryce and I.S. Ross, Oxford, 1980.

Lectures on Jurisprudence, eds. R. Meek, D.D. Raphael and P. Stein, Oxford, 1977.

Lectures on Rhetoric and Belles Lettres, ed. J.C. Bryce, Oxford, 1977.

Sorensen, V. *Seneca: The humanist at the court of Nero*, trans. W. Glyn Jones, Edinburgh, 1984.

Southey, R. 'Malthus's *Essay on Population*' in *Annual Review* 2(1803), 292–301.

'On the state of the poor, the principle of Malthus's population and the manufacturing system' in *Essays Moral and Political*, vol. 1, London, 1832.

Sperry, R. *Science and Moral Priority*, Oxford, 1983.

Spiegel, H.W. 'Adam Smith's heavenly city' in HOPE 8(1976), 478–93.

Spinoza, B. de *The Political Works*, trans. A.G. Wernham, Oxford, 1958.

Ethics, trans. R. Elwes, New York, 1955.

Stekloff, G.M. *The History of the First International*, trans. E. and C. Paul, London, 1928.

Stephen, L. *The English Utilitarians*, vols. 1, 2 and 3, London, 1900.

Steuart, J. *An Inquiry into the Principles of Political Oeconomy*, ed. A.S. Skinner, Edinburgh, 1966.

Stewart, D.K. *The Psychology of Communication*, New York, 1968.

Stigler, G. 'The development of utility theory' in *Essays in the History of Economics*, Chicago, 1965.

Memoirs of an Unregulated Economist, New York, 1988.

Strawson, P.F. *Skepticism and Naturalism*, London, 1985.

Swift, J. *A Tale of a Tube*, ed. K. Williams, London, 1975.

Taylor, A.E. *Plato: The man and his work*, London, 1960.

Taylor, C.T. *Hegel and Modern Society*, Cambridge, 1979.

Taylor, Rev R. *The Devil's Pulpit*. Containing twenty-three astronomico-theological discourses with a sketch of his life, vol. 1. London, 1831.

Taylor, W.L. *Francis Hutcheson and David Hume as Predecessors of Adam Smith*, Durham, 1965.

Teichgraeber III, R.F. 'Free Trade' and Moral Philosophy: Rethinking the sources of Adam Smith's Wealth of Nations, Durham, 1986.

Thomas, B. 'A plea for an ecological approach to economic growth' in *Contemporary Issues in Economics*, eds. M. Parkin and A.R. Nobay, Manchester, 1975.

Thomas, K. *Man and the Natural World*, Harmondsworth, 1984.

Thomson, A. *Materialism and Society in the Mid-Eighteenth Century*, Paris, 1981.

Tocqueville, A. de *Democracy in America*, trans. H. Reeve, London, 1862.

Tucker, R.C. *Philosophy and Myth in Karl Marx*, Cambridge, 1967.

Tucker, S.I. *Enthusiasm: A study in semantic change*, Cambridge, 1972.

Urmson, J.O. 'The interpretation of the moral philosophy of J.S. Mill' in *Theories of Ethics*, ed. P. Foot, Oxford, 1967.

Vartanian, A. (ed.) *La Mettrie's 'L'Homme Machine'*, Princeton, 1960.

Viner, J. *The Role of Providence in the Social Order*, Philadelphia, 1972.

'Bentham and John Stuart Mill: the utilitarian background' and 'Adam Smith and laissez-faire' in *The Long View and the Short*, Glencoe, Ill., 1958.

'Marshall's economics in relation to the man and to his times' in *American Economic Review* 31(1941), 223–35.

Voltaire, F.M.A. *Philosophical Letters*, trans. E. Dilworth, Indianapolis, 1961.

Whately, E.J. *Life and Correspondence of R. Whately*, vol. 1, London, 1866.

Whitaker, J.K. 'Some neglected aspects of Alfred Marshall's economic and social thought' in HOPE 9(1977), 161–97.

'John Stuart Mill's methodology' in *Journal of Political Economy* 83(1975), 1031–47.

Whitehead, A.N. *Science and the Modern World*, New York, 1928.

Adventures of Ideas, Harmondsworth, 1942.

Dialogues of Alfred North Whitehead, ed. L. Price, London, 1954.

Wicksteed, P.H. 'The scope and method of political economy in the light of the "marginal" theory of value and distribution' in *Economic Journal* 24(1914), 1–23.

Wiener, M.J. *English Culture and the Decline of the Industrial Spirit*, Cambridge, 1981.

Wightman, W.P.D. 'Adam Smith and the history of ideas' in *Essays on Adam Smith*, eds. A.S. Skinner and T. Wilson, Oxford, 1975.

Willey, B. *The Eighteenth Century Background: Studies on the idea of nature on the thought of the period*, London, 1965.

Nineteenth Century Studies: Coleridge to Matthew Arnold, London, 1949.

Williams, B. *Ethics and the Limits of Philosophy*, London, 1985.

Williams, R. *Keywords: A vocabulary of culture and society*, London, 1976.

Wilson, T. 'Sympathy and self-interest' in *The Market and the State*, eds. T. Wilson and A.S. Skinner, Oxford, 1976.

Winch, D.N. *Adam Smith's Politics*, Cambridge, 1978.

'Adam Smith's "enduring particular result": a political and cosmopolitan perspective' in *Wealth and Virtue*, eds. I. Hont and M. Ignatieff, Cambridge, 1983.

'Higher maxims: happiness versus wealth in Malthus and Ricardo' and 'A separate science: polity and society in Marshall's economics' in *That Noble Science of Politics*, eds. S. Collini, D. Winch and J. Burrow, Cambridge, 1983.

Economics and Policy, London, 1972.

Wittgenstein, L. *Culture and Value*, trans. P. Winch, Oxford, 1980.

On Certainty, trans. D. Paul and G.E.M. Anscombe, Oxford, 1979.

Wright, G.H. von 'Wittgenstein on certainty' in *Wittgenstein*, Oxford, 1982.

Yolton, J.W. *Thinking Matter: Materialism in Eighteenth-Century Britain*, Minneapolis, 1983.

Young, E. *Night-Thoughts on Life, Death and Immortality* in *Works*, vol. 2, London, 1802.

Young, R.M. 'Malthus and the evolutionists: the common context of biological and social theory' in *Past and Present* 43(1969), 109–45.

Mind, Brain and Adaptation in the Nineteenth Century, Oxford, 1970.

Young, J.Z. *Philosophy and the Brain*, Oxford, 1986.

Zeleny, J. *La Estrutura Logica de 'El Capital' de Marx*, trans. M. Sacristan, Barcelona, 1974.

Ziff, P. *Understanding Understanding*, Ithaca, 1972.

Index

249